Homer

Buck

April

AMERICA FACES THE FUTURE

AMERICA
FACES THE FUTURE

EDITED BY
CHARLES A. BEARD
Co-author of 'The Rise of American Civilization' and 'The American Leviathan'; sometime President of the American Political Science Association

BOSTON AND NEW YORK
HOUGHTON MIFFLIN COMPANY
The Riverside Press Cambridge

COPYRIGHT, 1932, BY CHARLES A. BEARD

ALL RIGHTS RESERVED INCLUDING THE RIGHT TO REPRODUCE
THIS BOOK OR PARTS THEREOF IN ANY FORM

The Riverside Press
CAMBRIDGE · MASSACHUSETTS
PRINTED IN THE U.S.A.

PREFATORY NOTE

No public question is of more importance than the issue raised by cyclical business disaster bringing misery to millions and threatening the security of the social order. The causes and consequences of such calamities and the projects advanced by thoughtful citizens for avoiding at least their worst evils, therefore, deserve consideration by all who hope to teach or lead in this generation. Hence it follows that, apart from the contributions of the Editor, this volume of papers on depressions and planning constitutes a highly significant document. The weight of the authorities quoted, the concreteness of their proposals, and the realistic character of their reasoning all combine to make the book an invaluable guide for current discussion and a permanent work of reference. To the gentlemen and associations whose papers are reprinted here and to Dr. Henry Goddard Leach, Editor of *The Forum*, the Editor of this volume owes debts that cannot be paid by mere words in a preface.

CHARLES A. BEARD

NEW MILFORD, CONNECTICUT
November, 1931

Contents

PART I

The New Intellectual and Moral Climate

PART II

Blue-Prints for a Planned Economy

AMERICA FACES THE FUTURE

PART I

THE NEW INTELLECTUAL AND MORAL CLIMATE

AMERICA FACES THE FUTURE

PART I

THE NEW INTELLECTUAL AND MORAL CLIMATE

CHAPTER I

CHALLENGES TO THE SOCIAL ORDER

IT IS the fashion of those who do not wish to be disturbed by the pain of thinking to face every crisis with the ancient formula: 'We have passed through similar calamities many times and have always come out improved in size and quality. History repeats itself. There is nothing new under the sun. Therefore, those who can afford it, confronting adversity, will betake themselves to their cyclone caves, close the doors, and let the gale wear itself out.'

For faith in this creed there is undoubtedly some justification in human experience, but on more than one occasion true believers, after a season of pleasant optimism, have found themselves in a major disaster beyond their control. The Bourbons, Hohenzollerns, Hapsburgs, and Romanoffs in their turn fondly imagined that, the more things changed, the more they had of the same good thing; that centuries of previous security had guaranteed perpetuity. Yet their expectations were not realized in the end. Certain phases of human affairs have a beginning, a course, and an ending.

The stubborn truth is that frequently something new does take place under the sun, and the most striking feature of the economic crisis which began in 1929 has been the expression of a profound conviction in high places that such disasters are dangerous to the whole social order, that in this world of interlinked economies they are not to be endured complacently, and that action akin to the heroic and prodigious must be taken to prevent their recurrence. Other panics have been generally accepted by the great and wise, as were plagues and famines in the Middle Ages, with prayers and resignation, but this disturbance is accompanied by a searching of hearts. Once it was said by economists that poverty and idleness were the fruits of improvidence, but now they are beginning to hunt for the social causes of these cruel curses. Once it was universally held by respectable thinkers that the cycles of expansion, prosperity, explosion, contraction, and ruin were the fruits of natural law operating in the moral world — law as far beyond the reach of human will as the imperative of gravitation. Now there are signs of doubt, of a positive conviction that, unless the intellect and will of man can prevent these calamities, the boasted progress of science and reason is a hopeless delusion.

This deep conviction, this constructive resolution is now possessed by leading citizens, by the representatives of great industrial corporations, by the official spokesmen of organized capital and labor. There were similar stirrings, it is true, during the depression of 1921, but today they have reached the uttermost borders of our confused civilization and are tossing high the waves of public opinion. This is something new under the sun, indicating a change in our intellectual and moral climate.[1] The

[1] For a terse and suggestive essay on the moral aspects of the economic crisis see a paper entitled 'Good Will and Prosperity,' by Arthur E. Morgan, in the *Antioch Notes*, December 1, 1931.

glacier of indifference thaws and moves. And it may very well be that a century from now the historian will discover, in the faded papers recording the proposals advanced in 1931 by our directors of opinion, the beginnings of drastic changes in the economy, ethics, institutions, and spirit of American democracy. It may be that this time those who try to warm their cold hands by the ashes of a dead past may freeze in the process.

Among those who are helping to create the new intellectual and moral climate, none has spoken more clearly, effectively, and courageously than Dr. Nicholas Murray Butler. America has too few men and women of independent position and commanding power who bring capacious minds to the study of public questions and fearlessly report their findings for consideration by their fellow citizens. While other leaders in education have been strangely silent, Dr. Butler has carefully formulated a verdict on the present state of national economy and has set it forth with an impelling cogency. He has issued a call for action and has gone beyond that — has indicated the line along which he believes action must be taken. In an address delivered before the American Club of Paris on June 11, 1931, Dr. Butler presented the challenge of the time to two hemispheres under the significant title, 'A Planless World,' and later in the same year he formulated a bill of specifications. The first of these great economic documents is reprinted in Chapter I (pp. 11–19) and the second in Part II, Chapter III (pp. 160–185).

In times of human distress the voices of religion are usually heard, urging benevolence and charity. Such messages are easily formulated, for guidance is furnished by a long line of precedents. Generosity may be praised without danger, indeed with a kind of soul-pleasing unction. But in the present calamity there has been an appeal to intelligence as well as to beneficence. The Pope, it is true, has called upon his faithful in the well-

worn phrases of the past, counselling mercy on the part
of employers and condemning socialism among employees, but the Protestant churches in America have
moved several inches beyond such generalities. The
bishops of the Protestant Episcopal Church invite employers of their communion to take steps to plan production in such a fashion as to give security to labor
(pp. 20–24). Still more boldly the Commission on the
Church and Social Service of the Federal Council of the
Churches of Christ in America indicts the prevailing industrial order and insists that our social and economic
life be reconstructed; that a system of 'national planning' be substituted for the heritage of chaos (pp. 24–
28). In the ferment of contemporary opinion, religious
leadership can no longer be content with evasion and
vague piety, save at grave peril to the Church as an
institution.

Hitherto during economic depressions captains of industry have generally taken it for granted that business
cycles are akin to the movements of natural forces, beyond human reach, and have refrained from inquiring
whether the capitalist system is fatally defective, at least
in important particulars. And the official leaders of
organized labor in the United States, while protesting
vigorously against the distress of unemployment, have
likewise kept within the lines of historic economics —
demanding, not a reformation of capitalism, but security
and higher wages at all costs, within the capitalist order
of production and distribution. In other words, although
accepting a scheme of economy which, as previously ma-
nipulated, produces periodical calamities, they have laid
upon it the task of assuring continuity of employment
and a high standard of life for labor. In the present crisis,
however, new notes are heard. Industrial managers in
high places, for example Mr. Daniel Willard (pp. 29–
32), express grave doubts about the absolute perfection

of capitalism and suggest modifications in the interest of employment, security, and social peace. At the same time such a conservative body as the National Civic Federation, speaking for both capital and labor, proposes to meet the five-year plan of Russia with a ten-year plan for America (pp. 33–43).

Even the principal laws of capitalism are now challenged. If experience in previous panics is a guide and no heroic measures are to be adopted this time to avoid their evils, it follows that the decrees of capitalist production must operate: the downward sweep of wages, prices, and standards of living must take its inevitable course until the bottom is reached, until deflation is completed, and until the ground is cleared of wreckage so that the upward swing may begin again. Yet one of the striking features of the cycle which opened in the autumn of 1929 has been the insistence of high and responsible authorities in politics and economics upon the maintenance of wage scales and a recourse to inflation as a means of liquefying frozen assets — assets which, in the absence of artificial stimulants, would sink in value to a realistic basis. President Hoover has repeatedly protested against wage cuts and has proposed measures of inflation to save property in peril of collapse. Many economists also have deplored attacks on the standard of living as likely to prolong the depression instead of accelerating the return to prosperity (pp. 44–56). Here, too, the discussion of the latest economic cyclone presents new aspects.

Another phase of the present moral and intellectual setting is the growth of popular misgivings about the prophetic and directive powers of our natural aristocracy of wealth and talents. There was a time when the leadership of opinion lay principally in the hands of the clergy, politicians, and editors. In the early days of capitalism, bankers and industrialists were men of deeds rather than words. They paid little attention to what the public was supposed to think and went on with their affairs through thick and thin. But many years ago a change was noted. Magnates of business suddenly became oracles of destiny and their opinions were sought by eager reporters on everything under the sun from prosperity to ping-pong. Newspapers were filled with their outpourings. When the whole country went into a frenzy of speculation in 1928 and 1929, these high counsellors, with a few honorable exceptions, were all on the side of more frenzy. As a result a double discredit fell upon business leadership: it had failed to lead and had given false counsel. So now the press, once filled with praise, is crowded with doubts about the capacity of old-fashioned business directors to think straight with respect to their own operations and to forecast the results of their own conduct. One example, given below (pp. 57–69), illustrates a library of current literature.

So far the scene has been viewed from above, from the standpoint of individuals whose former mode of life has not been destroyed by the cataclysm in which the nation finds itself. But there is another side to the picture. There are the nameless and unsung millions of unemployed at the bottom whose security has been swept away, whose savings of years have been lost, whose homes have been broken up, whose hopes for themselves and their children have been crushed to earth. What of them? Volumes of statistics have been compiled to exhibit their plight in the mass. Graphs have been drawn to indicate the curve of their degradation. Charity bravely comes to their rescue, with much trumpeting. But a steel etching is necessary to bring close to those who think lightly of efforts at planning the fate of men and women shelterless, toolless, and propertyless amid the cold and forbidding stone and brick walls of the great cities. Hence to the scene drawn by artists in elevated places must be added a microscopic glimpse of a single corner of the 'land of opportunity' viewed from the bottom level (pp. 70–85).

Inevitably the inquiries of distinguished citizens, the misgivings of religious leaders, the doubts of men of authority speaking for capital and labor, the uncertainty among economists, and the ribaldry of journalists have finally led to a fundamental question: 'Can Capitalism be Saved?' Or, to state it in another form: 'Can Capitalism Plan?'

In a letter from Moscow, published in the New York *Nation* of October 21, 1931, Mr. Louis Fischer, whose penetrating comments on current affairs have laid economists under a debt, flatly asserts that planning is impossible under capitalism. After making reference to various plans put forward in the West, including *The Forum* plan reprinted below (pp. 117–140), Mr. Fischer says: 'Mr. Beard and others assert that the Bolsheviks did not invent planning. "Hints of it," he says in the July *Forum*, "were discovered by Charles Babbage a century ago. There is nothing Russian about its origin." This is absolutely true, and it is this which proves the case against Mr. Beard. If planning is old, why did nobody try it before Soviet Russia did? I am sure the capitalists have economists and business directors at least as good as those of the Bolsheviks. Why did they not conceive the idea of planning? The answer is: they did. But planning was not adopted by capitalism simply because it could not be. Planning and capitalism are incompatible.'

Taking up this theme in *The Forum* of November, 1931, M. André Maurois explores its nature and implications (pp. 86–96), coming to the somewhat disconcerting conclusion that capitalism can save itself by transforming itself. Perhaps therein lies a paradox. In any case, the challenge to capitalism and the effort to meet the challenge by a combination of individual liberty and initiative with collective planning, control, and action seem to mark a new phase in the intellectual and moral development of mankind. Is it possible to evolve from the various plans contained in Part II of this book, supplemented by other proposals, a program of national procedure in economy? Or shall we continue to move, as a wit has put it, 'with bedraggled dignity from one calamity to the next until the dénouement of destiny is finally reached'?

For some, at least, it is impossible to accept either the gospel of despair or of complacency. It seems more reasonable to believe, with President Butler, that when the world comes out of this valley of distress, it will be upon 'a new upland, a new plane of endeavor and experience and of conduct personal and national.' For a period comparable to our own, as he says, it is necessary to go back to the distant past — to an age 'like the fall of the Roman Empire, like the Renaissance, like the beginning of the political and social revolutions in England and in France in the seventeenth and eighteenth centuries.' Our period, he continues, 'is different from them all; it is in some ways more powerful than them all; and it holds more of the world in its grip than any of them, but it certainly resembles them in its epoch-marking character.'

CHAPTER II

A PLANLESS WORLD [1]

By NICHOLAS MURRAY BUTLER

Mr. Chairman and Gentlemen:

You do me exceptional honor and give me exceptional pleasure in permitting me once again to greet the members of this club and their distinguished guests — finding here, as I do this morning, so many men, Americans and Frenchmen, whose names are known and honored on both sides of the Atlantic for public service and for constant acts of good citizenship....

When your chairman asked me some weeks since for a topic upon which I should say something this morning, I replied by taking the title of Henry George's famous book which is now about fifty years old: 'Progress and Poverty.' Lest I be suspected of plagiarism, I may say that a few days ago, in speaking to the graduating classes of Columbia University, I used the same title. There are so many things suggested by that title, so many questions which it raises in the mind of the intelligent observer of the world of today, that it offers material for a great many speeches by a great many different persons.

Henry George asked this question and answered it to his own satisfaction: Why is it that with all the progress which the world is making in so many directions, through scientific discovery and the applications of science, through advances in letters and fine arts, in every form of industry, commerce, transportation, why is it that there still exists so much distress, so much want, so much of all that which for lack of a better name may be summed up under the single word poverty?

[1] Address before the American Club of Paris, June 11, 1931.

Henry George asked that question fifty years ago with reference to a particular answer uppermost in his own mind. Today, everywhere in this world, East and West, North and South, in Europe and in America, in Asia and in Africa, that question is being asked. Why is it that with all that man has accomplished to his great satisfaction and pride in this last generation or two, why is it that the world today is in the grasp of the greatest economic, financial, social and political series of problems which have ever faced it in history? Why is it?

He would be a brave man who thought himself competent adequately to answer that question. But unless we make an effort to answer, unless we make an effort to understand, we shall not get on with the solution of these great problems. It is better to try to answer and be wrong than to sit negligently still and make no effort to stem the tide of dissatisfaction and unrest and want which is sweeping over this world from one end to the other.

There are those apt in social and economic diagnosis who are quick with their answer. They say this is just one more of those recurrent economic recessions and depressions with which different countries have been from time to time familiar, and as to which Americans in particular have had some four or five experiences within the lifetime of two long generations. I dissent from that view. I can see nothing either in the causes or in the probable effects of the present economic and financial situation at all comparable to those depressions which are recalled to the American mind by the naming of the years 1857, 1873, 1893, or 1907. Those gentlemen who come to us with their easy diagnosis, with their cures and their smug prophecies, will find no field or opportunity for the application of their theories in the present circumstances.

Why not? The reason which I offer, gentlemen, is that we are passing through one of those revolutionary periods in the history of the race which come at long intervals and which are the result of the operation of forces long accumulating which finally bring themselves to bear upon the life, the conduct, and the policies of men and of nations. The period through which we are passing and which it is so difficult fully to understand, and impossible, for me at least, adequately to explain, is a period like the fall of the Roman Empire, like the Renaissance, like the beginning of the political and social revolutions in England and in France in the seventeenth and eighteenth centuries. It is different from them all; it is in some ways more powerful than them all; and it holds more of the world in its grip than any of them, but it certainly resembles them in its epoch-marking character.

I suggest that when the world shall come out of the valley of distress and disillusion and disturbance through which it is now passing, the historian of one hundred or two hundred years from now will find that the world has come out upon a new upland, a new plane of endeavor and experience and of conduct personal and national, comparable to those great epoch-marking events which I mention in the historic past.

Why is this situation not only so acute but so widespread? Let me very briefly answer my own question.

It seems to me that three great sets of forces, causes, any one of which might have been adequate to bring about an economic and social epoch — that three forces have come cumulatively together and have begun to act and are acting, with their accompanying influences and effects, upon the lives of men and of nations everywhere.

The first of these is the result of the phenomenal destruction of the World War; the colossal loss of accumulated capital all over the world; the savings of generations and of hundreds of years, swept away, destroyed, in four short years or less, to say nothing of the complete disruption of the world's trade and commerce, the elimination of long-established habits of national and international intercourse in industry, and the bringing to a violent and tragic end of a system which had been building for three hundred years. That of itself would have presented to civilization a huge bill which civilization would have had very great difficulty in attempting to pay.

Cumulatively with that, there have come those influences which are due to the advance of knowledge and of science in their applications to industry and commerce and human endeavor, growing little by little, spreading their influence decade by decade, and finally bringing to pass a situation known sometimes as 'machine age,' or 'mass production,' which never could have been predicted by anyone. It is difficult for us to understand, save those who happen to be in immediate contact or relationship with some basic form of industry, how striking, how far-reaching, that change has been. When we talk about unemployment, we think of seasonal lack of occupation; we think then of the movement forward and backward in the adjustment of industry to labor which often lasts for weeks and months and readjusts itself automatically to the satisfaction of everyone.

But here is something entirely different. Here is a displacement of effort, of occupation, which is permanent because the forces which have brought it about are forces which it is economically advantageous for the world to use. We have just now had our attention called to its working in the field of agriculture. We have long been watching it in industry, in commerce, in transportation. We have recently had our attention called to it in agriculture, now that wheat-farming in the United States has become in part a great corporate enterprise. The corporate wheat farm can produce wheat and sell it at a price which bankrupts the individual farmer who, with his family, constitutes an army of nearly twelve millions of human beings in the United States living on the land.

With their power of consumption gone, you have sub-
tracted from the consuming power of the United States,
and therefore of the world, one of the great elements of
balance and prosperity in carrying forward on systematic
and satisfactory lines a great basic industry.

Students of agriculture tell us that while it took three
hours of human labor to produce a bushel of wheat in
1900, in 1930 three minutes of machine labor will do the
same thing. The relation is sixty to one. Somebody's
effort is superseded. Somebody's occupation is displaced.
We find ourselves facing this displacement, systematic,
basic, in accordance with the operation of fundamental
forces, which, of itself, I repeat, would have produced a
crisis in our economic and social life, but now cumulatively acting with the results of the vast destruction of
capital and the displacement of every organ of trade and
industry which were the result of the war.

And then, third, there has now come the development
of those political forces which have been operating in the
world for three hundred years and which we have in general terms described as the development of democracy.
Without stopping too minutely to define that term, you
realize that what it means, as I am now using it, is the
building-up of that social and political system in which
the final power of decision and authority rests in the
great mass of the population. When that movement
brought about the English revolution and the French
revolution, they seemed to convulse the world. But
what small convulsions they were compared to the convulsion which we are witnessing in this year of grace!

This convulsion extends to China, to India, to South
America, to the remotest parts of the civilized world; it
touches them all; it affects them all and through them
each and all touches us in France, in America, in Great
Britain, in Germany, in Italy, where you will.

These three great forces, cumulative, acting together,

are, if my observation be in any wise correct, the cause and the instrument of the whole vast world-wide economic, industrial, financial, social and political crisis which we are facing.

It is an interesting thing, gentlemen, and not very complimentary, to observe with what universal incompetence we are looking out on this situation. The whole world is waiting, like Mr. Micawber, for something to turn up; but somebody has got to turn something up! The world is suffering, as it has never suffered in history, from lack of competent, constructive, courageous leadership, political, social, and economic. We need personalities who are not anxious, like the jockey, to keep their seats in politics, but who are willing to tell the people the truth and to guide them toward a constructive, a liberal, and a progressive solution of these vast problems.

The universal answer of the office-holding class is 'Wait.' Gentlemen, if we wait too long, somebody will come forward with a solution that we may not like.

Let me call your attention to the fact that the characteristic feature of the experiment in Russia, to my mind, is not that it is communist, but that it is being carried on with a plan in the face of a planless opposition. The man with a plan, however much we dislike it, has a vast advantage over the group sauntering down the road of life complaining of the economic weather and wondering when the rain is going to stop.

There was a brief statement made to the press on Monday last, following the conference at Chequers between the German Chancellor and the German Minister of Foreign Affairs and the representatives of the British Government, a brief statement that contained two words, which I wish to emphasize in your presence. Those two words were 'international coöperation.' There I suggest is the door to be opened which offers approach to the path of greatest promise of advance and satisfaction.

We are trying to deal with these stupendous problems, with these new problems, with these problems of tomorrow, by using the ideas and the machinery of yesterday. We are trying, in the age of the electric light, to teach national economic progress with a candle. It cannot be done, gentlemen. We have got to recognize this fundamental fact, that economic boundaries are no longer identical with political boundaries anywhere in the world. The nation which thinks it can provide for itself prosperity, no matter what becomes of its fellows, is as foolish and as behind the times as the nation which thinks it can provide for itself security without regard to what becomes of its fellows. Prosperity and security have ceased to be national; they have become subject-matter for international coöperation. Selfish and self-centered nationalism is outworn and outgrown. The war both taught and witnessed the final collapse of competitive nationalism.

Did the world gain or lose by the great and quick development of the United States for one hundred years? Did the world gain or lose by the vast extension of British commerce and overseas trade following the Napoleonic wars? Did the world gain or lose through the development of science and industry in Germany beginning fifty years ago? Does the world gain or lose when France is active and prosperous and abundant in trade at home and abroad? The answer is not difficult. The world does gain at all such times. The moment we turn our back upon the invitation of the future, to look down the lane that leads to an abandoned past, we are making impossible that which we are so desirous to accomplish. We have not only got to face the front, but we have got to seize the instruments of tomorrow and put the instruments of the past in our museums.

What have we done?

The first thing that we tried to do, looking backward again, was to try to find out whether somebody could not pay for the cost of the great war. You might just as well try to make somebody pay the cost of the sunset. It cannot be done, gentlemen. That destruction was accomplished once and for all, and its cost cannot be repaid. It has got to be marked up to profit and loss, and the sooner the better.

And then, having attempted to pay the cost of the war, each nation has said to every other nation: ' Do not come near me with your goods.' In this plight we fell back upon the most vast extension of credit that history records — huge credits to meet the disbursements of the war, huge credits to meet the situation created after the war; and we have unanimously and universally done everything we could think of to prevent those credits being reduced or repaid and the nations concerned from again beginning to consume in order to produce. We have been children playing with marbles, and now, when we have occupied ourselves with that childish amusement for some fifteen years, we are more or less astonished to find that we are in the midst of a severe economic crisis. Do you wonder that the plan-making Russian smiles at us? Can he not afford to smile when we give him the field without competition and tell him to go ahead and show what he can do and that we will be very careful not to show what we can do? That is not the ordinary way in which a successful contest for supremacy is conducted.

Gentlemen, I am not one of those persons who worry about any more wars. Any more wars would come to an end so soon, and there would be so many persons who would not know that the war had begun before it had come to an end, that that fear does not very much concern me. But I have great concern for the man with a competing social and economic system and a plan, if we do not quickly plan to demonstrate the supremacy of ours. I have great concern for the man with a plan competing with a planless world.

We ought not to postpone a week, a month, those joint international undertakings, first, to diagnose accurately, and then to prescribe the first and simple steps of remedy for this economic situation. If France, if Germany, if Great Britain, if Italy, if the United States, if Canada, and the rest, each start to do this thing alone, they will get nowhere and they will leave the field to our Eastern European friends with a plan.

What I wish to point out is that in the midst of all this progress we are surrounded by all this poverty. We look upon persons in high political positions, we look upon men in high and responsible posts in the world of business, of finance and of industry, and find them without any competent suggestion of leadership, and without the courage to defy an uninformed public opinion by telling people the truth.

What I ask for, gentlemen, is a plan, a plan of international coöperation to solve the problems that have become international — not to sit and wait — not to stand and wait — not merely to abuse the people with a plan; but to present a better plan and to testify for our time and for the time that shall come after us that all the sacrifices that have been made for three hundred years all over this world to build institutions of liberty, of freedom, of political and economic opportunity, to build them into governments and social systems — that all that has not been wasted. We have not been on a false track, but we simply have been inconsequent in appreciating and in meeting the gravest situation with which our system of liberty has ever been faced. Let the world wake up. Let it demand of its men in public office that they either take constructive lead or make way for those who can — and will!

CHAPTER III

THE CALL OF THE PROTESTANT CHURCHES

A SIGNIFICANT sign of the age is the extensive discussion of economic issues which took place at the convention of the Protestant Episcopal Church at Denver in the autumn of 1931. A large part of the time of the clergy and the lay delegates on that occasion was devoted to a consideration of the challenge to morality and intelligence presented by the crisis in agriculture and industry and only the opposition of eminent members, such as the Honorable George W. Wickersham, prevented the whole convention from going on record as favoring a modification of 'rugged individualism' to meet the demands of a coöperative age. However, the House of Bishops which, it is interesting to note, was more radical in opinion than the laymen, drew up a heavy indictment of the prevailing social 'order,' if order it can be called in truth, and demanded that the employers in their communion labor for the adoption of a plan or plans 'which shall coördinate production and consumption, insure continuity of employment, and provide security of income to the workers of the nation.' In words that cannot be mistaken, the bishops of the Church, in the Pastoral Letter which follows, call upon the membership of their own communion to consider the gravity of the crisis, take measures of prevention, and substitute service for the profit-seeking motive.

To Our Brethren of the Household of Faith:
   We, your Bishops, in general convention assembled, greet you in the name of the Lord. We give thanks to God our Father for all the evidences of faith and courage

in the several parts of the Church, shown by simplicity and steadfastness of life, and by devotion to Christian worship and work in the midst of widespread indifference and hostility.

We are grateful for an increasing sensitiveness to human suffering, for the endeavor to understand better the complexities of human relationship and for the growing desire for such world adjustment as may promote universal good-will and well-being....

We are living in a time of extraordinary strain. The one word which describes best the present condition of society is 'confusion.' Uncertainty pervades every field of human interest, economic, political, and religious.

Poverty and wealth are relative terms and inequality of possessions is to be expected, but the contrast between individual want and collective plenty cannot be accepted as in accordance with the will of God.

The resources of the earth are unimpaired and the means of distribution were never so abundant, and the existence of world-wide involuntary unemployment and the fact that in every land multitudes lack not merely the comforts but the necessities of life and must depend upon doles and charities or starve is an arraignment of the present economic system under which the trade of the world is carried on.

An acquisitive society, as the modern age has been aptly called, stands bewildered in the presence of a crisis precipitated, not by earthquakes, droughts, floods, or any physical catastrophes, but, apparently, by the competitive, profit-seeking principles upon which, it has hitherto been assumed, general prosperity is based.

The obvious primary duty in the present crisis is the relief of the suffering which unemployment has created. We are confident that our people will give to the point of sacrifice for this purpose as long as the need exists.

But this is not enough. It is the duty of society to see that such a crisis does not occur again.

The Church cannot advocate a particular method, but we call upon the employers in our communion to labor for the adoption of a plan or plans which shall coördinate production and consumption, insure continuity of employment, and provide security of income to the workers of the nation.

Unemployment, however, is but a symptom of underlying selfishness. The Church must insist that every financial question is essentially one of human relations.

Until business is converted and is conducted as in the sight of God, who is the Father of all men, no change in technique will be of permanent value.

The profit-seeking motive must give way to that of service....

Economic distress and political unrest are aggravated by the present state of international relations. Progress here, in comparison with the amazingly rapid progress in other departments of life, has been painfully slow.

We, with the cave man, still depend upon force, the only difference being that his club has developed into vastly more efficient agents of destruction.

The peoples of the world are hungry for peace and ready to trust one another, while professional patriots in every land and all too many political leaders still adhere to prehistoric ways.

The reliance upon force is based on fear and mistrust, and it is for Christians to convince the leaders of the nations that the risk involved in trusting one another is far less grave than the consequences of mutual distrust.

The most hopeful step toward world peace ever taken is the agreement signed by fifty-eight nations to abandon war as an instrument of national policy. Yet the powers most active in promoting that agreement have shown a persistent disregard of its logical inferences and continue to put their trust in armed preparedness.

We covet for our country the courage to lead along the pathway of world peace by doing its utmost, even at the cost of risk and sacrifice, to achieve immediate substantial reduction of armaments and, above all, by more general and whole-hearted coöperation and conference with the nations of the world, especially through official participation in such existing international agencies as tend toward world peace.

We believe such a course would have far more weight with other nations and do more to restore confidence than any official utterance. It seems as if the point had now been reached when the nations must choose whether the pagan principles of force and deceit shall continue to determine their dealings with each other, or whether Christian principles of justice, mercy, and good-will shall prevail....

In all our thinking upon the conditions in which we find ourselves, it is necessary to see the world as a unit. Geographically, it has become such. The mountains and seas which once separated nation from nation have lost their meaning, and, in an area no longer divided into separate compartments, racial and economic barriers to intercommunication are doomed.

The spiritual barriers of prejudice and suspicion, based as they are upon the age-long habits of more or less self-sufficient groups, can be dissolved only by the will to recognize the unity of mankind.

No economic methods can meet the physical necessities of the people which are not conceived in terms of the whole.

No international relations can be stable which are not universal in their scope, no moral standards permanent which are not valid for all men. No salvation is possible unless it includes all mankind.

This world view has been the Christian attitude from the beginning. The ideal has never faded altogether, though the divisive influence of group loyalties and animosities has obscured it and prevented its realization.

But it must be evident now to every thoughtful Christian that we can no longer blind ourselves to the implications of our charter.

Here lies the justification of the missionary program of the Church. There is no such thing as foreign missions. If we really believe that God has made of one blood all nations of men to dwell on the face of the whole earth, we must follow the implications of this truth in all areas of human interest wherever it may lead.

How simple, yet how difficult; but nothing less is our Christian calling, and only by being true to it will we do our part to bring near that great day of the Kingdom of our God and of His Christ.

Brethren, may the Grace of God be with us all.

THE APPEAL OF THE FEDERAL COUNCIL OF THE CHURCHES OF CHRIST IN AMERICA

In September, 1931, the Commission on the Church and Social Service of the Federal Council of the Churches of Christ prepared a special message to be read in the churches on Labor Sunday. This document follows:

ECONOMIC SECURITY — A DEMAND OF BROTHERHOOD

During the past year we have seen millions of men and women tramping the streets looking for jobs, seeking help in churches and police stations, standing in bread lines, and waiting in the vestibules of relief societies. This army of unemployed has been composed, not merely of the inefficients of our industrial system, although they are the first to suffer, but chiefly of the manual and cleri-

cal workers upon whose competent labor we have all
depended for the necessities of life. Such conditions have
constituted a serious indictment of our economic organization both as to its efficiency and its moral character.

Comprehensive and reliable figures of unemployment
in the United States are lacking, yet we know that there
was a decrease of 750,000 in the number of workers employed in the manufacturing plants reporting to the
United States Department of Labor between October,
1929, and January, 1931. Employment on Class One
railroads declined seventeen per cent in the twelve
months following October, 1929, with a total eviction
from the industry during that period of nearly 300,000
men. The number of persons unemployed in the United
States last winter, according to the United States Department of Commerce, exceeded six millions.

PERMANENT PREVENTIVES OF UNEMPLOYMENT

The first need in the presence of such an emergency as
that of 1929–31 is, of course, relief. However, an intelligent, self-reliant society will exercise forethought and
take action to the end that the necessity for such relief
may be abolished. It will frankly face the fact that
twenty times since 1855 our country has passed through
business depressions. Eight of these may be classed as
major economic disturbances. Are we to continue indefinitely to drift into such situations through lack of
any adequate social planning?

In order to make progress toward a society organized
on the basis of justice and brotherhood, we need to raise
vital questions with respect to the present economic
order. When prosperity shall have returned, is it to be
the same kind that we have known in the past? History
indicates that a return to such prosperity will be only
temporary and that another depression with its human
suffering will follow unless fundamental changes are made.

It is not possible to treat, and we shall not attempt even to enumerate, here the many and complex reasons for business depressions. Many economists tell us, however, that one of these reasons lies in the present distribution of wealth and income. This phase of the matter is also peculiarly a problem of brotherhood and therefore of particular concern to religion. Five hundred and four persons in the United States, according to preliminary 1929 income-tax returns, each had an income of one million dollars or over. Thirty-six of these each had an income of five millions or over. The average income of this group of thirty-six was over $9,700,000. A careful estimate made by Dr. Willford I. King, of the National Bureau of Economic Research, indicates the following approximate distribution of wealth in the United States in 1921: one per cent of property-owners held thirty-three per cent of the wealth, while ten per cent owned sixty-four per cent of the wealth. On the other hand, the Bureau reports that the average earnings of all wage-earners attached to industries in 1927 amounted to $1205, or $23.17 a week. It is to be remembered that even these average earnings do not indicate the income of the least privileged, since millions must fall below the average. Such a distribution of wealth and income concentrates wealth largely in the hands of the few, while it leaves the masses of workers with insufficient income to buy the goods which, with the help of modern machinery, they are now able to produce. Hence we have what is called 'overproduction,' but which, perhaps, should be called 'underconsumption.' Purchasing power has not been scientifically adjusted to production. Apparently it can be thus adjusted only as we move in the direction of a more equitable distribution of income which Jesus' principle of love and brotherhood also calls for.

A NEW STATUS FOR INDUSTRIAL WORKERS

Unfortunately, business is so organized as to give greater security to investors than to wage-earners, the greater emphasis still being upon security of property. Reserves are commonly set aside in good years for the payment of dividends while in most cases no similar reserves have been made to stabilize the workers' income. In 1930, when unemployment was severe, the total dividends paid by industrial, traction, and railroad corporations, according to the Standard Statistics Company, amounted to $318,600,000 more than those paid in the prosperous year of 1929, while at the same time the index of factory payrolls of the Federal Reserve Board showed that total wage payments decreased about twenty per cent from the total paid in 1929.

That there are grave imperfections in an economic order which make possible the stark contrast of vast fortunes and breadlines is obvious. Society must turn its attention increasingly to the unsoundness of the present distribution of the national income, and to the control of the money-making spirit which lies behind it. Public sentiment must also turn against the amassing of property, especially through stock speculation, without regard for social consequences. New emphasis must rather be laid upon the Christian motive of service.

It is essential that we should have a new concept of the position and needs of all the workers and producers in the modern world. Society now treats millions of them, in times of depression, as if they were dependents, hangers-on, social liabilities. As a matter of fact, they are the very foundation of our economic structure. Justice, not charity, is the basic demand of the situation. That the worker is in theory entitled to a living wage is readily granted. But a living wage is generally conceived of as a sum that will purchase the necessities of life during

the time that the producer is at work. We must extend
the concept to cover all of a worker's life, including the
two periods at the beginning and at the end — childhood
and old age — when one cannot earn. This suggests an
ample wage during employment, stabilization of employment, and adequate protection against interruptions
in the opportunity to earn by methods which will preserve the initiative and independence of the worker, but
at the same time safeguard the family income by such
provisions as workmen's compensation, health insurance,
unemployment insurance, maternity benefits, and old-
age pensions.

ECONOMIC PLANNING

Before these great objectives can be fully attained, we
shall have to seek a new strategy in the organization of
society itself. Our economic life now seems to be largely
without a chart. The best minds of the nation are needed
for the reconstruction of our social and economic life on
sound religious principles. Our hit-or-miss economy is
noteworthy for its lack of direction and social purpose.
For this there must be substituted a system of national
planning, adjusted to world-wide trends. The world is
an economic unit. We do not live unto ourselves. Unless
the dawning recognition of this fact is quickly incorpo-
rated into our national policy, unendurable misery and
chaos will result.

The facts of the situation themselves constitute a
challenge to the churches to assume their rightful place
of ethical leadership, to demand fundamental changes in
present economic conditions, to protest against the selfish desire for wealth as the principal motive of industry;
to insist upon the creation of an industrial society which
shall have as its purpose economic security and freedom
for the masses of mankind, 'even these least, my brethren'; to seek the development of a social order which shall
be based upon Jesus' principles of love and brotherhood.

No MAN of large responsibilities in American life commands more respect in this country than Mr. Daniel Willard, President of the Baltimore and Ohio Railroad Company. In the midst of his pressing administrative duties he finds time to render public service in many directions and, what is even more important, to give thoughtful consideration to the currents of opinion that are carrying the nation forward to its future. On the occasion of the fiftieth anniversary of the Wharton School in the University of Pennsylvania, on March 27, 1931, Mr. Willard delivered a weighty address on the work of the School: 'Its Field in a Changing World.' In the course of his paper he dealt sagely with the function of higher education in our changing society and the problems awaiting solution at the hands of educational leaders. He emphasized especially the novel conditions of contemporary life and laid great stress on the necessity of making modifications in the capitalist system for the purpose of preventing the repetition of such disasters as broke upon the country in 1929.

THE VIEWS OF MR. DANIEL WILLARD

We cannot recall too frequently that we are living in a period of changing conditions, such as has probably never before existed. When I was a boy it seemed to me at least — and it seemed to be accepted generally by others — that most, if not all, of our fundamental institutions had been definitely determined and fixed for all time — how, I did not know, but at any rate fixed beyond discussion, almost beyond question. I have in mind, among others,

matters such as the following: The superiority of our
form of government, the status of the Bible as our rule
and guide of life, the place and authority of religion, the
so-called capitalistic system, based upon the right of
private ownership of property, the marriage contract,
which is the basis of our family life, the calendar and the
number of months in the year. I repeat — fifty years ago
these questions were generally considered as settled. Now
all these are under attack and all are slowly but none
the less surely going through a process of questioning and
of reassessment which may leave them better or worse,
but will certainly mean modification wherever and whenever it is believed by the majority of those affected that
change or modification will promote the best interests
of humanity. What the result of it all will be no one is
wise enough to foresee or foretell at the present time.

I do not suggest that all of these problems of human
relations fall within the scope of Wharton's field of activities, but I do believe that at least one of them does and
that, too, in double measure, because it involves, not
only a question of economics in its broadest sense, but
also a question of government, and the founder of
Wharton referred to each of these questions as being
within the scope of his vision.

The capitalistic system, which is the basis of our entire
political and economic structure, supplies the particular
problem which I have in mind. There are those who are
unceasing in their efforts to discredit it, to undermine it,
to cripple it, to destroy it. What are we who believe in
it doing to uphold and protect it? I admit that those who
seek to destroy or displace it may be as honest and well-
meaning in their intentions and beliefs as I think I am;
even so, I believe they are mistaken. With all its defects,
and doubtless there are many, the capitalistic system, in
my opinion, affords a better and fairer basis upon which
to build an economic structure than any other system so

far devised and tested by man. Feeling as I do, I am
deeply desirous that it should be perpetuated in order
that my children and their children shall be given the
opportunity of living under the same general conditions
that I have lived under, but made better and fairer
wherever possible to do so. We are deeply jealous of the
good name of those we love. We should be no less concerned in the welfare of the institutions under which we
live. We should be the first to recognize their defects and
should seek untiringly to correct them. While, doubtless,
there are many defects in the capitalistic system, which
is the basis of our political and economic institutions, I
shall refer to only two at this time.

A system — call it what you will — under which it is
possible for five or six millions of willing and able-bodied
men to be out of work and unable to secure work for
months at a time, and with no other source of income,
cannot be said to be perfect or even satisfactory; on the
contrary, it can be said to have failed in at least one very
important detail. I can think of nothing more deplorable
than the condition of a man, able and anxious to work,
but unable to secure work, with no resources but his
labor and, perhaps, with others even more helpless, dependent upon him. Unless he is willing to starve and
see those who justly look to him for support also starve,
his only alternative is to seek charity and, failing in that,
to steal. While I do not like to say so, I would be less
than candid if I did not say that in such circumstances
I would steal before I would starve.

The unemployment problem is not new, nor is it confined to this country, or even to times of general depression, but we have all come to see more clearly than ever
before that the mere existence of the problem presents a
serious challenge to our entire economic system. While
practically everyone agrees that the problem is a serious
and difficult one, no one apparently knows just how it

ought to be solved; at any rate, no one has yet announced a formula for its solution in such clear and definite terms as to carry conviction — hence your opportunity. First of all we must have the facts, and all of them. We must have a clear statement of what the problem really is, and what it will probably lead to if not corrected. This much having been done, and it has not yet been done, the rest should not be difficult. It is not now the duty of anyone in particular to find the solution of this problem, but it is the concern of all of us that the right solution should be found.

The second and the only other problem that I shall venture to discuss at this time is bound up closely with the first, and it may be indicated by the following statement: The United States is, perhaps, the richest country in the world in natural and humanistic resources. We have more coal, more oil, more copper, more iron, and more standing timber than we will require, if prudently used, for many generations yet to come. We can produce more wheat, corn, oats, cotton, and animal products than we can possibly consume, and we are holding millions of bushels of surplus wheat in elevators at government expense waiting for a market. We have a productive capacity in our mills and factories far beyond our own domestic requirements, and at the same time, and with all this surplus of wealth and resources, we have millions, so it is said, in dire need of food and clothing — in short, more of everything to eat and wear than we can possibly use, and at the same time millions of human beings hungry and cold. That is another problem, although closely related to the first, and the two problems together — unemployment and the distribution of resources — bring into question the very foundations of that political and economic system which the founder of this institution believed in and desired to perpetuate.

THE NATIONAL CIVIC FEDERATION ISSUES
A MANIFESTO ON PLANNING

If sober conservatism is an evidence of sanity, then the National Civic Federation is the sanest of our national associations. Composed of representatives of capital, labor, and the general public, it has long defended the capitalist system against all attacks from the Left and has been one of the most active bodies in ferreting out and suppressing radical opinions in matters economic. Nevertheless, on June 3, 1931, the acting president of the Civic Federation, Mr. Matthew Woll, also vice-president of the American Federation of Labor, in an open letter to the Honorable James W. Gerard, chairman of the Civic Federation's commission on industrial inquiry, asked that a national industrial congress be summoned to prepare plans for the stabilization of industry. In the body of his letter, Mr. Woll made the following comments on the economic crisis and measures of prevention and avoidance:

The great depression now upon us, after two years, has forced us to the conclusion that the time for action has arrived, so that the hopes of men may be translated into deeds of a character that will maintain for America that magnificent leadership in the whole field of human well-being that was asserted first in 1776 and that has never been lost.

It is not necessary here to attempt any diagnosis of today's lack of adjustment and it is not at all certain that we need at this time greatly to concern ourselves with too much detail regarding precisely what is wrong. It is much more important that we strive to create working machinery to promote social safety and economic stability.

If it can be agreed that there is maladjustment in industry, then we face the inevitable conclusion that the essential thing is to promote adjustment.

Knowing that there is maladjustment — or else we should not have idle factories, hungry men and women, bulging banks and shattered stock values — we must have in mind at the same time the tremendous fact of Soviet Russia and the parallel menace of social disorder within our own borders because of our own failures. We must have in mind also the fact that Europe is bound by traditions, jealousies, and limitations that compel us to go forward alone, as we so often have done.

It appears to me that bold measures are required — but mere boldness is not enough. We must have bold measures that are bold because they strike hard against what is wrong and promise sweeping elimination of maladjustment.

We may proceed with great safety upon the assumption that, if lack of industrial balance continues, we shall continue in our failure to feed our people, we shall continue in our failure to use our industrial capacity, we shall continue to have on one hand enormous wealth and on the other hand great valleys of want. This nation cannot in safety continue in that way.

There is a growing conviction that unless industry — using the term in its broadest and most comprehensive sense — finds and applies a remedy, the Federal Government will attempt to find and apply a remedy. It has been and is the conviction of organized labor in America that political government, valuable above price in its field, lacks the competency to govern industry. Industry must find and apply its own measures of guidance. And it must do this through correlations of its own essential parts or divisions....

The time has arrived for the conscious, organized development of coöperation in all industry, for the development of fundamentally democratic processes by which industry can bring about that balance which is essential to the welfare and perhaps to the safety of our nation.

All functional groups must come into ordered relationship with each other, developing legislative methods, contriving checks and balances, leading toward government of industry by industry, preserving within industry the opportunity for private initiative and profit, but marking out a greater goal for industry than it has ever known — the proper service to a nation of human beings.

To attempt to lay down a pattern or program would be discounting the capacity of industry for democratic functioning. The pattern must develop in the field wherein it is to be applied. It must come out of discussion, effort, thought, trial, and experimentation.

But we have proceeded so far along the road that it is not discounting the capacity of industry now to suggest that there be a coming-together for united effort, for the construction of a great new organized effort, knitting together the democratic efforts of many separated fields. The marvel of our time is that we have so large a degree of competent organization throughout industry, but so little coördination of that mass of organization. We have several hundred active, functional organizations within industry, but only to the most meager extent do they know each other or realize that they have a common problem upon which they must bend their efforts in unison and unity.

Our position is much as if we had forty-eight states, but no union of states — as if we had hundreds of communities, but no bond of government between them. We have in industry about the same chaos and misunderstanding and misapplication of energy that we should have in our political life if our various local community organizations were not brought together in an harmonious whole by a national system of government, or of working harness, developed out of practice and accepted by common consent.

I propose, therefore, that the time has arrived to begin the effort to create for the communities and the states and the sections of industry what our forefathers did when they wove a nation around the scattered, yet related, communities of our continent.

I see no sufficient gain to be derived out of anything less than a tremendous effort. I see no sufficient good to be gained through creeping with undue caution. The trials of our time do not permit long waiting.

We need, for example, to meet the cold-blooded communist five-year plan, with a warm-blooded ten-year plan of democratic idealism woven into the very pattern of our national fabric. We need to move with giant strides to put six million Americans to work, to start our machinery, to take out of our national economy the awful loss and pain of too much or too little. We need to take steps that will take as much account of the shameful fact that our average industrial wage is but a pittance of $1308 a year as we take of our million-dollar reserves and our brilliantly executed skyscrapers.

To avoid the merely showy thing and to get at the big and vital thing, I propose that the National Civic Federation summon a great American congress of industry, to be composed of representatives of all forms and characters of industrial organizations already in existence, to ascertain and evaluate all essential economic and industrial factors, to estimate our probable and normal industrial and commercial growth, say for the next ten years, to determine, as far as human knowledge and foresight permit, the tendency of new fields of industrial activity and changes within our present scheme of things, thereafter to seek coördination for the promotion of industrial balance and to begin that march toward permanence of machinery without which we cannot infuse into

industry that democratic urge and authority vital to
its life as a field of human endeavor and vital to its salvation from an onslaught of state political control that
cannot be avoided in the absence of self-control.

I propose that the National Civic Federation undertake the summoning of this great congress because the
National Civic Federation occupies a place unique in our
national life as the platform of employers and employed
alike — the one place where both have been able to join
in accord.

It is vital that such a congress be composed of those
who represent and who can speak and act for organizations. We should bring organizations together, not create
organizations. Let us call the industrial states together
that they may write the constitution of a new democracy
and provide ways and means by which all our economic,
individual, and commercial activities can be carried out
in an orderly manner, freed as much as possible from a
hit-or-miss basis, and inspired by the noble impulse of
having industry serve all our people and in a manner
calculated to benefit all and without destroying or vitiat-
ing the principles and incentives or destroying the voluntary institutions and organizations that have made for
our nation's growth and have gained for our people the
industrial leadership of the world.

A short time after the publication of the above letter,
Mr. Woll explained in some detail the purposes of his
communication in an address broadcast by radio on a
national hook-up. In particular he dwelt upon the possible functions of such an industrial congress as the Civic
Federation was about to call:

I have proposed that the principal aim should be to
begin the task of building a great national structure that
can function in accord with the fundamental principles

of democracy for the purpose of bringing about a better service to humanity on the part of American industry, using that term in its very broadest sense, for the purpose of finding and removing the maladjustment that has caused our present national suffering and for the purpose, in brief, of making things work as well as may be humanly possible.

It is proposed to bring about an authorized, representative gathering of persons who can speak for the economic forces of the nation; and to make a beginning in the voluntary adoption of rules of procedure and the initiation of operations which shall lead to the construction of a national scheme of economic operation. This must include industry, trade, transport, agriculture, labor, extraction of raw materials, credit and finance channels, and service equipment.

Such a plan of economic balancing should embrace the determination of the annual national human requirements in commodities and service, say for an ensuing ten years; the immediate visible supply of required commodities; the apportioning of required labor hours for the required production and handling, to point of consumption, of such commodities; the character and extent of industrial equipment required to guide intelligently the task of its design, construction, and installation; the immediate and continuing distribution of the necessities of life among the entire population, using all resources of employment, manufacture, and credit distribution requisite to that end; and the outline of legal enactments necessary and convenient to remove obstacles and to facilitate the operations of the suggested program.

It would be folly for me to set out a definite and all-inclusive program and seek to outline in every detail the method by which an organized economic world shall proceed to bring about balance and smooth functioning. I have faith in our democratic methods. We must have faith in the capacity of an organized world. We must have faith in the possibility of taking out of our life the uncertainty and the waste and the maladjustment that have produced panic after panic, depression after depression, and that have never yet found their way to do their best for humanity.

The congress of industry that is in mind should outline its own course and direct its own destiny. The institution should be permanent and the congress itself will have to work out its own plan for self-perpetuation. If there is not a permanent structure, there will be no cure, because the whole operation of our industrial and economic life is changing and with ever-increasing speed. We must be able to make adjustments all along the line whenever anything is definitely or materially changed at any one point.

An invention or a chemical discovery may wipe out whole industries and create new ones, sending dislocation along the line in one repercussion after another. The relation between output and primary effort is changing constantly. The relation between labor effort expended and output is changing constantly. There must be constant readjustment.

In my proposal to Judge Gerard I spoke of a warm-blooded ten-year plan based on democratic realism. If we can bring ourselves to look forward and to plan forward for as many as ten years, we shall, I am confident, never cease looking forward and planning forward.

American organized labor is committed to the fundamental philosophy underlying the proposal which Judge Gerard has forwarded to organized industry in all of its departments and phases. It offers what labor believes to be the basis of a sound social structure that will bring justice to our people and that will build its own defense against subversive movements. Revolutionists can make no headway against institutions that satisfy human needs, that deal justly with all people, and that derive their authority from 'the consent of the governed.'

Today we are desperately trying to recover from the penalty of not having planned forward. We are a nation in misery because of our lack of organized intelligence regarding future operations. Over our heads there hangs constantly the threat of dissolution unless we do better with the machinery at our command. We cannot afford to drift. We cannot afford any more depressions. We cannot afford any more armies of six millions unemployed and millions more underemployed.

It is more and more the belief of thinking men and women that we shall have to make democracy work in our economic life as in our political life. On every hand today there is loss and suffering. If labor is largely unemployed and underemployed, so is capital to a very large extent. If wage-earners are suffering, so too are a great many employers, driven to their wits' ends in a supreme effort to stay alive.

Why should not the various elements in our business, commercial, financial, and agricultural life welcome a movement to make for stability, permanence of prosperity, and an absence of the mountainous ups and downs of the past? We have at hand the machinery for a national life that can be made stable, satisfying, ennobling, and cultured as no national life has ever been in all history. It needs but the application of organized control, self-imposed and rooted in the philosophy of voluntarism, to bring that about.

Only a few days ago and since publication of this proposal Sir Arthur Salter, Director of the Economic and Finance Section of the League of Nations, advised American business that our present economic system, now on trial before the public of the world, has lost none of its power to increase productive capacity, but is more and more open to criticism as being unable to utilize that

capacity with a tolerable degree of justice. In pointing
to the need for collective leadership, he said:

We are in an intermediate stage between the automatic
adjustment of supply and demand through keen individual
competition and its deliberate adjusting by collective planning
and direction. In these circumstances we have the three
alternatives — chaos, collective control, or collective leadership.

Certainly, no one desires chaos. We have already had
too much of chaotic results. Unquestionably the over-
whelming majority of our people do not favor collective
control by the State. Soviet Russia presents a splendid
example of extreme control by the State. The only desirable and advisable choice left, therefore, is that of collective leadership. Unless we do arouse ourselves as a
people and put forward the superior claims and realities
of collective leadership in our economic and industrial
life, we may, even against our better judgment, be forced
to accept a modified form of collective control by the
State instead of chaos due to an extreme selfish, un-
bridled, uncontrolled, and leaderless individualism.

It is true that we, as a people and as a nation, have
before us boundless opportunities for further development and that there is no lack of raw materials, whether
mineral, textile, or foodstuffs, nor of mechanical equipment, capital, or human skill and labor. It is equally
true that we have a vast system of production and transportation created by generations of great productive
leadership.

It is likewise true that different industries have
planned and are planning for the future. And yet, despite
all these plannings and plenty and our remarkable system
of production, the mines, the mills, the factories, the
railroads, the workshops, and other places of employment
are standing idle with approximately six millions of men

and women unemployed and with probably a larger number underemployed.

While we are not lacking in materials, equipment, productive organizations, and economic opportunities, and while there has been some planning in some industries, there has been no collective planning and development of collective leadership in rationally coördinating these essential factors of civilization.

The leadership in this task of rationalization of America's resources cannot come from one man or any particular group of men. It must come from and be comprised of the efficient elements of intelligence in every field and quarter of our complex organism. Neither must such a process of rationalization be destructive of the fundamental principles and free institutions which have made for our greatness as a nation, and I cannot possibly conceive how thought, discussion, and conference, and the development of an industrial congress, free from state domination and control, can do other than produce improvement and give added opportunity for expression of choice and action to the individual.

Our people have taken the lead in all great economic movements for a hundred years, whether of production, of designing, of planning of equipment, of organization of industrial and commercial processes, of training and coördination of human labor. It is unthinkable that America can consent to face such a problem, with all of its physical, mental, and moral endowment, and permit itself to be found sitting idly, waiting for the 'ferment' to settle, quiescent, hoping somehow we will 'muddle through.'

The responsibility of conceiving, planning, and constructing a humanly rationalized arrangement and uses of the resources which stand between humanity and chaos is ours and we must look to ourselves rather than to the State to undertake this task.

There is nothing magical or mystical in the proposal offered through Judge Gerard. No questionable theory is involved. No grandiose picture of a people released from work is set forth. No 'ism' or 'itis' is included. We have before us just a very simple, very American proposal to carry organization into the great step, so that we may relate the various parts of our life, one to the other, in order that one may function in relation to and in harmony with the other.

If we can take this logical step, it is my very humble belief that the United States of America will give the world another blessing to stand beside and complement the blessing our nation gave the world when the states came together and united their fortunes in a common undertaking based upon government by the consent of the governed, establishing human freedom and for the first time making human happiness a national aim and a constitutional issue. For an enlightened people happiness is based upon freedom and justice. Our democracy will move forward to its logical destiny, if we can now bring about this step. And if we succeed, and succeed we must, our democracy will be forever unassailable either from within or without.

CHAPTER V

MUST WE REDUCE OUR STANDARD OF LIVING?[1]

By WILLIAM TRUFANT FOSTER and WADDILL CATCHINGS

YEARS ago, Thomas R. Marshall rescued his name from the obscurity allotted to most Vice-Presidents of the United States by announcing that what this country needs is a good five-cent cigar. Not to be outdone, the Governor of the Federal Reserve Bank of Atlanta, Eugene R. Black, has put in his claim for immortality by implying that what this country needs is a five-cent standard of living. 'I do not agree,' he has proclaimed recently, 'with those men who are saying that in America there must be no retrogression from the present high grade of living.... We have been living in an automobile, a Frigidaire, a radio era, and have been sitting in the atmosphere of a Corona-Corona. We cannot pay our debts and continue in that atmosphere. Let us not fool ourselves.'

But if it is good bankers' economics for us to use fewer automobiles, electric refrigerators, and radios, why not use fewer electric lights and go back to candles? Why not give up billion-dollar banks and go back to little strong boxes? Better still, why not emigrate to China in a body? China's standard of living ought to be low enough to satisfy anybody.

Before we take out our passports for China, however, we shall do well to ponder on this fact: we are perfectly able to produce all those automobiles, refrigerators, and radios which worry the Governor. There they are, already produced.

[1] *The Forum*, February, 1931.

By all means, let us not fool ourselves. If we reached a Corona-Corona level in 1929, it was not through wasted spending, but in spite of wasted productive power. Even at the heights of our so-called 'extravagance,' we were not consuming nearly so much as we were able to produce, or even so much as we actually did produce. Indeed, it was general overproduction, not general overconsumption, which worried the business world. Virtually every industry complained, as it still complains, that it had excessive creative capacity. Right now, we have enough productive power to maintain a Corona-Corona-Corona standard of living.

That being the unquestioned fact, it seems incredible that any man should advocate a reduction in the American standard of living. It would be bad enough if Governor Black were the only one who favored making progress backward, for even a single bank officer in high authority can do much toward achieving that end. But Governor Black does not stand alone. His conviction is shared by many other bankers. At the latest convention of the American Bankers' Association, John W. Barton, president of the National Bank Division, insisted that the only way out of the existing business depression is reduced consumption. 'It is folly,' he said, 'to expect to maintain our standard of living against the rest of the world.'

The Bankers' Association added an official word. Its new president, Rome C. Stephenson, announced that the Association would carry on an intensive campaign 'to induce our people to be economical and thrifty in the sense that the French nation is especially endowed.' This, again, means a drastic reduction in our standard of living. If wage-earners in this country bought no more than the people buy in France, they would thereby lose all the gains in real wages which they have made in the last thirty years. Production would fall far below even the present low level. So would employment and payrolls.

SAVING VS. SPENDING

Underlying these exhortations to spend less and save more is at least one fundamental fallacy. Usually it is not plainly stated, but always it is there. Now Thomas F. Wallace, president of the National Association of Mutual Savings Banks, expresses this common error in its baldest form. It is impossible, he says, for any country to save too much. He goes on, logically enough, to declare that the best thing consumers can do right now in order to assist in an economic revival is to put more money into the savings banks — in fact, all the money they do not need for 'necessities.' This, of course, means reducing their spending, and thereby reducing their standard of living.

The president of an association of six hundred banks, with deposits of nearly ten billion dollars, actually advocates less spending, when business activity is twenty-four per cent below normal chiefly because consumers have not spent enough. He advocates more saving, when at least three million of the unemployed are in that plight because consumers have saved too much. He urges the investment of more money in capital equipment, when at least twenty billion dollars' worth of capital equipment is idle because of slackened demand for the output. He advises us to turn over less money to merchants and more to savings banks, after we have increased savings deposits, in a single year, by $267,180,000 and decreased our spending by over ten times that amount.

Most incredible of all, Banker Wallace urges us to entrust the banks with still more money, when they are daily proclaiming, through the lowest interest rates in a decade of banking, that they cannot find responsible borrowers for the savings already entrusted to them. And the reason they cannot find borrowers is because nobody wants to borrow money wherewith to make goods for people who will save their money instead of buying the goods.

It will be a happy day for jobless men and women and their children when industry is freed from the strangling grip of the old fallacy that a country cannot save too much. Right now, the United States *is* saving too much. It is saving gold for which it has no use. It is saving money which will not be needed for increased capital equipment until enough consumers ignore the advice of these bankers and spend more. In fact, nothing in the whole distressed world of business is so obvious as the fact that the nation has already saved too many mills, mines, factories, foundries, tanneries, oil wells, railroads, office buildings, and power plants.

What do we mean by 'too many'? For industry as a whole, there can be but one meaning: too many in relation to reduced consumer demand for the products of industry. Yet the bankers whom we have quoted would still further reduce consumer demand in the process of reducing standards of living.

One cannot help noticing that it is never their own standard of living which the bankers propose to reduce. It is always the standard of living of the rank and file of the wage-earners. Or, if any banker does contemplate a lower level for his own family, it is a level far above the highest level ever reached by ninety per cent of American families. Even so, we should have to agree with these bankers if the United States were unable to produce enough wealth to maintain consumption at the level of recent years. But — we repeat — the United States is abundantly able. Not once since the war has our consumption of wealth even approached our capacity to produce wealth. Not once have we reached the standard of living which is readily attainable.

Nevertheless, Governor Black thinks that we have been wildly extravagant. This is an illusion that afflicts many bankers. It is a kind of occupational disease. Its proper name is financial myopia. As a matter of fact, the people of the United States *as a whole* have *not* been extravagant. Even in the prosperous period of which the Governor complains, the people *as a whole* spent too little. They saved too much — too much in proportion to what they spent, too much in the form of capital goods. In other words, as we have just observed, they put more savings into mills, mines, and machines than their rate of spending called for; they saved more productive equipment than they have since found any way of using. Every banker knows that.

WASTEFUL THRIFT

One of our readers, however, is from Missouri. 'You and Governor Black,' he says, 'flatly contradict each other. What are the facts?'

Here are the facts. In the first quarter of this century, real wages in all manufacturing concerns increased only thirty per cent, while productivity per employee increased fifty-four per cent. In other words, wage-earners produced far more than they had any means of buying. Most of the difference was saved in the form of capital goods, including the automobile, radio, and refrigerator factories of which the Governor complains. In order to find a year which gives any point to the Governor's charge of extravagance, we have to go back to 1919. By 1921, however, both the buying power and the creating power of wage-earners was seventeen per cent above the year 1899.

Since 1921, their creating power has far outrun their buying power. Production has exceeded consumption. In 1923, production was up thirty-eight per cent, but consumption by wage-earners was up only thirty-two per

cent. In 1925, production was up fifty-four per cent, but
consumption was up only thirty per cent. From 1926
until the crash in the stock market, production in general
continued to increase faster than consumption in general.
Not until after the stock-market crash did the reverse
process set in. In other words, it is precisely during these
last twelve months of excessive thrift that the country
has been extravagant, in the sense of using up wealth
faster than it has created it. Saving too much is extravagance.

These are the facts. If Governor Black, or any other
doubter, wishes to verify these facts, he need only consult
the standard work on this subject — 'Real Wages,' by
Paul H. Douglas — or, indeed, the Federal Reserve
Board itself.

If the people of the United States, as a whole, really
had been extravagant spenders in the two years of prosperity which preceded the stock-market crash, a rise of
commodity prices would have announced the fact. But
there was no rise. On the contrary, there was a marked
decline. There is always *inflation* of commodity prices
when dollars go to market faster than goods. That is
what happened during the years 1917–20. On the other
hand, there is always *deflation* when the flow of dollars
does not keep pace with the flow of goods. As a matter of
statistical record, the period 1927–29 was a period of deflation. Both prices and stocks on hand show that consumers as a whole were not buying wealth as rapidly as
they were creating wealth. By no stretch of the imagination can such self-denial be called 'extravagance.'

Even so, it is said, *some* individuals have been living
beyond their means: already they have spent part of the
wages which they hope to receive next year. That, of
course, is true. And it would still be true after we had
further reduced the standard of living of the country as
a whole. Indeed, the immediate effect of a further general

reduction of living standards would be an increase in the number of families who are living beyond their means.

In any event, it is stupid deliberately to penalize an entire nation because some of its citizens are extravagant. If easy-payment plans have been *too* easy for some consumers, let us consider what, if anything, should be done about that. If certain individuals will not, on their own volition, save enough to protect themselves and their families against illness, old age, and unemployment, let us accomplish the desired end by insurance. Let us not make the mistake of trying to change the habits of the improvident by reducing the standard of living of the provident.

But, exclaims Governor Black, 'We cannot have any permanent prosperity when there is a load of debt around our necks!' This illusion is another symptom of financial myopia. Of course some of our citizens owe money to other citizens. Of course some owe money to the banks; if they did not, the banks would have to go out of business. Of course millions of families still have payments to make on their houses; if the building of these houses had not been financed on credit, millions of them would not have been built at all, and unemployment would have caused even more suffering than it has caused. But the people of the United States, as a whole, are not in debt for so much as a single five-cent cigar. On the contrary, the *net* indebtedness of other countries to our government and to our citizens is over sixteen billion dollars.

Again we say, let us not fool ourselves: this country is perfectly able to produce and consume, on a sound economic basis, not only more automobiles and refrigerators and radios than the number which worries the Governor, but also more houses and pianos and vacuum cleaners and washing machines and tractors and all the other products for which now, as always in the past, some citizens are in debt to others. Many bankers agree with us.

It would be helpful right now if these bankers would carry on 'an intensive campaign,' not to lower living standards, but to raise them.

During the fifteen years prior to 1928, we *did* raise our living standards. Prosperity was real. The profits of capital were not mainly paper profits. The profits of labor were scarcely paper profits at all. During this period, as Professor Douglas has shown in his monumental study, the *real* wages of all workers in all manufacturing concerns went up about thirty-four per cent. In other words, for every *three* rugs, rings, ruffles — yes, and radios and refrigerators and other 'luxuries' — which wage-earners could buy in 1913, they could buy *four* in 1928. Even so, as we have shown, the country was not living beyond its means, for productivity increased much more rapidly than wages.

CONSUMPTION MEANS PROSPERITY

How did such prosperity happen? That question brings us to the basic fallacy in the argument of those who, in order to restore prosperity, urge us to cut down our buying of automobiles, radios, and electric refrigerators. For our greatest period of prosperity was precisely the period which saw over ninety per cent of the growth of the automobile, radio, and electric refrigerator industries.

Was there any connection? There certainly was. For these three industries expanded until, directly and indirectly, they put over six billion dollars a year into pay envelopes. Here, again, we must guard against fooling ourselves. If these six billions had not been paid as wages in connection with these new industries, they would not have been paid at all. If we had not made and bought and used the 'luxuries' of which the Governor complains, we should not, in their place, have bought more 'necessities.' We should merely have stayed on a lower plane of living. As a matter of fact, the expansion of bank credit and wages in connection with the expansion of new industries chiefly accounts for our prosperity. It is mainly in that way that we have contrived to *use* instead of *waste* our savings. We did not buy these 'luxuries' because we prospered. It is more to the point to say that we prospered because we bought these 'luxuries.'

But now, by a curious twist of thought, Governor Black and the bankers and business men who agree with him expect to cure bad times by curbing the very forces which made good times. These men are facing squarely in the wrong direction. Reduced spending is not the way back to good times. On the contrary, we shall not restore good times, *no matter what else we do*, until we spend more.

'But,' says the president of the National Bank Division of the American Bankers' Association, 'we cannot expect to maintain our standard of living against the rest of the world.' This is another illusion. During the present depression, it has become common. Not only Banker Barton but many other men talk as if there were something immoral about enjoying a standard of living higher than that of other nations. If not immoral, at least perverse and ungenerous; in any event, impossible.

Why impossible? What has the rest of the world to do with it, anyway? The rest of the world does not object to sending us as much wealth as it has sent in the past. On the contrary, it is eager to send more. It would like to begin by sending, in addition to current imports, about sixteen billion dollars' worth of goods in payment of its present debts. We refuse to accept the goods. To keep them out, we put up higher and higher tariff barriers. However, let us not confuse this matter with tariff theories. A higher standard of living *is* increased consumption of goods. And every nation is eager to have us consume more of its goods. It would profit thereby.

What, then, does Banker Barton mean when he says

that we cannot maintain our standard of living *against* the rest of the world? Why 'against'? Every prolonged rise in our own standard of living has brought higher living standards in every other part of the world. Nearly every nation has sent a commission to us to find out the secret of our prosperity; and we have sent abroad one of our citizens, by the name of Ford, to expose that secret in terms of scientific management, mass production, and high wages. In the past we have rendered other nations the conspicuous service of a conspicuous example. In the future, we shall best serve other nations, not by bringing our own standards down, but by bringing theirs up. 'Against' is a question-begging word. We can and should expect to maintain our standard of living, not *against*, but *for* the rest of the world.

LABOR LEARNS THE TRUTH

The position of organized labor with reference to standards of living used to be as unsound as is the present position of some of our bankers. For a long time, organized labor demanded a 'living wage.' Then came the demand for a 'saving wage,' and presently the demand for a 'culture wage.' But whatever it was called, it was nothing more than somebody's *opinion* concerning what was desirable. Committees were endlessly consulting and figuring, in order to determine 'how much it costs to maintain an average wage-earner's family in health, decency, and security.' The findings were merely opinions. These opinions, however, were presented by labor leaders as grounds for their wage demands.

Such demands have no sound basis. For practical purposes it does not matter how much income is necessary in order to maintain a given standard of living. It does not matter how high anybody *thinks* wages ought to be. The wages which a given concern, or a given industry, or a given country, is able to pay, at any given time and place, is a question of fact. Potential standards of living are determined by production, not by opinions. If, for example, money wages in China were doubled next week, the Chinese people would still be in poverty. The standard of living depends, not on units of currency, but on units of goods.

Five years ago, the American Federation of Labor abandoned its unsound position. Instead, it declared that the real wages of labor should increase in proportion to the productivity of labor. That was the most important decision ever made by organized labor. In making that decision, leaders of labor took a position which bankers and employers will have to take eventually. For capital, as well as labor, can continue to prosper only if real wages — that is to say, standards of living — increase at the same rate as the productivity of labor. In other words, employers of labor can prosper only if they can find a market for the products of labor; but for a market, employers must look chiefly to the laborers themselves.

Now that organized labor, after generations of struggle on untenable grounds, has taken a sound economic position, some of our leaders in banking are taking a position just as untenable as the position which labor has abandoned.

Have the bankers who advocate a lower standard of living considered precisely what that involves? Have they followed their proposal through to its inevitable consequences? What they advocate profoundly affects the happiness of forty million wage-earners and their children. For fifteen years these wage-earners have struggled successfully toward higher living standards. Their hopes have mounted high. Suddenly they are told that there *is* no hope. Progress is over. They must sink back toward the 'cesspool of poverty.' Surely officials of high authority would not lightly issue such a hope-killing decree. Surely they must have thought their way through to the bottom.

Where is the bottom? Where does their program lead? After they have greatly reduced the production of automobiles, radios, refrigerators, and other so-called 'luxuries,' what do they propose to do with the laborers whom they have thus thrown out of jobs? Are the discarded workers to be employed in making 'necessities'? Are they to produce more wheat and rubber, more lumber and leather, more copper and cloth, more boots and shoes, when all such 'necessities' are already overproduced, and after the market for 'necessities' has been further limited by reduction in the wages of the makers of 'luxuries'? No, there will be no hope for jobless men in that direction. What Governor Black really proposes is that we meet the present unemployment emergency by creating more unemployment. Under his plan, no doubt, we could reduce employment and living standards twenty per cent in six months. But how could we stop there? We couldn't. Where is the bottom? If we follow his lead, there isn't any bottom discernible.

Again, after we have reduced our standard of living, what are we to do with the great banking structure which we have created? Shall we put thirty per cent of it out of business? And what shall we do with all the fixed capital which we have laboriously created? At this moment we have every means of carrying on at least thirty per cent more business than we are now carrying on. We have proved it. We have the factories, blast furnaces, farms, mines, oil wells, trucks, railroads, power plants, lumber mills, tanneries, telegraph lines, office buildings, laboratories, and all the other fixed capital which we need. If we elect to reduce our living standards below the present level, we elect to render useless at least twenty billions of productive capital. Most of this capital has been created with the encouragement of the

banks. Much of it is owned by the banks. Now leading
bankers tell us, in effect, that there is nothing we can do
with this capital but to scrap it.

Fortunately, these bankers are mistaken. The way out
of our troubles is not to render existing capital useless,
but to create still more capital. The automobile, radio,
and electric refrigerator industries are not horrible examples. They are inspiring examples. In the future, as in
the past, we shall make real progress by increasing our
equipment for producing 'luxuries.' And buying more of
these 'luxuries.' And bringing forth more inventions.
And developing more new industries. And, in the process,
creating more bank credit and paying more wages. Thus
we shall *use* our savings, instead of *wasting* them. In
short, the way to go ahead is to plan to go ahead, and
not to plan to go backward. 'The emblem of the United
States is still an eagle, not a crab.'

CHAPTER VI
PROPHETS WITHOUT FORESIGHT [1]
By EDWARD ANGLY

ONE of a thousand ways in which the American business executive differs from his counterpart in foreign lands is to be found in his penchant for making predictions. He may be a bit cagey if you ask him how business is, but he isn't likely to toss away an invitation to speak on how he thinks business is going to be next year, or just as soon as it stops being what it is now. I refer to the business man who is big enough to rate a seat on the dais at organization dinners, or who is sufficiently well known to be pestered and flattered by reporters.

Even a casual study of these crystal-gazers of commerce will embed the conclusion that when business is good they generally predict that it will keep on being that way, and that when business is ailing, they confidently say it will recuperate about the time of the next equinox or solstice.

With so many business men talking into microphones and reportorial ears, the presumption must be that the ultimate consumers — the common people and the almost somebodies who hear and read their predictions — find in them sufficient aid, comfort, inspiration, and encouragement, if not guidance, to make it worth the big man's while, and their own, and that of the gentlemen who foot the bills for ether waves and printers' ink. Is it not strange, though, that the custom has not been adopted in other busy, gold-grubbing lands?

Unlike our own eager-eyed and willing-eared populace, the small-fry of Europe work and worry along without

[1] *The Forum*, May, 1931.

much economic enlightenment from on high. The subjects of King George, for example, haven't the slightest
idea what the Right Honorable Montagu C. Norman,
Governor of the Bank of England, thinks business conditions will be in the spring. The citizens of the French
Republic pursue their labors and their pleasures without
any notion of how sound their smiling President, M. Gas-
ton Doumergue, may consider fundamental conditions to
be. M. Emile Moreau of the Bank of France rubs his
hands as the gold pours in, and says nothing. M. Citroen
makes automobiles by day and splurges at baccarat by
night, and if he has a formula for general prosperity, the
Gallic public doesn't know the nature of it. Since S.
Parker Gilbert closed up shop in Berlin, there has been
a similar silence in Germany. It is the same in Italy,
Il Duce excepted, and it is the same in Spain and elsewhere this side of the Red paradise.

Public predictions in the European economic field are
pretty much confined to Soviet Russia, where the ambitious architects of the Five-Year Plan have figured out,
even unto the third and fourth decimal point, the future
of everything — real wages, production, the cost of commodities, the decline of illiteracy, the world demand for
caviar, and the domestic consumption of vodka. If Ivan
Ivanovitch Ivanoff doesn't like it, he may lump it, but
he cannot get away from it. While the big man in capitalistic America and communist Russia is telling the little
man what is going to happen to him and his pocketbook,
people everywhere else seem content to mind their own
business, keep their own counsel, and let the other fellow
guess for himself as to what the future may hold.

For a good many months now, our business prophets
have been telling us that this depression cannot go on
much longer. In many instances these assurances come
from the same authorities who used to get their names in
the papers by explaining why prosperity was going to

continue forever and ever in the United States, whatever might happen in the shabbier, more pedestrian parts of the world. We are told now that people simply must start buying very soon, and the men who say so are those who used to tell us that such a thing as a saturation point no longer existed.

That business men should go on airing their predictions in public seems the more amazing when one considers what happened to the predictions made by them during the seven fat years. In those bright and bustling times there grew up a theory that the business cycle had ceased to exist so far as this country was concerned. The once inevitable loop that old-fashioned economics professors had told us was made up of prosperity, crisis, depression, and revival had been 'ironed out' by American business genius until nothing was left of it except prosperity. We began to hear that every American laborer was becoming a capitalist. Then we read that there was no such a possibility as overproduction.

The newer theory seemed to be that consumption would keep up with production so long as Americans continued to demand a higher and higher standard of living. And breathed there an American with ambition so dead that he would be content to sit under an unmortgaged vine and fig tree, like a lazy European, utterly unwilling to get out and hustle for more and better things for the wife and kiddies? No, a thousand times, no!

The point was simple. One merely had to induce people to crave more commodities and comforts — radios, two-car garages, prismatic bathrooms, whatever else the neighbors possessed. Thus would consumption keep up with production. The stimuli of advertising and the blessed boon of buying on installments would keep the ball rolling merrily along. American mechanical efficiency would maintain the country in high speed even in a shrinking world that was climbing in low or second gear up the long, long hill away from the slough into which the war had bogged it down.

Mass production, involving the use of machinery on a scale of which Europe had never dreamed, was permitting the American industrialist to pay his workers from three to five times the foreigners' scale. Still he was able to deliver his product in world markets at a cheaper price than his backward competitor. Thus the foreigner would remain a good customer, whatever his sentiments against the tariff. The cotton planter of the South and the wheat farmer of the West might be complaining, but the Machine Age was helping everybody else to get richer. And if a machine slowed down, one could merge it with a faster one. Everything was hotsy-totsy and the sky wasn't half way to the limit.

USHERING IN THE MILLENNIUM

One evening, at the start of this, the second winter of our discontent, I bought an apple at a Fifth Avenue corner from one of the workingmen-capitalists of whom I had read. Thus fortified, I entered a library where the prophecies of business men are embalmed for the edification of economists yet unborn. I sought to recapture the spell of the optimistic days.

There they were, those wondrous speeches and interviews of the seven fat years. They began to grow in eloquence about the period when the country was recovering from its return to normalcy under the amiable Warren Gamaliel Harding. By the time my journalistic *confrère*, Mr. Calvin Coolidge, had been in the White House a year, board chairmen the country over were as stuffed with optimism as Mr. Charles M. Schwab. Year by year things were on the up and up. In 1926, all records for production, for wages, for earnings, and for general prosperity were broken. The price of many of the soundest stocks in the country had almost tripled in five years.

Santa Claus that Christmas surpassed all his previous achievements in distribution, and it was noised about that here and there in Wall Street bonuses had amounted in some houses to as much as one hundred per cent of the recipient's salary.

When 1927 arrived, even Colonel Theodore Roosevelt was remarking that 'the country has gone prosperity mad.' E. G. Wilmer, president of Dodge Brothers, Inc., had favored the newspapers with a New Year's message in which he said times were going to get even better still. He laughed at the few bears who were not hibernating, and brushed aside the warnings of the pessimists with the gladsome news that modern business men were 'seeking and finding the solutions of business panic and business depression.' His competitor, Mr. Myron E. Forbes, of the Pierce-Arrow Motor Car Company, assured the nation just one week later that 'so long as people want and are willing to strive for better homes, better clothes, better food, and better recreation, just so long will consumption keep production at growing levels.' And, he added, 'There will be no interruption of our present prosperity.'

The spring of that year brought disastrous floods in the Mississippi Valley, and a strike in the union soft-coal fields, but the steel industry again exceeded all its previous production figures and other industries were riding it out. Europe didn't seem to be doing so well, but that did not worry such Titans of foreign trade as Mr. Victor M. Cutter, of the United Fruit Company. A new era was dawning, he said, which would give to North and South America not only the industrial and economic leadership, but also the cultural leadership of the world.

About that time there was a stock-market slump, but Mr. Mellon drove the bears back into the woods with an *ex-cathedra* bull. He held that brokers' loans were not too high and predicted a growth of general prosperity, whereupon the market rose again. Magnus W. Alexander, president of the National Industrial Conference Board, assured the nation there was 'no reason why there should be any more panics.' The chief economist of the Board, Mr. Virgil Jordan, took a poke at doubting Thomases by saying that 'it was difficult for some economists to abandon the reassuring rhythm of the business cycle.... This favorite cradle of the economists no longer rocks so regularly as it used to.'

The tons of ticker tape that cascaded into Broadway that summer during the receptions to Lindbergh, Chamberlain, and Byrd all recorded higher altitudes for stock prices. In September, Roger Babson, prophet emeritus, admitted he was a bit puzzled by a condition that had never existed before since the keeping of business statistics had become a vocation. Interest rates and commodity prices had gone downward together. Mr. Babson told a group of go-getters who had come to one of his inspirational conferences that declining interest rates had never brought on a panic, and that declining commodity prices had never been followed by good times. In such a situation, Mr. Babson confessed, it was pretty hard to predict what was going to happen next. He recommended caution until the portents became less paradoxical.

A month later, Mr. Melvin A. Traylor, then president of the American Bankers' Association, wrote of 'The Changed Business Cycle.' He told the bankers they need not fear a recurrence of conditions that would plunge the nation 'into the depths of the more violent financial panics such as have occurred in the past.' He remarked that 'more widely prevalent business intelligence, efficiency, and effective facilities for financial coöperation and control on a nation-wide basis tend to reduce the danger of speculation and other excesses bringing about general unsound conditions.'

From Minneapolis, almost within earshot of the bucolic

bellyachers, there came winging over the wires, on the last night of 1927, two tidings for a happy future from Mr. R. B. Sheffield, head of the Commander-Larrabee Corporation. 'The problem of distribution is being solved rapidly,' he said. And then he brought the millennium almost within view of the naked eye by adding: 'The laboring-man is becoming a capitalist.'

Mr. Alexander, too, had a happy forecast that put to shame those who dared suppose Americans would ever have their fill, even temporarily, of motor cars, radios, and other modern blessings. 'The potential demand for manufactured goods is elastic and well-nigh inexhaustible,' he wrote. 'While per capita production and consumption of food have actually declined since the beginning of the century, production of manufactured commodities has increased ninety-one per cent per capita of population. There is no reason why this pace should not be maintained; in fact, it is hard to see how it could be restrained.'

The White House and the Treasury took another squint at the economic skies and assured the country that flying conditions were still perfect for the business kite. A few old conservatives wagged their heads, but their warnings were drowned in a rising crescendo of cocksure optimism. Even Mr. E. H. H. Simmons, who was then president of the New York Stock Exchange, departed from the silent tradition of that office to preach against the pessimists. Talking to the Engineers' Society of Western Pennsylvania, assembled in convention at Pittsburgh, he said: 'I cannot help but raise a dissenting voice to statements which we are hearing today that we are simply living in a fool's paradise, that a saturation point in industry and finance has been reached, and that, having passed its peak, prosperity in this country must necessarily recede and diminish in the future.'

SOME MINOR CHORDS

On a cold, wet day in February, a day provocative of gloomy ruminations, even Mr. Alexander began to speculate whether, after all, the thing wasn't too good to last.

'We must all pause to wonder,' he said to a dinner gathering, 'if this so-called prosperity is of an enduring character.' Unemployment was increasing, especially in the Mid-West. Business was described by the experts as spotty, and was showing signs of hesitancy. Brokers' loans had risen the previous month to almost four and a half billion dollars and, as in 1927, there had been a brief break in the market which the bulls had quickly repaired. This time it was the thrifty Mr. Coolidge who assured the country that he did not consider brokers' loans too high. By April the market was rising again. Even higher interest rates and an outward flow to gold couldn't stop it.

In May, the *American Bankers' Association Journal* said the earnings statements of leading industries had emphasized the impression that a new business cycle was prevailing. But it did not consider that anything 'approaching a general depression' was likely.

In July, candidate Hoover, speaking in California, could see that the outlook everywhere on earth was for the greatest era of commercial expansion in history. The rest of the world, he said, would become better customers of America. In September, Mr. Mellon again assured the country there was no cause for worry and that the high tide of prosperity would continue.

After Mr. Hoover's election in November had guaranteed a full gasoline tank to every citizen for four more years, the previously optimistic Mr. Virgil Jordan began to fear that the rapturous situation was 'rather a state of mind than a fact.' He pointed out that basic industries which were providing people with their fundamental requirements had not shared in the prosperity to the extent enjoyed by the makers of luxuries. But Irving T. Bush pooh-poohed such pessimism as soon as the reporters found him. 'We are only at the beginning of a period which will go down in history as the golden age,' he said, and proceeded to predict ten years more of grand and glorious prosperity.

Even a twelve per cent money rate couldn't dislodge investment holdings as 1928 approached its close. A decline in stock prices in December was followed by a quick recuperation. New Year's Day brought pages and pages of happy predictions from brokers, industrialists, chain-store czars, and business men. The big fish swallowed the little fish in an orgy of mergers, and the innocent bystanders and deposed vice-presidents were kept contented with four-to-one splits in stock.

The story of 1929, with its joy-ride of nine months and twenty days, must still be fresh in the minds and check-stubs of the twenty million workers who were to become capitalists by the simple process of having a broker.

In the gladsome month of May, 1929, Mr. Harry Culver, president of the National Association of Real Estate Boards, pepped up a reunion of realtors by telling them they had 'better get ready for one of the greatest waves of prosperity that this country has ever known.' In June the *American Bankers' Association Journal* figured that the unprecedented pace of business would probably continue even though high money rates had curtailed the flotation of bonds, 'so much so in the case of foreign bonds as to constitute a threat at the country's export trade.' Even in the dog days of midsummer, business was on the boom. That moved the Secretary of Commerce, Robert P. Lamont, to remark that the 'greater foresight of business men in producing and selling commodities had brought about a reduction even of seasonal variations in industrial activity.' Why, there wasn't even a seasonal cycle any more, let alone any thought of a whole long-range business cycle with a down as well as an up!

On August 23 — less than two months before the wonderful new era exploded — an Englishman, Mr. T. E. Gregory, of the London School of Economics, made bold to say that 'the miracle of American prosperity was in part unreal and illusory, a mirage produced by a naïve and undiscriminating optimism.' He made his statement at the Williamstown Institute of Politics. A New York newspaper promptly reminded him that America had learned to accept gratuitous criticism from visiting English lecturers with a pinch of salt and a smile.

A 'creeping bear market' set in with the first frosts of October and reached a crisis stage on October 21. On that day Professor Irving Fisher of Yale, the great proponent of prohibition as a guarantor of prosperity, told the New York Credit Men's Association he believed the breaks of the few preceding days had already 'driven stocks down to hard rock.'

'I believe that we will have a ragged market for a few weeks,' he confessed, 'and that then we shall see the beginning of a mild bull market that will gain momentum next year.' The Professor felt that the investment trusts that had become so popular in America would 'stabilize' the market by buying heavily should the market become unsteady. The next morning, sure enough, prices capered upward again, and Mr. Charles E. Mitchell arrived home from Europe. The Wall Street reporters trooped into the office of the president of the National City Bank to see what Mr. Mitchell had to say. He told them that the decline in stock prices had gone too far 'in certain important directions,' and he 'deplored' the importance attached by the country in general, and Wall Street in particular, to the size of brokers' loans.

The next day, October 23, came the first crash. More

than five billion dollars in lovely paper profits perished, and one hundred and eighty-one stocks reached new lows for the year. The following day nearly thirteen million shares changed hands, but Mr. Mellon said business was 'steady,' and the bankers boasted that they had checked the decline. The next morning President Hoover informed the nation that 'the fundamental business of the country — that is, the production and distribution of commodities — is on a sound and prosperous basis.'

That night, in New York, Mr. Schwab told the American Iron and Steel Institute members that prospects had never been brighter. No, never! 'If the equilibrium between production and consumption is maintained,' he went on, 'there is no reason, in my opinion, why our present prosperity should not continue indefinitely.'

But an awful thing happened to the equilibrium just four days later. In five frantic hours 16,410,030 shares of corporation stock were pitched onto the floor of the Exchange. The new era was all over.

THE POLLYANNAS

But the prophets live on. The new year of 1930 was welcomed by Mr. Mellon with 'every confidence that there will be a revival of activity in the spring.' The Democrats felt the same way about it. John J. Raskob also thought on New Year's Day that 'by early spring business ought to be going ahead at its regular rate.' On January 22, 1930, President Hoover, after a series of conferences with the business leaders of the land, had a vision in which he saw the 'employment trend' already turning for the better. On March 3, the eve of the first anniversary of the administration that was to perpetuate prosperity, Secretary Lamont assured the country that business would be normal in two months. Five days later, Mr. Hoover predicted that unemployment would be ended in sixty days.

The sixty days were up on May 7. About a hundred hours before the deadline, the President, on May 2, made an address in which he expressed the conviction that the worst was over, and that 'with continued unity of effort, we shall rapidly recover.' Railway earnings went on dropping, however, steel prices slipped downward, and the stock market got worse instead of better. When summer came, Mr. Hoover said business would probably be 'normal' by autumn. The dog days of August found cotton and wheat prices tumbling deeper and deeper, but the Secretary of Labor, John J. Davis, visualized the nation as 'on the road to recovery.' Mr. Babson predicted a revival for the autumn, and Mr. Harvey S. Firestone said the country would soon be enjoying the greatest prosperity it had ever known.

On September 22, when the Weather Bureau announced that autumn had arrived, Secretary Lamont said it looked as if the business decline had come to an end. As the press associations were scattering his message to the country, wheat sold in Chicago that afternoon at 77⅛ cents a bushel, the lowest price since July, 1914. The next morning Washington had an explanation. It seems the dastardly Bolsheviks were dumping wheat on the capitalist world.

Down in Virginia, Governor Pollard took an afternoon off to deliver a funeral oration over 'Old Man Depression' and 'Old Lady Pessimism,' who were made to walk the plank of the S.S. *Virginia Lee.* Mr. Ford, on sailing for Europe, expressed the quaint notion that laziness had caused the slump. Mr. Babson, remaining at home to keep an eye on his charts, blamed the depression on a 'general moral relapse.' They both said it would soon be over.

In October, the tradesmen of Philadelphia started a 'Buy Now' campaign, and Mr. Dwight W. Morrow, who used to go about the country telling people to save their money, endorsed it. On October 21, within three weeks of the elections, President Hoover appointed Colonel Arthur Woods to direct employment 'relief' throughout the nation, and the business prophets decided to postpone the return date of prosperity until the spring of 1931.

Finally, in December, a great light dawned upon the Presidential mind. Mr. Hoover sent a message to Congress which contained this ringing phrase: 'Economic depression cannot be cured by legislative action or executive pronouncement.' It did not pass entirely unnoticed that the disillusioned President spelt executive with a small *e*.

Not long ago in a French industrial center, where one must go indoors to buy an apple, a French manufacturer was telling me of his visits to America, in good times and bad.

'We French are perhaps old-fashioned,' he said, 'but we long ago learned, Monsieur, that the sun is not going to shine brightly every day. And if a politician promises us to make the sun shine every day, we have the power, under our system of government, to kick him out at the first drop of rain.'

Chapter VII

DOWN AND OUT IN DETROIT [1]

By Charles R. Walker

I

In 1914 an extraordinary thing occurred in America. An automobile manufacturer in Detroit announced that he was raising wages for common labor to five dollars a day. Newspaper headlines in Detroit went a little crazy; the streets of the city and of the little town of Dearborn were packed with workmen fighting for a chance to work at the new wage. And automobile manufacturers of Detroit and elsewhere raged and gave out desperate interviews prophesying doom. Detectives came to Detroit to investigate Henry Ford. But above all, workmen from all over the United States bought railroad tickets and boarded trains for Detroit. Among the latter was John (once Anton) Boris, American citizen of Slav descent, father of a family, who had ambitions to be a 'miller-wright' and needed cash for an expanding family. He had been a logger in a Michigan lumber camp, then a worker in an Ohio steel mill where he earned from two to three dollars a day. With thousands of others, he now came to Detroit.

'In dose days work was hard all right at Ford's, but dey treat us like mens.' One day the straw boss fired a workman in anger. The employment manager stood between the boss and the workman. 'You can't discharge a man out of spite,' he said. 'I am putting you back to work — both of you — in different shops.' Boris remembered the episode a long time. Another day a boy in his department suggested over their noon sandwiches that

[1] *The Forum*, September, 1931.

they should have a union at Ford's. The boy was a skilled worker with a good record. The next week he did not appear in the millwrights' gang. When Boris asked where he was, his companions raised their shoulders. Boris remembered this, too. He decided not to listen to men talking about unions even though they were 'good miller-wrights.' He decided not to talk about unions himself.

John Boris's wages at Ford's rose steadily as the years passed, till he was making eight dollars a day. His young wife, whom he had found it a delight to cherish as he had promised the priest, had borne him eight children, five of whom were living and going to Michigan schools. One day a letter arrived from a friend in a Texas oil field, saying to come out there for a good job. 'I think I go all right,' he told me, 'can get twenty dollar a day.' But his wife expressed other ideas. 'You stay wid Ford; here steady job — better dan big money for you; las' all de years what you live.' Boris stayed at Ford's.

'The American way,' said the automobile manufac-turers in 1927, 'is to pay wages sufficient to guarantee the workingman not only subsistence, but the comforts and some of the luxuries of life. Let him buy a car, a radio, and an American home!' The children wanted a radio, so John got one; but he resisted his foreman's appeal to buy a car, even though American salesmanship did what it could against his Slavic conservatism. Public advice to 'buy a home,' however, appealed to an instinct. The real estate agent made out his contract. There was a five hundred dollars down payment and fifty dollars a month. He started payments and moved in. The house seemed in a sense to be rounding out his millwright's career for him; and better, he thought, than a car — even though the neighbors boasted of both.

It was in this house, under the shaded light of the 'parlor lamp,' that Boris the other day gave me in his own words the final chapter of this history. The house was subject to foreclosure in default of payment, but the furniture was still intact. The radio stood at the left of the chair where Boris sat; a double door led into a pleasant dining-room.

'Fourteen year,' said Boris, leaning forward, 'I work for Henry Ford. All kin' jobs... millerwright, danger jobs; I put in all my young days Henry Ford. Las' July, what you know, he lay me off. When I go out of factory that day I don' believe; I don' believe he do such ting to me. I tink trouble wid man in de office who don' un'erstan'.' His voice ceased and he took a deep breath which was expended in the earnest emphasis of his next words: 'I tink,' he said, 'I go Henry Ford *pers'nally!* But what you know!' He looked like a boy whom a drunken father had whipped into physical submission. His voice was angry, but with a deep hurt at the core of it. 'I can' get close to him,' he cried, 'I can' get clos' even employment man. De guard say, "We got your name in dere all right, we let you know when we wan' you." Nine mont',' he concluded, 'I go no work.'

II

Figures show that 14.2 per cent of Detroit's normally employed are out of jobs. Other cities follow close, with Cleveland at 13.8 per cent and Chicago at 13.3. The distinction of Detroit, however, is not that she has been hardest hit in the depression, but that she has done something to buck it. Municipal and community leadership — not the manufacturers — are doing what they can.

During the first of his workless periods, Boris was able to support his family and to continue regular payments on his home. Against public pressure he had exercised thrift, and had in reserve a few hundred dollars. But misfortunes did not attack him singly. His wife fell ill and an operation for tumor was demanded. Boris met the emergency and hired the best doctor he could find.

A kidney operation on the woman followed the first, running up medical charges for hospital and doctor to eight hundred dollars. Somewhere during this epoch the son of John Boris, who had gone to an American school and could put matters clearly in written English, composed a letter to the welfare department of the Ford Motor Company.

An 'investigator' arrived promptly, and took the chair, Boris informed me, in which I was sitting. 'Investigator say, "Boris, employment have no right do that to you. You get job back right away. Seven o'clock tomorrow morning you go employment; he put you back on job; tak' this slip."'

Going back the next morning through the high mill gate, with the slip tightly held in his fingers, Boris found delightedly that he was admitted to the office. 'We cannot give you your old job,' they told him, 'at eight dollars a day, but we will give you a new one at six dollars for three days a week.' 'Yes, all right,' said Boris. Lay-off and rehire with a dock of a dollar or two a day is common in the automobile industry. It enables the manufacturer to give the appearance of 'maintaining wages' while effecting the needed economies in his payroll. The same work is performed on 'the new job.' Boris was glad. 'Hard times for everybody,' he explained, 'sure, I take.' The employment manager continued courteously: 'After you work sixty days, you will receive seven dollars a day.'

Walking into the mill after that, he felt light-headed. The roar of it, and the smell of oil, brought tears to his eyes. All day he busied his head over the eighteen dollars, buying food with it, paying the doctor, earning back a small brick house in Highland Park. The smoke from Bessemers as he left the mill was a deep ruddy gold. He hadn't noticed the color since first he worked at Henry Ford's.

On the sixty-first day, Boris received the promised

seven dollars. On the sixty-third his foreman fired him.
'You're finished, Boris,' he said. To Boris it seemed clear
that he had been dropped because he was 'making too
much money.' And because there were thousands waiting
to take his job at minimum pay. But he repressed this
resentment and went to the office. 'Anything wrong wid
my work for comp'ny?' he asked earnestly. No, the employment man assured him; his work was satisfactory.
'Wid my records for comp'ny?' he persisted, knowing
that in hard times a man's record is his friend. 'No,' said
the employment man, 'you have a good record with the
company. But there is no longer any work for you.' The
office then stated that this was not a lay-off, but, as Boris
had expressed it, 'finish.' Boris then exploded. In remi-
niscence of what he had said, his voice came somewhere
from the middle of his chest; it was compacted of fourteen
years of exploded loyalty.

'I haf' no money now,' he cried, 'lose my home quick,
what I do chil'ren, what I do doctor? Fourteen years!' he
returned to his original cry, 'I work Henry Ford!'

The employment man looked at him. 'That is a long
time; you should have saved money, Boris, to take care
of you in your old age.'

Boris trembled. 'You say dat to me!' he cried, struggling for possession of himself. 'I give up my strength to
you; I put in all my young days work good for Henry
Ford — you can' do dis to me now!'

'Why did you spend all your money?' asked the employment man.

'For why? I tell you. I spen' money for house,' replied
John Boris, 'to raise fam'ly, to sen' my chil'ren school,
to buy foods, *dat's how I spen' money* ——'

'Your children are your own business,' said the other,
'not Henry Ford's.'

III

Even in recollection of this episode which terminated his career and hastened the break-up of his family, I was struck by the special character of Boris's resentment. It seemed clear that he was torn as terribly by the blasting of his workman's loyalty as by the enormity of his personal loss.

'I go out from mill,' he continued. 'I try tink what I do help mysel'. Who I go to? I use tink,' he cried, 'if something come like dis, go to Henry Ford yoursel'. But I tell you no workman beeg enough see Henry Ford! Well, I go lawyer — I happen to know him once — who knows ting like dis more what I do. I say: "What can I do now?" He say: "Nutting, John, ain' nutting you can do!"'

John Boris refused to accept the dictum of the lawyer that there was nothing he could do. In accordance with the formula that 'there is plenty of work in the world if a man be willing to take it,' he buried the pride of a skilled maturity, and found a few hours' work in a cushion factory, accepting a wage twenty-seven and one half cents an hour less than Ford's minimum rate in 1914. But long before he managed this, his daughters had taken jobs in the same factory to which he came ultimately. They carried and are still carrying the bulk of the family load.

These latter items make the story of John Boris a relatively lucky one. The family enjoys a small income from wages; John Boris is not, and except only for a few weeks between the time of 'finish' at Ford's and the cushion factory job, has not been rated as one of the unemployed. And he is lucky enough to have escaped charity.

As I was sitting in the Boris parlor, the two girls came in from work. It was nine o'clock. He introduced his daughters to me; they excused themselves and went to the kitchen. John Boris explained: 'Only when they work late, comp'ny give time for supper.' Work begins at seven-thirty; lunch at twelve. 'How late do you work?' I asked the younger girl, when she reappeared. 'Sometimes till nine o'clock,' she answered, 'sometimes till ten. One night last week we worked till eleven-thirty.' I checked up on this and found that in the smaller concerns which have sprung up in the wake of depression, no regularity prevails: the workmen are expected to finish the work available, which sometimes takes five hours, sometimes ten.

'Alice, Louie's girl,' said one of the girls, 'said she felt faint tonight' — it seemed to me that Miss Boris thought Alice a little silly for it — 'so I sent her upstairs to my coat where I keep cookies.'

John Boris had been silent a long time. He moved his shoulders restlessly and looked down at the thick fingers of his hands. 'Las' July,' he said, 'I was good man.' He raised his eyes slowly. 'I ain't man now,' he said.

With some effort I looked into the work of the Ford employment office and of the welfare department of the Ford Motor Company. A comprehensive stagger system I found had been organized to spread work among the largest possible number. Further than this, a sincere effort was being made everywhere to give jobs to the neediest. Boris was dismissed, I am ready to believe, not through carelessness — but because relatively worse cases needed his job more. In fact the wealth of data put before me by the mayor's unemployment committee of the city of Detroit confirms me in the belief that his particular case, in which job, savings, and home were wiped out, was one of the lucky ones.

In addition to Mr. Boris's case, there are 227,000 men totally unemployed. Let us consider some of these. Out of the number, fifteen thousand are reported homeless. Boris as yet is not of this class and will probably escape it by living with relatives. These men are now housed in the 'emergency lodges,' better known as 'flop houses,' which are maintained at the city's expense. What are they like? Take the 'Fisher East Side Lodge.' It is a huge unused factory building lent to the city by Fisher Brothers and housing, when I visited it, sixteen hundred men. Here I found bank tellers with twenty to thirty years' experience, traveling salesmen, expert toolmakers, a vice-president or two, and workmen of every variety.

The mayor's committee estimates that of the 'homeless men' on their records, about ten per cent are chronic vagrants who would be looking for hand-outs in fat times as well as lean. The rest are *bona-fide* unemployment cases with a large white-collar sprinkling. Fifteen thousand homeless is considered large for the size of the city and is generally attributed by manufacturers I talked with to the army of unmarried men attracted to Detroit by the high wages and short hours of the automobile factories. But I discovered that over ten per cent of the homeless group are married men. These are perhaps the least fortunate cases, as contrasted with the relatively fortunate who, like Boris, still command resources of a sort. What is their history? What, for example, becomes of the wife, and what happens to the kids? The story of the married homeless averages as follows. (I am omitting the cases of suicide and actual starvation.)

A majority of the men are automobile workers; the average age is thirty-eight. Fifteen years ago they came to Detroit attracted by the good wages. A considerable number are college men; as skilled workers, tool designers, and engineers, they made from ten to fifteen dollars a day. They laughed at their white-collar classmates making forty per — and obliged to 'keep up appearances.' The ordinary workers among them were making five dollars a day, or six dollars, or seven dollars, with steady jobs. They married, bought a car, and ultimately started payments on a 'home of their own.'

About six years ago the 'inventory period' of the manufacturers began to stretch. From two weeks' 'vacation' in summer — without pay — it edged up to a month. 'Changing tools' for the new model, repair periods, 'reorganization,' sliced another week or two from the winter months. As a rule the single man didn't care; for him it *was* a vacation. But his married brother got fidgety. He hadn't rigged his budget for a ten-month year. Then among Ford men came the five months' shutdown in 1927. This wiped out a good many surpluses. The surpluses were not large. Why? Most of the men had bought a car, had taken out insurance, and begun payments on the 'home.' By 1929, the family men were worried. Not in a panic, but thinking hard. They still had their homes, they still had the car, but their savings were gone. The expanding vacations gave them an increasing sense of insecurity.

IV

Then descended the first months of the depression a year and a half ago. They were caught in the lay-off which everyone from their employers to the President of the United States assured them was a temporary dip in the cycle of prosperity. The first act of the conservative householder was to sell his car — the purchase of which a year before had been all but compelled by company salesmanship. 'It is your duty,' the married man had been told; 'it will guarantee your job.' Two months passed. Just as the newspapers agreed that the 'worst was over,' the married man borrowed four hundred dollars on his furniture. This to keep his end up, to continue payment on his home, pay his insurance premiums, buy food, and keep the boy at school. At this point he had adopted his employers' optimism. 'Things *must* pick up. In another

month I'll be back at work.' But the month passes, and
the furniture goes to meet the loan.   However, there is
the hundred dollars which Alice hasn't told him about.
With it he manages one more payment on the house, hoping that the rumor about a 'pick-up' at Fisher's will come
true. It doesn't.

In a Michigan 'land contract' the owner holds the
deed; in case of the tenant's default, payments go to the
deed-holder. At this point his contract is foreclosed, and
with the house passes forever the three thousand dollars
paid to date toward ownership. The children, who have
been denied milk for a couple of months, are now sent to
grandmother's, or parked around among relatives. The
married man and his wife move into two rooms in the suburbs she had always scorned. With the change there
passes into discard the emotions which cling to a united
family, and to the home as a physical possession, somehow defensible.

The married man, however, at this point is really just
beginning to fight. He tells his wife this in as many
words. With the burden of the kids off his mind, and
with no payments to make on the lost home, he is ready
for any kind of work at any pay. It is the mood endorsed
by so many well-wishers who themselves are in more
fortunate positions. And he gets the work. Any number
of young men found a month's neighborhood work, repairing the front steps, trimming hedges, mowing the
lawn, or cleaning out the furnace — at a dollar a day, or
two.

But this permits a physical subsistence only; it doesn't
constitute what the married man hopes for and desires
passionately — the beginnings of rehabilitation. After a
couple of months the odd-job market is exhausted, and he
has learned either to pity or to despise himself. The mental attitude of his new employers is, I find, almost without exception a compound of self-interest and charity.

They demand two things of the ex-tool-maker who has asked the privilege of tending furnace for them: first, that he take a rate lower than they would pay an ordinary workman at the job; second, that he show himself abundantly grateful.

At some point during this odd-job epoch, the wife goes back upstate to live with her mother. She suggests he come too. But in the group I am considering, when the man's nerve is still strong, the husband answers: 'No. You go ahead, but I'll stick it in Detroit. This has been our home since 1918, and I certainly can find something. Before you know it I'll be sending for you.' He tries another six months, paying five dollars (a month) for his room. Finally pawns his overcoat, his watch; applies at last to the Welfare for an old pair of shoes.

You and I can call on him today at the Fisher Lodge, where at the moment the city will be able, if tax receipts hold up, to expend twenty-two and a half cents a day on him. Out of this comes a clean cot, clean laundry, and two meals a day. And he — with most of his fellows with whom I talked — is still looking for that job, working a week or two without pay for the city to pay for the winter's board.

V

This has been the briefest inspection of the human power plant under the hood of the Detroit motor industry. Besides the rust and wreckage, it is important to remember the municipal response of Detroit which hardly has precedent in the history of American cities.

Here are a few of the city's achievements since the mayor's employment committee dug in actively last September. Actual placement on jobs, 23, 417. Men fed and lodged daily, 12,000. (The other 3000 are absorbed by private charitable institutions.) Number of people clothed by the city, 168,510. Number of families on city welfare, 46,000 — at a cost of $2,000,000 per month. School-children served crackers and milk daily, 9000. Car tickets furnished school-children, 216,000.

The policy and point of view underlying this activity is as important as the achievement itself. The mayor declares flatly it is *not* charity. It is a municipal enterprise. He regards the task as much as a matter of city business as the building of schools or the cleaning of streets. Its emergency character is of course recognized, and more permanent solutions are under way — such as the provision this summer of ten thousand gardens for unemployed workers, large enough to provide that many families with the bulk of next winter's provisions. However, the mayor's real problem is, as one worker puts it, to provide 'meat now — and not spinach next summer.'

The 'production department' of the American automobile industry is one of the greatest engineering achievements of all time. And many of the modern plants in Detroit are remarkable, not only for productive machines, but for such devices as tubes which suck noxious gases out of workrooms, ventilation systems, 'scientific' light, and clean machinery. On my recent trip to Detroit I was courteously shown the salvage department of the Ford Motor Company. It aroused my enthusiasm. Here drills were sharpened and files renewed, aluminum scrap from the Lincoln factory was cut into squares to make labels, the vitals of broken-down dynamos torn apart and distributed among new mechanisms, second-hand Ford upholstery sewn into support belts for window-washers.

And everywhere I found intelligence and order and an absence of dirt. I shan't forget the rolling mill. Here were men with dusters cleaning off the girders! My guide conducted me through 'the largest machine shop in the world.' It was not running — the primary human power being shut off Thursday, Friday, and Saturday, but on a raised gallery I watched squads of tool-makers repairing the machinery.

The whole process of intelligent salvage, the evidence everywhere of plant care and tool care impressed me deeply, and I shared a hearty enthusiasm with my guide. But after we passed the gate a man stopped me with his hand. His face carried hardy American features weakened by hunger and he wore a coat held together at the neck with a safety pin. 'I have been out fifteen months,' he said. I asked him if he was married. 'No,' he answered, 'thank God!' I gave him a quarter.

All over the country opinion grows that the manufacturer should join the municipality in tackling the emergency of unemployment. In Detroit itself taxation gives a special emphasis to this demand. Last May the *New York Times* editorially put the situation as concisely as possible:

The winter and spring of 1930–31 have been among the hardest in Detroit which any city has known. Its rapid growth, and the depression of the motor-car industry, filled the city with unemployed workers, of whom, at great outlay, it has taken remarkably good care. But twenty per cent of the welfare costs, according to Mayor Murphy, have been expended on laid-off members of Mr. Ford's organization. His companies have a rule against contributing to local charities, and this has been extended to include the winter's welfare work. He pays his taxes elsewhere, and the municipality is devoting forty per cent of its relief expenditures to people dropped from the rolls of the Ford Companies and of other factories just outside the city limits.

Not only in the case of the automobile industry, but everywhere the ordinary citizen feels more and more that it is the industries' job to look after their own.

VI

I sat down in one of the glass-partitioned offices of the Ford Motor Company. Through the transparent wall I could see Edsel Ford enter the next room. Henry himself was in Washington. Facing me was an official who is close to Henry Ford — if anyone can really be close to Henry. Speaking for himself, he said some extraordinary things. One was: 'If this is the best our industrial system can do, I don't think it's worth saving.' He continued: 'I believe, however, that we're only in the stagecoach stage. Something better will follow.' Speaking of the depression, he warned me not against pessimism, but optimism. 'We might as well face the facts,' he said. A little later: 'There have been more homes lost in Detroit through this depression than were lost as a result of the World War.'

Many persons in Detroit, I found, were very bitter about the 'big shots' — meaning all presidents of banks, the heads and high officials of the automobile companies, and of course Mr. Ford. I was frequently told that they were peculiarly heartless individuals barbarously delighting in the misery of their employees. They are of course ordinary men who in economic relations confine their attention to their own interests, which inevitably makes them brutal toward the mass of mankind, but who in their human contacts are as human as the rest of us. The point is that attention to their own interest plus gentleness in private life is not enough to apply to a major business depression. I can illustrate the point by a Ford story — a true one.

About a year ago while Henry Ford was out in his car, he found a lad of eighteen or twenty heading for Detroit. The boy was afoot and, being partial to boys, Henry invited him into his car. The two of them got to talking, and the boy told Henry that he had come to Detroit to get a job at Ford's. The owner of the Ford Motor Company asked if he knew anyone there, and the boy said, 'No.' Henry remarked that *he* did — a man who worked at Ford's. He'd speak to him about it. A little later the employment office was primed. And the next day the boy got his job. Henry was curious about it all and called up the employment manager. 'Who did he say sent him?' 'Oh,' said the other, 'just an old man that he met driving a Ford.'

Unfortunately, through this generous impulse of Ford's, the boy was hired at roughly the same time that Boris lost his job, his faith, and his home. Kindness in private life is not enough.

VII

Since writing the above record of unemployment misery and the gallant effort of the municipal government to combat it, a drastic change has come over the picture in Detroit. A barrage of criticism against the mayor and his policy of relief finally succeeded in causing the closure of *all* public 'flop' houses in Detroit. The city found itself heavily in debt, and further expenditures were bitterly opposed by certain powerful interests. Henry Ford hired private detectives to prove that the city's funds had been misused, in order to break down the scheme of relief and the hostile publicity which was accruing to the Ford Motor Company. An ultimatum was finally delivered by the city's banking interests: a loan to be granted the municipality with the proviso that no more than eight million dollars be spent on relief this coming winter. An expenditure of twenty-two million last year brought the imperfect alleviation of misery recorded in this article. A third of this will be spent this year to relieve a situation at least twice as severe. The lesson which the financial interests of Detroit seem bent upon driving home is that both private enterprise and democratic government in Detroit have failed. The masses of starving workmen in Detroit who last winter trusted in the city and still hoped for aid from the manufacturers are turning to other sources for leadership and hope. I attended a meeting of unemployed workers on the outskirts of Detroit in the local schoolhouse. The speaker was telling about Soviet Russia. A little man behind me kept shouting in my ear: 'They've got a better system than we've got.' I turned around and looked into a strong American face. 'Are you a communist?' I asked. 'Hell, no,' he said, 'I'm a Roman Catholic; how can I be a communist? But they've got a better system than we've got.'

'Where do you work?'

'Work?' he said, 'I've been out fifteen months. I've got four children,' he added, his eyes narrowing, 'and I'll fight before I'll see 'em starve — wouldn't you?'

I said I would.

CHAPTER VIII

CAN CAPITALISM BE SAVED?[1]

By ANDRÉ MAUROIS

I

IF, IN 1240, one had described to the Norman or Breton peasants those institutions which now seem so natural to us — independent farms, estates without men at arms, justice rendered in the name of the people by official judges — they would have been amazed to the point of incredulity by such a picture. Likewise if, outside of socialist or communist groups, a writer had discussed before the war the chances for the survival of capitalism, he would not have been taken seriously. The system of private ownership seemed then to be one of the necessary consequences of human nature. A leader of industry did not question his rights to his factory any more than a feudal lord questioned his rights to his fief.

Will capitalism and private ownership be relegated to an obscure museum existence along with the archaic institutions of feudalism and manorial rights? A whole party believes so, and already one nation, Russia, is seeking a new economic system. Has she succeeded? Has not capitalism still got before it years or centuries of vigorous life before it finally yields place, like all human creation, to other forms engendered by itself? Is it a young institution which has reached a period of crisis in its growth, or is it a system crumbling and already doomed? What action should the capitalist nations take to remedy infirmities which may become mortal? Such are some of the questions which, in 1931, inquiring minds must ask.

[1] *The Forum*, November, 1931.

Certainly none of these questions would be so urgent were it not for the Russian experiment. Not that it is easy, today, to give an honest judgment concerning this experiment. It is one of the most curious phenomena of the day that impartial men (or those who believe themselves to be so) find it impossible to get dependable information about conditions in the new Russia. The existence of a censorship renders suspect the testimony of the Russians themselves, and even of the foreign correspondents living in Russia. The brevity of their stay, their ignorance of the language, the watchful supervision of their guides, destroy much of the value of the accounts given by travelers. They are committed almost completely to preconceived ideas, favorable or unfavorable, which, consequently, they wish to verify.

Despite this ignorance, or perhaps because of it, communist Russia excites the imagination. We do not know if she is succeeding, but we cannot ignore the fact that she is continuing in her ways. Her leaders, who are adroit, are ingeniously maintaining an impression of success. Their Five-Year Plan was a windfall, a lucky hit. There is in this formula a mixture of precision and mystery which troubles and satisfies the mind.

Furthermore, it is not merely a formula. Engineers and capitalist manufacturers who have been in Russia for as much as a year come back, not converted, but surprised. Themselves builders of factories, they cannot help admiring those giant plants which Russia is constructing. It is true that it is not difficult to build; that the problem is not to create equipment, but to make use of it under conditions of output and salary scale superior to that of the capitalist régime; and that finally it has not been proved that this last problem will be solved. No matter. At a distance, the effect produced is impressive.

II

For two years the capitalist countries have been undergoing a formidable crisis. The machine seems to be out of order. The number of the unemployed is mounting. The necessity of caring for them is forcing the nations to live on their reserves. It is natural that communism appears as a refuge to two groups of human beings. First, there are the unfortunates who, having lost their money or their jobs, blame their personal mishaps on 'the system.' Next, there are the intellectuals who, shocked by the impotence of capitalism to organize production and distribution on a rationalized basis, are seduced by the apparently rigorous logic of the Russian scheme. For these two types of malcontents the U.S.S.R. is a nucleus of crystallization. The existence of a communist Russia gives a new, dangerous, and profound character to the crises of overproduction and unemployment. On the other hand, it is certain that since the war these crises have themselves seemed to assume a more serious and far-reaching character than before. One is obliged to seek out the reason.

The right of a proprietor, on condition that he respect the law, to do what he wants with his possessions and to accumulate them without check is a very old system which, on the whole, has produced admirable results. Human civilization has been founded on this right in almost all places and throughout the course of history. The hope of gain, the will to increase one's power, the less selfish desire to bequeath it to one's children, have produced a zest for labor and a philosophy of thrift to which are due the prodigious accumulation of capital that, in the form of houses, cultivated fields, livestock, furniture, works of art, and all other property, constitutes the framework of our spiritual civilization. At the present time one may be either an enemy or a defender of capitalism. It seems to me impossible for an historian not to recognize the magnitude of its results in the past.

In the nineteenth, and later in the twentieth century, the system of private ownership was radically transformed by the development of the machine and by the concentration of large industries. This story has often been told. I wish to stress here only two points.

First, the great profits realized during this period have created a new form of feudalism. Industrial or commercial dynasties hand down their family businesses like fiefs. Millions of workers have accepted as overlords the employers who give them their jobs. Until 1880 (and even, in some countries, until 1900) the working-classes abandoned, in effect, all political power to these leaders. The heroes of the banking world, of business, and of industry, devoted themselves to Homeric combats in which defeat entailed failure and frequently suicide. Like all quarrels between great estates, these combats cost the hovel-dwellers dear. The public, however, delighted in these jousts, and there were great employers as there were formerly great overlords. In the United States, where business feudalism is still primitive and strong, the masses, up to the recent crisis and in spite of the fact that they had often been wounded by the blows, admired the fine thrusts and strategy of the jousters of Wall Street.

Secondly, the development of certain industries has been so rapid that the isolated capitalist no longer finds, in private profits, the new capital which is indispensable to him. Hence the growth of joint-stock companies, and a complete transformation of the nature of property. In the days of Balzac, a Père Grandet owned poplars, fields, houses, gold, and, as a part of his fortune, government stock. Today a Parisian clerk will have shares in an Amsterdam oil company, in a copper mine which he believes to be in Spain and which is actually in the Argentine, in a rubber plantation whose trees ooze forth in

Java or Sumatra. This participation of the small-fry in big business has led superficial observers to talk of the democratic régime of ownership. Actually, the system resembles political democracy in this respect — that both are plutocracies. Big business is administered by a small group of men who remain all-powerful, who sign contracts and fix dividends, and who, by the very multiplicity of the stockholders, are free from any serious control.

The consequences of this transformation in private ownership have not been happy. They are: the discontent of the small capitalist, who has lost all feeling of confidence and security; the anarchy of a feudal society in which, with each individual seeking only to increase his own business and profits without regard for the general needs of the market, overproduction is inevitable; the accumulation of immense revenues in the hands of a few men who, unable to spend them on their personal needs, divert these forces from the normal economic cycle and use them to multiply still further the already too numerous means of production; periodic crises of depression, which are perhaps inevitable, but the severity of which could have been diminished by more intelligent control of speculation and production; finally, unemployment, a grave symptom which automatically follows overproduction.

The evils created by abandoning to its own devices so complicated a mechanism could have been predicted in the nineteenth century. Then, however, the symptoms seemed harmless and capable of being overlooked. The expansion of markets had given the illusion of a possible continuous growth of production. The war, by closing down a large number of these markets, by transforming into industrial nations countries which formerly had been purchasers, by multiplying customs barriers in Europe, so increased fluctuations that it has become difficult for a bourgeois civilization to sustain them. Two attitudes remain possible. The first is to believe that these ills are not a necessary consequence of the system of private ownership, and that the introduction of certain corrections in the formulas of our economic structure would suffice to reëstablish the efficacy of the system. The second attitude, that of the Russians, is to affirm that every capitalist society necessarily produces these evil consequences, and that the sole remedy is communism.

III

What are the elements of strength in communism? The first is that it is an economic dictatorship. We have, in the capitalist world, had experience of such methods. People often forget that the first great economic experiment in international socialism was made by the Allies from 1915 to 1918. During this period the Inter-Allied Shipping Board controlled the world's shipping and, in America, the War Industries Board under Bernard Baruch established an economic dictatorship. The results were prodigious. Why? Because individual interests, which are always at odds, were subordinated to general interests. A coördinated system replaced anarchy.

How was such self-denial, such abnegation, wrested from rebellious human nature? A strong emotion, patriotism, had subdued envy, vanity, and greed. A certain mysticism had been created, and the individual, worshiping a force beyond himself, had accepted the sacrifice.

The second positive factor in communism is that it, too, has a mystic faith to offer. It is blended with patriotism. Russia is playing a lone hand against the world, and many Russians who do not believe in communism wish nevertheless to see their country triumph. But, for the members of the Party, the active force is a mysticism characteristically communistic: a complete abandonment of the individual to a task and to expectations which are greater than he. It is this mysticism which enables a cruel and exacting dictatorship to endure. The strength of the governmental system seems to lie in police and military power — as in fact it does — but no régime of force can long survive if it is not sustained by faith. In the Russian Communist Party, and particularly among its younger members, this faith exists.

Will it suffice? I do not believe so. The number of individuals capable of true sacrifice and of disinterestedness is certainly not negligible. It cannot be large enough to keep a whole nation at work. When one reads contemporary Russian fiction (as, for example, Pilnyak's fine novel, 'The Volga Falls to the Caspian Sea,' one sees that more human passions supplement disinterestedness. I have always asked myself what incentives, in the communist system, could take the place for vulgar, unregenerate people (and one must admit that such people exist in Russia as elsewhere) of that desire for personal profit which is the motive force of the capitalist system. Pilnyak's book, like Calvin B. Hoover's 'The Economic Life of Soviet Russia,' and, more recently, Stalin's speech on necessary inequalities, have shown me clearly what those incentives are.

In the first place, the idea of profit has not been entirely discarded. 'One cannot,' says Stalin, 'allow a locomotive engineer to be paid like a stenographer.' Even when the question of profits does not come up, ambition takes its place and produces almost identical results. In Soviet Russia a man can, if he is a good technician, become a foreman, a superintendent of a factory, an engineer — and consequent upon these duties he enjoys a way of life, a type of dwelling, and a prestige in the eyes of his wife superior to those of the ordinary workman. Hoover, like Pilnyak, shows that economic-political intrigues, maneuvers for advancement, and denounce-ments calculated to overthrow the superior who blocks one's path, play as large a rôle in Russia as the lust for profits in the capitalist world. One reëncounters the instincts which underlie all fanaticism, hidden under the mask of virtue. Stalin's communists are like Cromwell's puritans — though puritanism and ambition are perhaps more subversive of social harmony than the love of money, a form of power which is anonymous and exchangeable. I do not know whether humanity would gain much by substituting the god Power for the god Money, and calumny for competition. I do not believe so.

But another and more noble emotion crops up in the novels of New Russia. It is the joy of action. In all pioneer periods the man who, by unceasing labor, models a virgin nature in his hands, has been a happy man. For two centuries America knew this optimism of the pioneer. Now Russia is giving free rein to the 'Men Who Would Be King.' An article by an American engineer employed by the Russians expressed this emotion perfectly. 'I am not a communist,' he said, 'and I have no interest in all the communist doctrines. I only know that here I can build the largest and finest electric plant. What does the rest matter? I am happy.' Read the little primer which the Soviets distribute to their school-children. You will see that the Five-Year Plan is represented to them as a great, an heroic adventure — in a style which is reminiscent both of Rudyard Kipling and Walt Whitman. It is natural that the country has been able, by such methods, to awake the enthusiasm of youth.

Are this enthusiasm and this mysticism likely to last? Here, as always, one must beware of the dangerous rôle of prophet. It is, however, fine intellectual sport to study possibilities. One of these would be the rapid disappearance of communism. The Five-Year Plan might fail; the Russian working-class, weary of an abnegation shown by its results to be barren, might drive out its masters. This solution seems to me unlikely. The Five-Year Plan will not produce ideally happy conditions in Russia and it will leave the Russian workman in a position still inferior to that of his French or American counterpart. But it will better his position, and the change will be radical enough so that it will be easy, with the aid of faith, to persuade the Russian masses again to put their trust in a new plan — which this time it will be wise to extend over a period of ten or even fifteen years.

Possibly, during these fifteen or twenty years of planned economy, the Soviets will gain much ground over the capitalist nations (providing the latter do not alter their methods). The Soviets are working in a new country, whose needs are immense and whose natural resources are very great; German or American engineers have given them the benefit of their technical skill; they exercise absolute power. By imposing privations on their people, they are accumulating reserve capital more rapidly than the capitalist world. There seems no reason why they cannot create a great industrial civilization. The Pharaohs built the Pyramids, a much more absurd enterprise, and yet the people did not revolt. Even if, at the start, the output of communist production is mediocre, it is probable that with the aid of foreign co-operation on the one hand, and a system of coercion on the other, the Russians will, after a series of partial failures, learn to correct their mistakes.

IV

The real difficulties of Russia will begin with the advent of success. 'Nothing fails like success.' Assume that at the end of thirty years the Soviet régime achieves for its people a mode of life equal or superior to that of the capitalist workman, or even the petty bourgeois. It is natural to suppose that one may then look for the following phenomena: First, the mystic urge will weaken —

because all human emotions lose their strength when they no longer have the prestige of novelty; because victory will wipe out the thrill of combat; and finally because the desire to build and create will no longer be gratified. The pioneer clears the ground, and his destiny is to destroy the environmental conditions and the obstacles which are the basis for his happiness. On the day when he replaces hostile nature with the human hive, he is at once triumphant and dispossessed. The Russians of 1960 will have a dull time of it, like the Americans of 1927.

Secondly, Russia will undoubtedly try, like America, to prolong the pioneer period. Then, in her turn, she will experience overproduction. Exportation will be difficult, for it is unthinkable that other nations will not defend their own workmen. 'But how,' people will ask, 'can there be overproduction under a communist system? Cannot the Soviets increase their wages indefinitely, improve the standards of ordinary living, and cut down working hours?' One must admit frankly that this could, indeed, be the superiority of the communist system over an unreformed capitalist system — that a greater share of production could be put back into circulation. It is not, however, true at the present moment, because Russia needs, and will still need for a long time, to create a working capital.

Finally, a permanent betterment of standards of living will again build up a bourgeoisie. The Soviets will be brought to the point of distributing such diverse commodities that they will be obliged to accord their wage-earners the right to choose between the goods offered and to dispose of their money as they please. From such a right to the rebirth of savings, and then of wealth, the road seems easy and the descent swift. Toward the end of the twentieth century, a Russian will discover the theory of private property — which will seem like a great and revolutionary novelty. Prosperity will bring with it the reappearance of a form of capitalism, which will nevertheless be different from the old. The cycle will have been completed. This is, at least, one of the possible directions which world history may take; it may not be the one which will be fulfilled. If, however, it is very naïve to suppose that capitalism is impregnable, it is equally naïve to see in communism the true religion, a perfect and logical form into which human economics will crystallize for all eternity.

It is also a surprising intellectual weakness to pit individualism against socialism, and capitalism against communism, as if one were concerned with clear-cut concepts and sharply marked frontiers. Reality is living and complex, and historical evolution causes human societies to vibrate from one system to another without allowing them a permanent resting-place in either. If our epoch can boast any original philosophy, it is one of absolute relativism. It is not immoral to be a capitalist; it is not criminal to be a communist; but it would be intelligent to perceive that every doctrine is harmful if it is too rigid.

There is no absolute economic truth, or rather there is an economic truth for each moment in time. As the scholar revises his hypothesis in accordance with the dictates of experience; as the military leader, if he is wise, accepts the schooling of facts, so economic leaders should have a doctrine only so that it may provisionally coördinate their actions. Capitalism may avoid a revolution, and I hope that it will do so. It can save itself only by transforming itself.

Chapter IX

THE RESPONSIBILITY OF BANKERS

By James Truslow Adams

[A LARGE share of the responsibility for the frenzied expansion that preceded the explosion of October, 1929, must rest upon the bankers, particularly those engaged in the investment business. That the panic would have come had bankers been more conservative cannot be doubted, for it is the bitter fruit of the capitalist process as historically endured, but undoubtedly the oscillation would not have been so violent nor the losses so heavy. Nor would the aftermath have been so ruinous — the failure of great banks, enormous dissipation in savings, and widespread distrust of banking methods, morals, and honor. Perhaps it is the imponderables that count most here as elsewhere. Some of the banking and investment houses, by no means insignificant concerns, were guilty of practices more worthy of the racketeer than the man of character. And the righteous indignation which their conduct has awakened in the minds of thousands of citizens not given to radical opinions is eloquently voiced by Mr. James Truslow Adams in the following pages taken from *The Forum* of August, 1931. Those who are thinking about attempts to reduce the anarchy of capitalism to a reasonable degree of order and stability will of necessity have to consider the place of centralized and controlled banking and credit in the scheme of planned economy.]

Scarcely any of us can escape a banker. If we have luck we may go for years without consulting a doctor. Many of us go for a lifetime without consulting a lawyer, except perhaps to draw our wills. But the banker enters into the life of all of us, rich or poor, at every nook and cranny. This ubiquitous dependence, direct or indirect, makes the subject of sound and responsible banking one of intense and legitimate interest to the public. Indeed, banking is a 'public utility' of much greater delicacy and social importance than such enterprises as are usually so classed. The banker can no longer regard his business as private or as primarily the concern of his stockholders. Their interests have been transcended by those of the public.

The banking situation deserves to be treated without gloves, and if I do so it is without any wish to write a mere muck-raking article. The righteous discontent of the average citizen today with the way the banker performs and regards his public function demands an attention on the part of bankers themselves that unfortunately it is far from receiving, as is evidenced from the proceedings of the Bankers' Convention this spring. The business men of America are organized in multitudes of bodies, and presumably can take care of themselves. The ordinary men and women of the country are not, and it is for them and of their relations that I speak.

A banking account is a necessity for all but the lowest in the financial scale. For great numbers of us, busy all day within the confines of a single neighborhood in a city, or living in a small town where there is only one bank, it is a practical need to deposit our money in a bank which is near at hand. In any reputable banking system, we should be able to be sure, when we have saved the money and deposited it, that it is absolutely safe except for the rarest of colossal world panics or scandalous defalcations. The Englishman or the Canadian can be thus sure. We in the United States cannot. In 1930, 1326 banks failed, of which only 138 were able to reopen, the total final suspensions tying up nine hundred million dollars of depositors' money. Translating passbook entries into human terms, who can estimate the crushing amount of anxiety, of suffering, of hopes deferred or blighted, that the above figures indicate? Nor was this the situation only in a year of business depression. In the past decade, the prosperity of which our government has so blatantly proclaimed, about sixty-five hundred banks closed.

Leading bankers try to minimize this scandalous record by saying that practically all the closed banks were small and unimportant. To this it may be rejoined that no bank is unimportant to the community whose money is in it and which has its economic life dislocated or ruined by the failure. Nine hundred million dollars, mostly in small communities, is not an unimportant sum to have been taken from the people, even temporarily, in one year.

When a large New York City bank, with four hundred thousand depositors, fails for the largest sum in American history, we are again told it was an unimportant institution, apparently because Wall Street bankers 'in the know' had considered its management dishonest, and because its clientèle was mostly made up of 'foreigners.' What the State Banking Department was doing all the time we may discover in the investigation of the unsavory mess now under way, but why 'foreigners' should be considered as less entitled to have their money conserved safely than native Americans is a mystery that is not yet resolved. As a matter of fact, plenty of Americans lost their money also — college professors, doctors, and others who found it convenient to use the neighborhood branch of a large bank which was presumably being regularly examined and checked up by the state.

COMMERCIAL BANKS AS SAVINGS BANKS

Commercial banks in the past few decades have sought to widen their opportunities to make money by trespassing on fields which before were occupied by specialized bankers, notably in their handling of savings funds, in competing with trust companies for trust functions, and in taking over the business of underwriting and issuing of investment securities. None of this business has been forced upon them. They have gone after all of it solely to make money, and at the possible risk of making the people's money less safe.

Unfortunately, in 1914 the Federal Reserve Act practically allowed a commercial bank to function as a savings bank, and many were quick to seize the opportunity. So far has the movement gone that at present there are 1,500,000 persons in the State of New York alone who have 'thrift accounts' in commercial banks. Throughout the country at large in the past five years, such savings accounts have bulked large in the deposits of all insolvent institutions. Savings depositors have been said by a high authority to have borne the brunt of the losses. The average savings depositor has not realized the difference between depositing his savings in a savings bank or in the 'thrift department' of a commercial bank; and the commercial banks have been at no pains to point it out to him. A busy individual has found it much more convenient to carry both checking and savings accounts in the same near-by bank, and this has accounted for a huge growth in commercial bank deposits, wholly at the risk of the savings depositor.

This has not only directly jeopardized the savings of millions of citizens everywhere in our country, but has had a distinctly detrimental effect on savings banks proper. In some states these have secured legislation lowering the safety to increase the return on legal investments so as to meet this unfair and dangerous competition. It is needless to point out that a commercial bank, free to discount commercial paper and to engage in many lines of banking denied to a savings bank, can average a much higher return upon its deposits than can the latter, properly limited to the highest grade of legal investments for trust funds.

Attempts to correct this abuse, notably in the battle recently waged by Governor Roosevelt in New York for the segregation of 'thrift accounts' by commercial banks, have made it fairly clear that, with some exceptions, the bankers have cared more to retain, with the least trouble to themselves, a profitable business than to safeguard the public whose confidence they invite. Unfortunately, in national legislation, banking is a political subject; and in the leadership of bankers themselves it is all too apt to be a question of the profits of their particular institution. Between the two, the ordinary man or woman who asks for safety is but little considered, in spite of the nauseating talk about 'service.'

The situation with regard to the permanent investment of savings has altered greatly in the past generation or two. Even I can remember when not only in villages and small towns, but even in cities so large as New York, it was the usual thing for almost all but the poorest to own their own homes. Interest in Wall Street investments was comparatively slight among the ordinary people of the country, as old lists of daily transactions on the Stock Exchange will indicate. Today all that is changed, for various reasons. Within the confines of a city like New York, for example, it is extremely difficult if not impossible for a man of small means to own his own home. We are, moreover, living in a period of large units and of corporate forms. Circumstances, reënforced by all the psychological pressure of modern salesmanship, have made the small man, as well as what used to be termed a 'capitalist,' the owner of securities.

Formerly the conservative small investor, the widow, and what a recent writer has termed the 'investment illiterates,' usually bought bonds. For some years pre-

ceding the late *débâcle*, under the slogan of 'buy equities'
they were urged to invest in stocks — with disastrous
consequences. In many cases here in the United States,
for example, and even so far away as Chile, I have found
people who were urged to buy, as something exceptionally choice, the stock of a banking institution then
absurdly selling at around five hundred which is now
below one hundred.

INSECURE SECURITIES

The term 'investment illiterates' is a little misleading.
Modern business has become exceedingly and perplex-
ingly complex. This is in part due to changes in business
itself and in part to consolidations and juggling. Forty
years ago there was a comparatively simple business
structure for the investor. In most cases, moreover,
speaking broadly, the capital structure of the enterprises
themselves was simple. One could readily compare the
operations and earnings of one year with those of another. Today the situation confronting the small investor is utterly bewildering. Not only are there literally
thousands of so-called 'securities' among which he is
urged to make his choice, but the conditions making for
success or failure in an industry change rapidly.

In addition, though the balance and earnings sheets
of our vast modern consolidated companies would be
almost impossible for a layman to analyze in any case,
the stock split-ups, the stock dividends, the constant
amalgamations, and other factors make it even more impossible for him to compare the condition of a company
in one year with that in past years. The position of the
average investor today is not so much that of an 'illiterate' as it is that of a person who is well-educated,
but who is expected to master a highly technical scientific subject in which he has had no training whatever,
and which, not seldom, is so complicated by his in-

structor as to make it still less capable of being understood.

In the old days, a group of neighbors could build a wooden bridge or put up a barn. Now we have to count on the technical experts to build a Holland Tunnel or a skyscraper. In the same way, most men and women are today utterly dependent on the bankers, by which I mean also the 'investment bankers' as they call themselves, for technical expert advice. This advice they wish on two topics, when to buy and what to buy. On neither count, it seems to me, can the technicians take much pride in their work in the past few years. I was in the Stock Exchange and investment business for thirteen years, and I assuredly do not expect any banker to be able to predict the price movement from day to day or even from month to month, but that is very different from considering the long swings or not seeing danger when the signals have been set for months past.

With the statements of Mr. Mellon, whom the public looked up to as an eminently successful banker and Secretary of the Treasury, with presumably all possible information at hand, I have already dealt elsewhere. Let us take another distinguished example. Mr. Charles E. Mitchell, as president of the largest banking institution in America, the National City Bank of New York, was naturally assumed by the public to be a man of unusual banking ability and of sound judgment. On October 9, 1929, the *New York Times* reported him as saying in Berlin that 'the industrial condition of the United States is absolutely sound and our credit situation is in no way critical.' A few days later, in London, where I happened to be at the moment, he made a similar statement. Yet even before he could reach New York the crash had begun, and by the twenty-ninth the *Times* was reporting the crumbling of values to the extent of fourteen billion dollars; and six of the leading bankers of New York, including Mr. Mitchell, were in conference in Mr. Morgan's office to try to save the country from a complete cataclysm. In the eyes of the public at large, there are, or rather were, no more eminent bankers than the two whose advice, to say the least, had hardly been found helpful.

Most of us have to rely upon the published sayings of our leaders. It is not often that a widow is so fortunate, apparently, as to be able to have her investments made for her by a partner in one of the very greatest of American private banking houses or by one of the highest banking officials of the Federal Reserve System. I happen to know of two who were. In the first instance a number of the lady's investments are at present worth less than fifty per cent of what she paid for them. In the second, the official, whose name is one of the best known in America, stated that the investments would be of the widow variety — that is, that the first and most important principle guiding him in making them would be safety. He bought bonds, and *within five months* two of the various blocks had defaulted on their interest. Such episodes are as unnecessary as they are inexcusable.

SPECULATION AND INVESTMENT

To a very great extent the commercial banks have begun, in recent years, to compete with private bankers in underwriting issues of securities to offer the public. The subterfuge of maintaining a separate 'securities company' is, of course, flimsy. In the case of one bank, of which I am a stockholder, and I think this is true of many others, the same certificate covers my interest in the bank and in the affiliated security company, and the same dividend check covers profits from both legally disparate concerns. The advantage to the public of having its banks engaged in this line of business would seem to me to be doubtful, and the competition with the old private houses of issue unfair, but I am not here concerned with those points; and as both providers of the public's supply of investments call themselves bankers, I shall not here discriminate.

It is needless to say that the great majority of securities sold to the public by 'reputable' bankers pay their interest, if not always their dividends, for some years at least after being issued. The business could not continue otherwise. But it would be a doubtful endorsement of an engineer to say that the majority of the bridges built by him did not *immediately* collapse. The responsibility of the engineer is clear. What is the responsibility of the banker?

There are several things to be said as to that. It is quite true that we could not continue to widen the scope of our business activity as a nation, that we could not develop new undertakings, if some among us were not willing to take chances with capital for the possibility of securing large profits or income yields. This is an age of coöperative endeavor, and the banker is performing a useful and necessary function when he collects the balances awaiting investment from many small scattered sources and unites them into such a sum as shall suffice to build up or assist a large-scale industry. This is, as I see it, a legitimate function even when the undertaking and the security representing it are of distinctly a speculative nature; that is, when the investment is an uncertain and risky one.

As I also see it, however, three heavy responsibilities rest upon the banker. One is that he should assure himself that the investor has some chance from the start before securities are sold to him; the second is that no specific issue of securities should be forced upon anyone; and the third is that such information should be given as to allow an investor to judge of the risk — in a word, that speculative geese should not be advertised in the same terms as investment swans.

As an example of the first point, I well recall a number of years ago an extreme case of what should not be done. One of the largest and most notable banking houses in America brought out an issue of bonds. From the day of issue, apparently, they were not worth the paper they were engraved on. Not only did they never pay even the first coupon, but a client of mine has never since been able to realize ten cents on a block of five thousand dollars which he bought. The total issue, as I recall, was $1,500,000 and the money was as completely wiped out as if the owners had put their bank-notes in the fire. Not a word of regret or explanation could ever be got from the house, which is still going on merrily as one of our great houses.

On another occasion a man I know was sold twenty-five thousand dollars' worth of bonds by a banking house. Before the first coupon was due, the company went into the hands of a receiver. As it happened, the purchaser was sufficiently important in Wall Street to enable him to force the bankers to refund the purchase price, but if he had been an ordinarily obscure citizen, or a widow without influence, the loss would have had to be taken. My readers can doubtless supply a sufficient number of other such incidents.

Whatever mistakes, to take the most charitable view of it, the private banks of issue might make as to the real security of the 'securities' brought out by them, there was one important difference between such houses and the security companies of the big banks. The former could not force anyone to buy from them. The situation is different as between a big city bank and, say, its out-of-town correspondents. The president of a country or small-town bank has nothing like the information at hand that the president of a big city bank has, but instead of selling 'an issue' of bonds to 'the public,' he sells one or two bonds to his neighbor Tom Jones. The relation, being personal, at once becomes different.

Not long ago such a president of a small bank asked a friend of mine, who had recently been in a certain foreign country, for all the information he could give about it. Surprised at such a thirst for facts, my friend asked the reason. This proved to be that the securities affiliate of the country bank's city correspondent had brought out an issue of government bonds of the nation in question. The country bank had been forced to take its small share of the issue. The country president did not believe in the bonds and declined to sell them to his friends Tom Jones or Bill Smith. His bank was therefore carrying them, at a heavy loss, hoping eventually to get out.

The other day an officer of a bank in a city of five hundred thousand inhabitants remarked that he hoped to heaven his New York correspondent would not force any more securities down their throats for a while, for his bank already had far more than it ought to have of securities it both would not and could not sell. On the other hand, if the bank did not take the amount allotted to it by its correspondent of *every* issue brought out by it, it would never thereafter have a chance at any issue, and business men do not have to be told of how pressure can be brought to bear in various other ways.

Having scores or hundreds of such outlets through the country greatly facilitates the city bank's underwriting and disposing of bonds. It would be quite consonant with human nature, however, that such a certain market for a large proportion of *any* issue underwritten would tend to make the underwriters somewhat less careful as to quality than they would be if their customers were free to scrutinize and reject such issues as they did not believe sound.

FOREIGN BONDS

The billions of foreign bonds floated in the past few years have given peculiar opportunities to underwriters, and entailed corresponding obligations on them. As a people we had had no experience whatever with foreign bonds. As a great creditor nation it was essential that we should learn how to invest surplus funds abroad to finance trade and international obligations. Today our people are extremely gun-shy of foreign bonds. I think the reason is that the bankers who brought them out thought more of selling them than of educating the public. The bonds which have been sold have run all the way from thoroughly first-class investments to extremely dubious speculations. To altogether too great an extent, the advertisements have failed to distinguish between them for a public ignorant as to the whole subject. I do not mean to say that a single banker of standing has made a willfully false statement, but the public can get a wrong impression from carefully selected facts, *and omissions*, as readily as from false statements. One or two instances illustrate my meaning.

On July 21, 1925, we made our first loan to Australia, which was oversubscribed two and a half times within an hour. The bankers offering the issue made a most impressive list, J. P. Morgan and Company, the City and First National Banks, the Bankers' and Guaranty Trust Companies, and others. In the offering not a single false fact was stated or any true fact twisted. But the knowledge of the average investor throughout the country as to the financial stability and credit of Australia was presumably of the haziest. He trusted to the facts given and to the reputations and colossal aggregate resources of the issuing bankers. Most investors did have some idea of our neighbor Canada. The prospectus read: 'the Commonwealth of Australia is comparable with the Dominion of Canada in area, resources, and importance to the British Empire.' Of course, almost any two things may be said to be 'comparable.' What the investor, however, would naturally take the words to mean would be that Australia was about as safe for his money as Canada.

Nothing was said of the real nigger in the woodpile, which was the difference in character between Canadians and Australians, and the extreme labor views and socialistic experiments among the latter. It was precisely this important and unmentioned factor that has forced Australian bonds down in the fifties, with danger of default, whereas Canadians are still well above par. I do not suggest misrepresentation. All I say is that in buying Australians the prospective investor might well infer from the advertisement that he was making much the same sort of investment he would have been had he bought Canadian bonds.

Four years ago, on March 16, 1927, two groups of bankers brought out respectively $6,000,000 Pernambuco 7's at 97¾ and $15,000,000 Peru 7's at 96½. Both advertisements read well for the ordinary uninformed investor. Both, as it happened, stated that the income to cover charges was three and one half times the amount necessary. Today the Pernambucos are selling at 17½ and the Peruvians at 38. Investors are facing heavy losses in both.

It must be remembered that there are today vast numbers of people who have money to invest, little or much, but who have no knowledge whatever of how to do it. These are not only widows and orphans, but professional men of all sorts, and even, in the growing complexity of life, business men whose daily work gives them no insight at all into investments. In innumerable instances throughout the whole country they have no access to financial works of reference, to Moody's ratings, and other things that they would not know how to use if they had. These people have to a considerable extent bought on the recommendation of bankers. If the bankers make no effort to distinguish between sound investments and questionable speculative ones, the public is bound to make mistakes, and to blame the bankers.

It is natural, in our American business world, that when a man has something to sell, he will make it look as attractive as possible, and leave the buyer to find the flaws. It may seem absurd to ask the bankers, when they offer a security, to tell the public whether it is gilt-edged, moderately good, or highly speculative. Yet is it so absurd? In a few months after issue the agencies which give rating to securities will have listed the newcomer as AAA or what-not, all the way down the scale. When the temporary support given to the market has been withdrawn, the bonds will find their own level, often making a sudden drop not understandable by the unfortunate holder. But then it is too late for him to discover that he has been speculating when he thought he was safely 'soaking away' a few thousands.

It may be said that an investor should not trust himself to buy from the advertisements of even the most reputable houses, but should consult his own banker. One answer to this is that of our twenty-three thousand banks, the vast majority are so small as to preclude even their presidents from having much knowledge of investments. Another answer is that even in larger banks, the information received is often discouragingly wrong. I have cited above the instance of the two widows with their exceptionally highly placed advisers, and can add that much of the poorest information I have had in the past two years has come from New York bankers. Why this should be, I frankly do not know. I do not blame bankers for not making fortunes for their clients. I do blame them for so frequently and tragically not being able, when asked, to give them safe investments.

As I made a very modest sum and lost nothing in the wild days of the past four years, I may say that none of this article is flavored with sour grapes or personal resentment. Such resentment, however, I find in America today on every side. For example, I was talking yesterday with a professional man who knows nothing of investments and trusted to his bank for information, a good one in a large city. This bank told him that the Bank of Kentucky was perfectly sound and its stock a good investment. Today the man is facing not only the loss of his money but the possibility of an assessment besides. As a result of this and other like experiences, he remarked, 'What is the use of trying to save from a salary when it is impossible to find out how to keep your money when you have saved it?' This man, like many others I know, has relied solely on bankers' advice, only to lose money over and over again.

TRUSTEES AND MERGERS

There is another factor in the present banking situation, as it has been developing for the past few years, which is causing very deep anxiety to the public. The banks, in many cases having swallowed trust companies, advertise on every hand asking that they be made executors and trustees. The arguments they advance against the use of individuals for that purpose are perfectly sound, especially so in this day when people move about from one locality to another so frequently, and when active business men are as apt to die in the fifties from heart disease or a stroke as they used to be to live to eighty.

There is, however, one point which gives, apparently, a great many others pause as well as myself. We pick, let us say, after careful thought, the X.Y.Z. Bank and Trust Company to execute our will and to invest and handle our estate for our widow and children. But when we have done so, we have not, in reality, the faintest idea *whom* we have made trustee. We may have picked the X.Y.Z. because we consider it to be ably managed, to have a personnel and a tradition of the sort we would like to trust our widow or child to, and then, perhaps the very day after we have signed our will and paid the lawyer his fee, we pick up the paper and find the X.Y.Z. has been merged with the 'Steenth National, which is the last bank in the world we would ever have named, and the whole personnel and policy of which we hate as the Devil hates holy water.

One of my legal friends, not so long ago, met me one day with a 'Thank God I am still alive.' I inquired the reason for the pious but somewhat cryptical ejaculation, and was told that, the night before, the trust company which he had made trustee of five hundred thousand dollars for his widow and children had been merged with a bank that he would not trust with a nickel, and that he was about to change his will as fast as possible. Had he been dead, there would have been no way out. Another lawyer told me at luncheon the other day that since he had made an irrevocable trust fund less than ten years ago, the bank has been through three mergers, and that the resultant institution was one he would never have dreamed of selecting.

I have myself made a New York institution executor and trustee, yet I am haunted by the question of who will really be in charge of the investing of the funds twenty years — or even one year — hence. The banks which solicit your business as trustees will sell you out, without notice, whenever it suits their purpose to do so, and leave your shade in Hades to watch an entirely different institution and set of men handling the affairs of your widow.

There are other aspects of the banking situation that are giving the public deep concern, but I have touched on enough to indicate some of the reasons why resentment against bankers is rapidly growing. There have been several periods in our history when such resentment has been extremely deep and has had far-reaching effect. The present wave of feeling is, in one respect, different from any of the preceding ones. Hitherto the anger against banks and bankers has been voiced by the poor and debtor classes; today the strongest feeling I find is among the well-to-do classes.

This is a new phenomenon, and one well worth pondering by the bankers. It is needless to say that I have no intention of indicting every member of a most important profession. I am at the moment well content with my own banking connection, although of course I have the uncomfortable knowledge that I may find in the newspaper any morning that a merger has completely altered everything. There are able, public-spirited, conscientious bankers, but I think the criticisms made above of conditions in general are all fair, and that the public is wholly justified in its present belief that the banking fraternity is unsocially lacking in sense of responsibility as to how it performs functions now vital to everyone.

In the old days, when business was comparatively simple and almost every American man was in business, we overdeveloped our theory that each could look after himself, and the business philosophy of *caveat emptor*. Today conditions are wholly different. In every department of our life, the responsibility of the technical expert is increasing in proportion to our growing and necessary dependence upon him. As I have pointed out elsewhere, one of the most sinister influences now at work is the breaking-down in law, medicine, and other professions of the professional spirit as contrasted with the business spirit. This is occurring just at the time when more than ever the professional spirit has got to permeate all our activities unless society itself is to break down. In no business or profession is that spirit more needed at present than in banking, nor will that spirit interfere with legitimate profits.

Many years ago in a money panic, the rate for money

on the Stock Exchange rose to one per cent a day, three hundred and sixty per cent a year, before all money disappeared. My father needed fifty thousand dollars to avert failure. As a last resort, he applied to J. P. Morgan and Company, and Mr. Morgan, though a stranger, let him have it. Asked what the rate would be, Mr. Morgan said 'six per cent. Morgan and Company never charge more than that.' Others of the banks charging their hundreds of per cent that day, have failed. For the forty years or so since, Morgan and Company have been on the whole the symbol of strength and ability, and the chief reliance of the bankers themselves in every period of stress. If, on the other hand, most of the leading bankers find the public — as it is — with regard to them, anxious, distrustful, cynical, resentful, they have only themselves to blame, and will have until they have cleaned their houses and shown by their acts that they have come to a full realization of the heavy social responsibility which rests upon them.

PART II
BLUE-PRINTS FOR A PLANNED ECONOMY

IF THE vast literature of discussion and opinion that has been poured out in this season of economic distress were limited to expressing discontent with calamity, it might be expected to vanish with the return of prosperity even though it has the sanction of high civic leadership. But there is more than discontent in the complaint. It is more than a protest against unemployment and the suffering of millions. This literature contains an acute analysis of causes and an array of doubts respecting the possibility of continuing indefinitely the economic and political methods chiefly responsible for the violence of business oscillations — an analysis and an array of doubts that will penetrate deeply into the consciousness of those who do any thinking on political economy in the future. This literature of protest which furnishes a new intellectual and moral climate for America is accompanied by concrete proposals bearing on the prevention of ruinous fluctuations in business. And these proposals for the stabilization of production and employment all look in the direction of a more highly integrated and consciously planned economy. The documents thus form a part of the intellectual record of our time and they also furnish the substantial basis for a discussion of the issues involved in national planning. For this reason several of the most important papers are collected here and arranged, as a rule, for convenience of reference, in the chronological order of their appearance.[1]

[1] Besides these papers, special reference should be made to the plan presented by Mr. Stuart Chase in *Harper's Magazine*, June, 1931.

PART II
BLUE–PRINTS FOR A PLANNED ECONOMY

CHAPTER I
A 'FIVE–YEAR PLAN' FOR AMERICA [1]
By CHARLES A. BEARD

Is THE concept of national planning merely another transitory fad, an idle fantasy born of day-dreaming and destined like a thousand others to pass away tomorrow or the day after? The answer seems to be an inescapable negative. All Western civilization is founded on technology, and of inner necessity technology is rational and planful. The engineer must conform to the inexorable laws of force and materials. Technology cannot begin anything without first establishing a goal, a purpose. To proceed at all, it must stake out a field of work; then in execution it must assemble materials and engines and carry on its operations according to blue-prints until it reaches its predetermined ends. With irresistible might it strides across the wild welter of unreasoned actions, irrelevant sentiments, and emotional starts and fits which characterize historic politics, agriculture, and industry. As technology advances, occupying ever-larger areas of productive economy, there will be a corresponding contraction of the spheres controlled by guesswork and rule-of-thumb procedure. This means, of course, a continuous expansion of the planned zone of economic activity.

[1] *The Forum*, July, 1931, referred to in this volume as 'The Forum Plan.'

Rational in method and planful in procedure, technology is also centripetal in operation. Systematization and unification are inherent in its very processes. Every advance in the chemical field, for instance, involves contacts with other fields — the use of electricity, the exploitation of coal, and spinning, dyeing, and weaving. Wherever technology works in industry and transportation, it contributes powerfully to the concentration of productive activities — to the integration of small plants — thus running counter to the individualistic and free-will methods prevailing in the days of handicrafts and simple agriculture. Horizontal and vertical trusts and interlocking directorates are the inevitable outcome of technical rationality functioning under its law of efficiency. If technology, now young, is to go forward — and it will under the drive of mass demands for the comforts and conveniences of civilization — then the area of economic life controlled by planning will widen. The only question is: under what institutional auspices?

In this there is nothing new. Hints of it were discovered by Charles Babbage a century ago. There is nothing Russian about its origin. Indeed, planning of economy was anathema to the Bolsheviks until, facing the task of feeding enraged multitudes, they laid aside Marx, took up Frederick Winslow Taylor, and borrowed foreign technology to save their political skins. There is nothing in the concept that is alien to American experience. Our giant industrial corporations, though harassed by politics, bear witness to the efficacy of large-scale planning. From industry the idea spreads to politics. Its progress is symbolized in the rise of the budget system, in the work of the Bureau of Standards, and in the growth of city planning. At the present moment, two thirds of the American cities with more than twenty-five thousand inhabitants have planning boards or commissions, and collectively they have in course of execution projects of great magnitude.

City planning is represented by a national association, a magazine, a national conference, university chairs, a practicing profession, volumes of statutes and ordinances, and achievements of no mean proportion. State planning for power, agriculture, highways, and other branches of economy now looms large in governors' messages. Fragments of national planning are already scattered through the agencies and establishments of the Federal Government and await the touch of engineering genius to extend them and tie them into a consistent organization for efficient functioning on the national stage. Planning is already here; it is inherent in our technological civilization, which is now as American as the individualistic agriculture that held the center of the economic stage for two centuries during our early development. It would have gone forward inexorably, even if the Russian revolution had not borrowed it and dramatized it.

It is merely accentuated today by an industrial paralysis which promises to be deeper and more prolonged than any previous crisis of the kind. The American people now stand aghast at the paradox of wheat piled mountain high and shoe machinery rusting while millions willing to work go hungry and unshod. This paradox is no longer pointed out by a few 'long-haired agitators.' From the top to the bottom of our civilization a searching of hearts is proceeding with startling rapidity.

A business leader as experienced and practical as Daniel Willard openly informs the Wharton School of Finance and Commerce that 'A system — call it what you will — under which it is possible for five or six millions of willing and able-bodied men to be out of work and unable to secure work for months at a time, with no other source of income, cannot be said to be perfect or even satisfactory; on the contrary, it can be said to have failed in at least one very important detail. I can think of nothing more deplorable than the condition of a man, able and anxious to work, but unable to secure work, with no resources but his labor and, perhaps, with others even more helpless dependent upon him. Unless he is willing to starve and see those who justly look to him for support also starve, his only alternative is to seek charity and, failing that, to steal. While I do not like to say so, I would be less than candid if I did not say that in such circumstances I would steal before I would starve.' Evidently we have gone a long way from the day when an ex-President of the United States could fling back the cry 'God knows; I don't' to a workingman asking what he should do in the face of unemployment and starvation.

But the issue transcends the present crisis. The crisis will pass. Still the waste of our natural resources, the neglect of our opportunities, the failure to use our marvelous material endowment efficiently will be pointed out by technology with increasing emphasis. Awareness of the necessity of planning will spread. Projects and work in hand will force the gates of the future. And there is good ground for predicting that other crises, more devastating, will return with rhythmic regularity, until science takes the place of rule of thumb and the untrammeled acquisitive instinct. Herein lies the problem: How to go forward along lines already made clear by the lamp of experience and engineering rationality?

PLANNING — OUR ONE SOLUTION

When the question is asked: What shall be done? three answers come at once, the easiest at the outset naturally, for all love ease. First there is the answer: Do nothing at all; return to *laissez faire*. This is the counsel of despair; like the peasants of Europe in the presence of the Black Death, we should lie down and accept fate. Besides being repugnant to reason, the philosophy of *laissez faire* has been tried and has failed to fulfill its promises. It is also obsolete, having been abandoned by technology and business enterprise. Condemned by experience as a pledge of security and prosperity, it cannot be revived; children burned and blackened in that fire will not return to it again. Even if attractive as a theory, it has been rendered impossible by the march of events beyond the reach of any person, functionary, or class.

At the other extreme, we are offered a dictatorship — of politicians either in their own name or in the name of the proletariat. Both are a form of verbal legerdemain, but owing to their prominence in current discussion they deserve consideration. The former may be adapted to Italy with her meager resources and her vast mass of illiterate or semi-literate peasants; it may have improved slightly at least the economic lot of the Italian people — which is debatable; but to talk of forcing such an iron régime of despotism on the citizens of the United States is to betray a woeful ignorance of their history, their traditions, their ideas, and their wilful way of life. It is to adopt the fanciful philosophy of the French revolutionists, who thought they had a creed good always, everywhere, and for everybody. To expect dictators who have never before managed anything as complicated as a chicken farm to manage a vast technological system of industry with success is to expect the impossible, even though evangelistic fervor be enlisted.

The same criticism applies with equal force to the Russian remedy. It has lately been associated with the concept of planning, but that was an afterthought and never would have been even partially realized had it not been for the technological assistance of Western capitalism. Nor is the Russian plan really a plan in the sense of a definite stereotype for action. For more than ten years the Russian Government has pursued a zigzag course, trying one expedient after another; and it is still constantly changing the inner organization of its industrial machinery in a desperate effort to make it work efficiently. It has renounced one proletarian policy after another in order to make its wheels turn, and what will be the outcome of its labors either in terms of organization or performance, no one can vaguely guess.

One thing, however, is certain; it rules by tyranny and terror, with secret police, espionage, and arbitrary executions. The system may be adapted to a people who endured tsarist despotism for centuries, but to suppose that it could be transported intact to the United States, even if deemed successful in its own bailiwick, is to ignore the stubborn facts of American life and experience — the long practice of self-government in towns, villages, and states, the traditions of personal liberty, the established public school system, and a thousand other elements that stand out like mountains in the American scene. If capitalism were cursed with all the evils ascribed to it by communists (and it has plenty to its credit), still the American people, on a fair and free count, would vote one hundred to one for keeping it rather than enslave themselves to the kind of political and economic despotism regnant in the land of the former tsars. This does not mean, of course, that they will not soon see the necessity of recognizing the right of Russia to work out her own destiny and put their trust in the mollifying effect of reasonable intercourse rather than in barricades and blockades.

In the third place, we are offered palliatives. Some hopeful economists propose the four- or three-day week in industry, blandly overlooking agriculture, which would be called upon to pay the bill for that generous luxury, assuming that it is feasible for manufacturing. It is also suggested that children be kept in school until they are twenty-one years old. This scheme ignores the fact that thousands of children do not want to be in school and, in truth, should not be there, after they are fifteen or sixteen years of age. Were the idea practicable, its execution would be demoralizing to millions of young people, unless the whole system of education were geared into a planned national economy. Standing alone, the proposition is absurd.

Under the head of palliatives come schemes for elaborate public works, especially to employ the idle in times of depression. Within limits such a building program is undoubtedly desirable, but it has perils, for it may withdraw millions and billions from fruitful capital investments and waste them on enterprises which add nothing to the nation's economy except expenses for upkeep. The history of federal waterways appropriations affords a tragic warning.

Finally, there are various projects of insurance. Here, too, is a device of restricted utility. Governing persons may prefer to give doles to idle working-people rather than to have them upset the fair pageantry of state, but the practice extended over long periods of time is ruinous to economy and morals. It represents the imbecility of defeatism. Besides, it displays the kind of intellectual cowardice which led the Romans to seek safety in supplying bread and circuses to the pullulating multitudes of the Eternal City. It is a foe of, not a substitute for, planned economy.

In the fuller realization of that type of economy, the stubborn heritage of American civilization must be kept in mind. Planning cannot ignore the human elements in the situation — the traditions of personal liberty (though often violated), the inventiveness and experimenting spirit of individuals, long-continued institutions of local government, ways of living, standards of life, and easygoing democracy of customs. It must conserve the dynamics of enterprise which has been so marked in the conquest of this continent. It must reward efficiency from the top to the bottom — a truth which the Russian Government is learning by bitter experience. It must leave wide areas of life and economy open to ingenuity. It must reckon with the resolve of vast masses to have more than the minimum subsistence now tolerated by millions in Europe and the Orient. It must avoid the red tape and sterility so common to large government undertakings — though not so common as often imagined in interested quarters. It will lop off the deadwood of our futile plutocracy, so sinister in its influences on politics, culture, and rational living, without at the same time destroying the prudence of husbandry.

Planning on a large scale in these circumstances, and in fact in any circumstances, is a hazardous industry, but it must be faced, and attempts must be made to cut a way into the dim future under such light as we have. It is not given to any mind to conceive a blue-print of the whole field, and the present project is submitted with the thought that it may be more of a target for concentrating fire than a beacon to the lampless. Yet in human affairs a target has its utility. As James Madison explains in *The Federalist*, 'it is impossible for the people spontaneously and universally to move in concert toward their object'; hence in time of stress and strain changes must be 'instituted by some informal and unauthorized propositions made by some patriotic and respectable citizen or number of citizens.' In this spirit the following plan is sketched to the limits of the space allowed.

A NATIONAL ECONOMIC COUNCIL

The first step in the program is the institution of a National Economic Council, under the authorization of Congress. In organizing the membership of this Council, Congress will take into account all the great industries which have reached a high degree of concentration or would be easily consolidated were it not for the hampering barriers of the anti-trust acts. The groups thus affiliated will certainly include economic agencies concerned with transportation, communications, fuel (oil, gas, and coal), iron and steel, lumber and building materials, electrical utilities, textiles, packing, and perhaps a few others. Also represented on the Council will be the several organizations in agriculture, wholesaling, and retailing. In addition, labor, organized and unorganized, will have its spokesmen. The exact weight to be assigned to each element will be a matter of great delicacy, but criteria can be evolved and in the process the experience of Germany with economic councils may be studied with profit.

In short, there will be established for the fundamental industries of the country — covering the prime necessities of food, clothes, and shelter — a small national body charged with the function of coördinating these divisions of economy and working out the project of their inner relations — financial, operative, and distributive. At the outset it will serve as a kind of economic convention, like that of 1787, to draw up an economic program to be submitted to the country for approval. It will naturally propound any changes in the Constitution and laws deemed necessary for the realization of planned economy.

To facilitate this immense operation, the Sherman and Clayton anti-trust acts will be repealed. All industries included in the National Economic Council, and other industries not yet ripe for affiliation but approaching a high degree of concentration, will be declared to be national public service enterprises 'affected with public interest' and subject to the principles of prudent investment and fair returns. In all this there is no departure from concepts now well established in American law. Billions of dollars' worth of gas, railway, communications, and electric property is already within the scope of this declaration. The Federal Coal Commission, which examined the coal problem in 1923, reported that the mining of anthracite was 'affected with public interest.' In sustaining an act of Colorado pertaining to strikes and lockouts in such business undertakings, a state court declared years ago: 'We must take judicial notice of what has taken place in this and other states, and that the coal industry is vitally related, not only to other industries, but to the health and even the life of the people. Food, shelter, and heat before all others are the great necessities of life and in modern life heat means coal.'

Well may the informed commentator, R. E. Cushman, add: 'This is a line of reasoning which raises the query whether the courts may not yet come to the point of defining businesses affected with a public interest in simple terms of human necessity.' Whatever the courts might say with respect to such a principle, it would be supreme if established by constitutional mandate. At one stroke the billions of capital now within this category will be widened to cover all enterprises fundamental to a high standard of American life, and the process of regularization, standardization, accounting, and control can be immediately set going. If a great deal of water went under the bridge, it could be later squeezed out painlessly by inheritance taxes, and the proceeds devoted to amortization of capital.

Associated with the National Economic Council will be a Board of Strategy and Planning, with appropriate divisions, each headed by a production engineer. Here points of reference can be found in the War Industries Board and other federal agencies created during the Titanic effort to mobilize men and materials for the World War. The prime function of the Board of Strategy and Planning will be to make a survey of the resources and productive facilities of the country and forecast the production of consumers' and capital goods, starting with obvious needs and proceeding to the possible boundaries of wealth creation under a system of efficient technology.

After this survey will come an allocation of productive and distributive activities with respect to the requirements of the plan. Procedure here will be in keeping with that already followed by large corporations in the United States — simply on a vaster scale and subject to economic, not legal, restrictions. The central concern will be not only the maximum output of goods in each division, within the limits of constantly expanding requirements, but also a steady raising of the standard of life by increasing wages and reducing prices. The tempo of the production machine will be, as our philosophical engineer, Ralph E. Flanders, says, 'a question of values. As we value goods more and leisure less, we will lengthen our work days. As we value leisure more and goods less, we will shorten them.'

Closely affiliated with the Board of Strategy and Planning will be the Bureau of Standards in Washington, which will be strengthened by a concentration of industrial research agencies, as far as centralization will work for the elimination of duplications. Whenever it is necessary, for industrial or geographical reasons, to attach research laboratories to particular plants or, as in the case of agriculture, to experiment stations established with reference to climate and soils, there will be a planning and allocation of work at the center, under a planning staff, with a view to intense specialization and the solution of problems with the least motion. In connection with its work, the Bureau of Standards will extend its present activities to include the standardization of all commodities produced under the jurisdiction of the National Economic Council; and goods produced outside of that jurisdiction will be subjected to the same tests as to weights, measures, composition, and quality. These will be, of course, the fundamental goods. A large part of so-called 'quality goods,' calling for distinctive taste and æsthetic characteristics, will continue in private hands, but with the decline of the plutocracy the production of articles for the *demi-monde* will fall off.

SYNDICATED CORPORATIONS

So much for the general overhead of the new order of technological efficiency. Now let us turn to the internal structure of the great industries associated with the National Economic Council. Each will be a syndicate of affiliated corporations, in the form of a holding company, analogous to the present Electric Bond and Share Company, with large directorial and service powers. Perhaps in time a closer union will be effected, but the more freedom at the bottom the better for initiative and prompt action.

The syndicate will have its own board of strategy and planning, geared into the grand Board of the National Economic Council. The syndicate will consist of divisional or geographical corporations, or both, as the case may be, and the various plants under each corporation will be operated by corporation managers. Operating standards and efficiency tests for all plants will be set by syndicate production engineers, and competitive principles will be established, with National Service Medals and graduated bonuses as rewards for valorous soldiers of the forge and lathe. Since the profits of each syndicate, as a public utility, are to be limited, such surpluses as may arise will be due mainly to unexpected efficiency, and will be divided into two parts: one to go to bonuses and the other to reserves for contingencies, including unemployment arising from accidents, temporary shutdowns, changes in machinery, crop failures, and depressions, if any.

In the precise form proposed for each syndicate and corporation, there will be nothing foreign to American experience and practical achievement. Numerous examples are to be found on every hand. There is, for instance, the Inland Waterways Corporation under the management of the War Department, which operates fleets of vessels in the carrying trade between Minnesota and the Gulf of Mexico, as well as along the Gulf from Alabama to New Orleans. Though a business concern making regular charges for its service, it is entirely public in nature, the Government of the United States holding all the stock in it. Another illustration is afforded by the Federal Land Banks, in which the Government owns part of the stock and closely supervises the issue of bonds. Possibilities are to be found in the limited-dividend corporations established for housing projects under the laws of New York.

Hints for development may also be drawn from the proposed corporation to take over transit companies in New York City, involving property worth approximately a billion dollars. Under this scheme the outstanding stocks and bonds are to be transformed into other securities, bearing a low rate of interest, and the amalgamated concerns are to be operated by a quasi-public directorate representing the city and the constituent companies.

From fragments gathered from holding companies and organizations mentioned above, illuminated by imagination, ideal forms for the syndicates and corporations to be established under the National Economic Council can be readily brought to blue-print, without violating a single American economic tradition. Indeed, a far more tender regard could be paid to stock- and bond-holders than is usual in cases of bankruptcy and reorganization under private banking auspices.

Now let us consider the problem of financing. In the beginning, the financial readjustment necessary to the establishment of each syndicate or corporation might be left to private arrangement, as in the case of railway and utility enterprises under federal and state commissions.

Principles conceived in the public interest with due respect to private rights are now a part of the laws of the land. Since the new syndicates to be organized under the National Economic Council will be public utilities, it will be relatively easy to work out the financial readjustment on the basis of prudent investment and fair return. In time, however, it may be found desirable to reduce the capital charges by substituting consolidated first mortgage bonds drawing three per cent interest, gradually extinguishing the outside stock-holding groups, and providing safe investments for small savings.

Doubtless, as indicated, a lot of water would flow into the capital set-up, causing a huge outcry among political democrats, but since the water could be effectively reduced by taxation, it would be better to allow a generous freedom than to stall a grand plan in a quarrel over details. As a part of the program, it would contribute to efficiency if a large amount of stocks were kept afloat, with graduated dividends based on efficiency in operation and production, especially if these stocks were distributed among the directors, managers, and employees of the several corporations. Thus the private stockholder, who ordinarily does nothing for industry but sign proxies and grumble when dividends are reduced, would be eliminated in the end, and vested interests turned over to engineers and workers, leaving the bondholder with his three per cent and liable to a stiffer inheritance tax than is now imposed. It would also be advantageous if the proceeds from inheritance and income surtaxes were all turned over to capital account for amortization purposes or new construction, leaving the politicians to raise their current revenues from other sources.

From what has been said it is apparent that no confiscation of property is contemplated here. On the contrary, the examples set by the abolition of three or four billion dollars' worth of property in slaves during our civil conflict, and the destruction of millions invested in the liquor business by prohibition, are put aside as highly undesirable methods of operating in a technological society. It is one thing for peasants to seize land belonging to their lords and go ahead tilling it as of old; but the arbitrary seizure of property employed in complicated technical operations is an entirely different proposition. An acre of land is an acre of land, and corn or potatoes are easily produced on it. A factory or railway is, to be sure, a collection of objective utilities, but the amount of wealth it can turn out depends fundamentally on the interest, skill, and loyalty of those who manage and operate it. The loss of a few months of chaos may be equal to the entire capital value. It has been estimated that the entire productive outfit of an industrial nation could be reproduced in ten years.

Everything hangs on management. Violence and tyranny cannot create a spinning machine or operate one after it is built. A few years of civil conflict in a technological society, even if carried on by political methods only, might well destroy more wealth than could possibly accrue to present vested interests under the generous reorganization plan suggested above. Cave-man methods on the part of capital and labor in a technological civilization indicate a lack of common-sense, if not a want of humor, to say nothing of justice and humanity. If the American economic system could be run full blast on principles of efficiency for five years, the surplus alone would probably extinguish half of the capital obligations, especially if coupled with a moderate use of the taxing power.

FARMING

Since American industries are far advanced along the road of technology and concentration, it is not necessary to attempt here a closer picture of the syndicate plan proposed above. But something must be said about agriculture, which is still in a primitive state of development in large sections of the country. Agriculture ought to be especially emphasized in connection with national planning, for city dwellers are woefully ignorant of the land and seem to care little for the conditions under which their basic industry is carried on. Yet it is fundamental. If agriculture perishes, as in parts of China, civilization sinks down in ruins. Rome likewise furnishes an example; our scholars well know the intimate relations between the decay of Roman agriculture and the decline of the Empire. There is also another side to the problem. The overgrown urban agglomerations of the United States, with their millions pounding pavements, toiling listlessly in poorly lighted offices and factories, and living in sunless tenements need more of the country, not less. And a rational system of industrial planning will dissolve the absurd and unwholesome slum areas of cities, carry industries out into air and sunlight, and institute a fine balance of rural and urban life.

But is it possible to plan for the individualistic anarchy of American agriculture? There are great difficulties in the way; yet they are not insurmountable to intelligence and will. Governor Roosevelt, of New York, propounded last winter, in a statesmanlike manner, the beginnings of an attack on this problem. Recognizing the fact that immense areas of marginal land are now being tilled, yielding only poverty and distress to the tillers, he proposed a survey of all the agricultural resources of the state, a classification of land according to fertility and uses, and the reforestation of enormous sections now under futile cultivation. Fair compensation would be made to the owners and a recovery of outlay effected in the long run by the production of lumber. Collaterally, a great mileage of back-country roads would be closed, materially reducing the burdensome taxes now imposed on farms for maintenance. The abandonment of dirt roads could be accompanied by the extension of improved highways throughout the fertile regions according to a rational plan, thus providing rapid transportation to market and raising the standards of country life. Along the improved highways high voltage lines could be built for the transmission of electricity, furnishing cheap power and light for farms — power to facilitate production and light so indispensable to civilized living.

Under the Agricultural Syndicate, to be formed under the National Economic Council, plans along the above lines will be worked out for the whole country and carried into execution through federal and state coöperation. This would, of course, be merely a start, important, no doubt, but still a preliminary.

With regard to the millions of individual farms and plantations under cultivation, all is not formless and void. Powerful associations in cotton growing, wheat raising, dairying, fruit culture, and other branches are operating today in connection with the Federal Farm Board and the Department of Agriculture. Standardization, the introduction of scientific methods, and coöperative marketing are in rapid process of development and, great as are the difficulties ahead, they are by no means baffling.

But this is not enough. A more thoroughgoing rationalization is demanded by the exigencies of our industrial civilization. Efficiency calls for a concentration in certain branches of agriculture as in manufacturing and transporting. To proceed on the assumption that wheat can be profitably raised on small farms, costing sometimes two hundred and fifty dollars an acre, in competition with gigantic enterprises such as T. D. Campbell conducts in Wyoming or Hickman Price in Texas, is to pursue a delusion bound to be ruinous in the end, no matter how much money the Farm Board pours into the bottomless wheat pit. It simply cannot be done and heroic measures will be necessary to meet the situation created by technology in agriculture.

What is the way out? At best it is dimly seen, and only guesses can be made here. Yet one thing is certain: the ruthless conquest and exploitation of peasants by the urban proletariat practiced in Russia is impossible in the United States or, if possible, a violation of every human decency cherished by the American people. There are, however, methods of collective action which are compatible with individual rights and long settled traditions. In the first place, the syndicate and corporation idea to be applied in industry is applicable to important branches of agriculture — is, in fact, already applied on some scale. Hence the Syndicate of Agriculture, established under the National Economic Council, will proceed as a public utility to acquire large areas of land which cannot be profitably tilled by historic methods and will work them by machinery under special corporations. Individual farmers, without surrendering their local interest, can come into a corporation on specific conditions, just as individual manufacturing plants can be taken into an appropriate industrial corporation.

In addition, one large agricultural corporation in the national syndicate could undertake large diversified farming. It might acquire by purchase thousands of farms in different parts of the country and tie different branches into one enterprise. For instance, it could operate corn farms in Iowa and dairy farms in Connecticut, shipping its feed by the trainload from the West to central depots in the dairy district, employing improved highways in detailed distribution. Agents stationed at central points could supply standardization and efficiency methods and exercise supervision over individual dairymen. Machinery could be used coöperatively in convenient districts; insurance and other services rendered.

Farmers owning their land might come under the scheme, keeping individual initiative and yet deriving the benefits of a collective economy.

In conjunction with the industrial syndicates a distribution of power and minor industries can be made in such a way as to employ farmers during the winter season, supplying local and even national necessities, perhaps wooden articles from neighboring forests. As a further guarantee of efficiency, the system of bonuses for performance, prevailing in industry, will be applied to agricultural corporations. As far as the system works, agriculture will be brought under the régime of planned economy.

MARKETING AND FOREIGN AFFAIRS

On the marketing side immense difficulties will be encountered and it will be the duty of the Marketing Syndicate under the National Economic Council, representing wholesaling and retailing interests, to work out the plan. Chain stores and mail-order houses point one way of development. The establishment of great storage houses and refrigeration plants, with branches, and the integration of those now under federal and state supervision will eliminate wastage in haulage and handling, curtail the sphere and profits of middlemen, and open the direct routes between producers and consumers. Here, too, as in other divisions of planned economy, individual merchants may affiliate themselves with the Marketing Syndicate's corporations. In the end, however, with respect to all staples, the area of this hazardous occupation will be materially restricted, without closing the doors upon merchants dealing with specialties and objects of æsthetic enjoyment.

Now we come to foreign affairs, which, strictly speaking, is a department of industry and marketing. Since an immense domestic market will be opened under national planning and attention will be directed primarily to the enlargement of this market, the feverish and irrational methods of unloading and dumping goods on foreign countries will be reduced to a minimum, if not discontinued entirely. The industrial countries of the world cannot live by taking in each other's washing. Here also is the most fruitful source of international rivalries and wars — the source of most burdens for diplomacy. Once rationalized, foreign exchange could proceed on the basis of reciprocal trade in necessities not well supplied by domestic enterprise.

Under the plan here proposed the foreign commerce of the United States will be carried on by a syndicate of exporting and importing corporations organized along the lines now laid down in the Webb Act of 1918 for the export trade. In this field as elsewhere there will be nothing new — merely an extension of principles and practices well established under prevailing legislation. The purpose of the syndicate, however, will not be to force firearms and trinkets on African savages, but to carry on a rational trade with other countries in such a way as to secure, on fair and favorable terms, the goods needed by the United States. It will not proceed on the assumption that the nation can get rich by dumping goods abroad at less than the cost of production. The syndicate will also control the issue of foreign securities in the United States. It will stop the reckless habits of financiers in making loans to irresponsible governments to be wasted in unproductive enterprises — a custom ruinous to American investors and a curse to the peoples of the borrowing countries. Naturally the syndicate will also be a powerful aid to diplomacy, bringing the reason of commodity exchange to bear on the vagaries of ministers plenipotentiary.

As a phase of foreign policy associated with trade, American diplomacy will proceed on the basis of the

Kellogg Pact. It will recommend adherence to the World Court. It will frankly coöperate to the fullest extent in the economic conferences and conventions of the League of Nations, as it does now in a furtive manner. It will advise a cancellation of European debts on condition that the armed forces of the world be brought down to a police basis. It will abandon the Coolidge theorem that the army and navy of the United States must be big enough to protect any American citizen who wants to make ten per cent on the bonds of Weissnichtwo or sell cornflakes, shoe-horns, and collar buttons to the inhabitants of the world willy-nilly. For the policy of dominating the world, American diplomacy will substitute that of strict and adequate national defense — defense of the land and people of the United States — by universal military service, if Europe stubbornly refuses to come to terms on disarmament.

AMERICA TOMORROW

All this, it may be said, is too large, too general, too remote, and offers no help in the present emergency. That complaint may be faced, although it is sometimes better to suffer in an emergency than to do more harm in an effort to get out of it. While the program outlined above is being put into execution, expedients may be devised in line with its provisions.

Let the President summon Congress in a special session to organize immediately two of the syndicates to be ultimately fitted into the grand scheme — one for agriculture and the other for building materials and housing. The first of these, with the consent of state legislatures, will begin immediately to carry into execution in each state the plan proposed by Governor Roosevelt of New York, alluded to above, namely, buying up marginal land, reforesting, constructing highways, and building electric transmission lines (with or without the coöperation of private companies as circumstances may dictate). In each state the syndicate will also proceed to organize one or more agricultural corporations to establish corporate farming as outlined above on a large scale, in that way covering thousands of acres of public and private land with grand model enterprises.

The Building Materials and Housing Syndicate will proceed at once to a survey of the slum and submerged areas of great cities, make regional plans, and prepare a gigantic housing program. It will entrust construction to limited dividend corporations in each locality or, where this is not feasible, form special corporations for the purpose. It will enroll an army of two or three million men to tear down and build cities decent to live in and delightful to the eye, summoning to its aid the best architectural talent in the country. As each housing project will be directed by a special corporation, matters of management, rentals, and ownership will be left to local circumstances. Until the general system of productive and distributive economy is organized, there will be many difficulties and hazards, but after that consummation housing will be geared into the development of industry. It should then work out smoothly.

These two undertakings will be financed by Freedom Bonds and sold with the zeal of war issues. And they will sell. If the hysterical governments of Europe should get into another war and the United States were drawn into the conflict, who would protest against the sale of a hundred billion dollars' worth of consols to pay for killing ten million boys? Not a single patriot. Then will it be said that we cannot float one tenth of the sum, if necessary, to save five or six million American citizens from the horrors of unemployment and pauperism — and enrich the country at the same time by adding grand capital works, wealth-creating enterprises? After a war, the people, that is, plain citizens, are poorer than before;

after this heroic national effort, all will be richer in goods — and still more important, in patriotic spirit. It ought not to be difficult to arouse enthusiasm for such a cause.

Let the worst be said. Let it be prophesied that these agricultural and housing works will not 'pay.' Doubtless some money would be lost, but in the end there would be millions of acres of model farms and thousands of houses fit to live in. If the scheme fails, the properties can be sold on better terms than, let us say, unused munition dumps and the boats of the Emergency Fleet Corporation. Should they all fall into ruin, still they would be the noblest monument to human endeavor ever erected since time began, making America at doomsday unique among the civilizations of the earth.

But the project is not utopian; it involves the extension of practices already in effect; and brains and materials are available. If such a program were officially announced, its immediate effect would be to give the people of the United States assurance for the future; they would begin to spend where they now hoard against direful uncertainty; and the outcome would be confidence in the will and power of the nation.

In summary, the scheme here outlined is no foreign concoction or importation. It is a purely native product. Even now it lies partly completed before us. It may be merely American destiny foreshadowed. In any case, it makes no break with American institutions and traditions. On the contrary, it integrates and accelerates processes already unfolding under our very eyes: according to the estimates of Gardiner C. Means, two hundred corporations, managed by fewer than two thousand directors, control between thirty-five and forty-five per cent of the business wealth of the country, and they are growing three times as fast as the small corporations. Are they to be great aggregations of wealth selfishly administered or public service corporations operated on a basis of prudent investment and fair return? That is a fateful question, soon to be asked in tones of thunder, even if planned economy be rejected as chimerical.

But it is not chimerical. It is practical, for America has the intelligence, the organizing capacity, the engineering skill, the material endowment, and above all, men and women willing to make immense sacrifices for their children and their children's children. They have faith in the mission of their country. And in due time America will arise, shake off her lethargy, and put forth powers like those of our ancestors who founded this nation and conquered this continent. If to the aged of little hope, planned economy appears remote and impossible, it must be said that it is not as remote and impossible as the very United States today would seem to the little band of men and women who landed under wintry skies at Plymouth three centuries ago. To take counsel and to dare, again and yet again, this is the true American spirit, and out of daring will come achievement far beyond our dim, chill imaginations.

CHAPTER II
UNEMPLOYMENT[1]
BY NICHOLAS MURRAY BUTLER

ON THIS eve of Labor Day, a holiday set apart in recognition of the fundamental and most honorable place which work holds in organized society, it is becoming to turn earnest attention to that problem of unemployment which now confronts every nation throughout the civilized world. A problem so universal, so fundamental and, if left unsolved, so full of danger, cannot have arisen from any merely national, much less local, cause, but must be traceable to tendencies, influences, and conditions which are everywhere at work.

For something more than a century we have been living in a rapidly developing and rapidly expanding industrial age. Agriculture and all forms of handwork have declined in relative importance while machine production, transportation and commerce over wide areas and long distances have multiplied many times over. So far as the wants of men have been diversified and increased to keep pace with this rapidly expanding and multiplying production, all has gone fairly well. In recent years, however, the effect of the displacement of hand labor by the machine, of the complete overturn of existing industrial and commercial undertakings and arrangements by the Great War, and of influences arising from changes in the value of the accepted standard of the world's monetary system, have combined to bring about a situation in which it is estimated that there are nearly, if not quite, thirty million human beings in Europe and America who

[1] An address delivered at the Parrish Art Museum, Southampton, Long Island, on Sunday evening, September 6, 1931.

are able and willing to work but who are not able to find gainful occupation. One need not attempt to emphasize the significance of so grave a happening. It speaks for itself. First of all it challenges, with peremptory directness, the social and economic system which gives rise to it and permits it. In the second place, it may easily and quickly lead to an organized expression of deep-felt discontent that would seek the overturn of political systems which now seem well established, on the ground that anything is better than the continuance of life without steady employment, without hope and without protection against disability and old age. What shall be done about it?

Despite its present urgency, this is no new problem. Wise economists and students of human affairs have for years past seen it coming upon us. It has brought into existence a large and most instructive literature scattered through a dozen languages. Committees and commissions, official and unofficial, have examined it and made recommendations concerning it. Fifty years ago the keen eye of Prince Bismarck perceived the relation of this problem to the German State and presented it to the Reichstag in an impressive speech marked as much by vision as by wisdom.[1] Germany, which has always been in the forefront of those nations with a firm grasp on social problems, moved forward to deal with this question under Bismarck's leadership. Smaller nations followed, and then Great Britain, whose government has for a century been quickly and increasingly responsive to public opinion and anxious to satisfy public needs, made its contribution. Various states of the American Union have dealt with some of what may be called the outlying aspects of this whole subject, but the main question itself yet remains to be grappled with in the United States.

[1] Bismarck: *Die gesammelten Werke* (Berlin: Stollberg Verlag, 1929), XII, 236–49.

Signs are not wanting that under the impulse of emotion and pressure of immediate need courses of public action are likely to be proposed which, if adopted, will only increase the difficulties of the situation which now exists, as well as bring new and unsuspected difficulties in their train. We must prepare ourselves and our public opinion to approach this vital question from the viewpoint of sound principle and along the path of wisdom rather than that of uncritical emotion.

It will help if we get back for a moment to fundamentals. Everyone lives by his own labor or by that of someone else. No one but a beggar, as Adam Smith pointed out more than a century and a half ago, chooses to depend chiefly upon the benevolence of his fellow citizens.[1] It is a fair inference that somewhere and somehow the social and economic system which regulates men's lives must find place for the willing labor of everyone who is not incapacitated by infancy, by disability or by old age. Society has been organized and developed on a basis which uses the family and property as its foundation. Therefore the family grows up about and depends upon the labor of its chief worker, and any property which he may accumulate is statedly made available for the support and protection of those immediately dependent upon him both during his life and after his death. So far so good. What shall be done, however, when, by the operation and influence of those causes which have already been mentioned, or others less important and less widespread than they, the willing worker finds no place to which he may take his willingness and his capacity to work?

Our vast working population of the present day may be divided into three groups or classes: first, those who are able and willing to work and for whose labor the social

---

[1] Adam Smith: *An Inquiry into the Nature and Causes of the Wealth of Nations* (London: Henry Frowde, 1904), I, 16.

order must find some opportunity and make some provision; second, those who are able but not willing to work, who may be described as social derelicts; and third, those who, while willing to work, are not able to do so and therefore become social dependents. Our chief concern at the moment is with the first-named group, namely, those who are both able and willing to work, but who can find no remunerative occupation.

ORGANIZATION AND RATIONALIZATION OF INDUSTRY

Obviously, there are two different and complementary ways to attack this problem. The first is through social organization and control of industry, the establishment of such balance between production and consumption — all of which might well be known as rationalization — as will reduce the number of unemployed as much as possible. The second is the provision of ways and means by which the irreducible minimum of unemployed may be statedly cared for on principles and by methods that are sound both in morals and in economics. If, as one suspects, the first of these steps is made doubly difficult by economic and financial conditions which are under human control, then we should lose no time in addressing ourselves to these.

It appears to be admitted, as the English economist, Mr. J. A. Hobson, asserts, that almost everywhere productive power is held in leash, everywhere unemployed labor confronts unemployed machinery and other capital, because markets are not sufficiently expansive to purchase either the consumable goods or the capital-goods which could be produced.[1] It is essential, then, to expand the purchasing power and so to distribute it among the entire population that it will have a tendency to remain in balance with the power of production. It would begin

[1] Hobson, J. A.: *Rationalism and Unemployment* (London: George Allen & Unwin, 1930), 6.

to appear that we may have been moving in the wrong direction by our endeavors to stimulate unlimited competition in production and to prevent combinations in restraint and control of trade. It may perhaps be that the Sherman Act of 1890, then hailed as a long step in advance for the protection of the small producer and merchant, was in reality a step backward in the light of all that has happened since. It begins to appear that what we really need are many combinations in control of trade — in restraint of trade, so to speak — all interpreted, as the United States Supreme Court would have it, in terms of the rule of reason, and so supervised by official authority that they cannot be used to establish privilege or to permit discrimination and persecution.

To put the matter somewhat differently, what appears to be required is that the several great basic industries of the nation should be so organized in the interest of the general public as to control production within the limits of a proper balance with an expanding power of consumption. Should something like this be effected and work well, it would then be practicable, as several writers of competence have pointed out, both to stabilize and to regularize employment within the field of each one of a considerable number of large industries which are easily susceptible of regional or nation-wide organization.

The next step would be to make each one of these organized industries feel responsible for the employment and care of its great body of workmen. When a new enterprise is undertaken and new capital is sought, every consideration is given to studying the estimated production of the factory or mine or oil well in order that a satisfactory return upon the money invested may be assured. Why should not an equal amount of study be given to the problem as to how many work-people are statedly needed for the enterprise and as to what provision can be made for their security within the limits of

the ordinary fluctuation of the rise and fall of the production of the business? In other words, why should not
the care and protection of the employed be made as much
a part of the policy of any great business undertaking as
are the care and protection of the money invested? Why
should not the question, Is it human? be put beside the
question, Will it pay?

This point of view opens large possibilities and offers
various suggestions. There is, for example, possible provision from this source for the retirement of work-people
who through age or disability are no longer competent to
work, as is done in the case of the best administered American universities. There is the whole field of insurance
which has already been entered upon, but which can be
much more fully occupied to the very great advantage of
the great mass of work-people. Were organized industries
to accept such a policy as this, there would quickly grow
up among them a new sense of social responsibility and a
new sense of satisfaction which would have their beneficent and profitable practical effects in public approval
and public support. Moreover, it is quite conceivable
that such a policy carefully studied and sagaciously
worked out would actually, as the president of the General Electric Company suggested some months ago, lower
taxes levied in order that a portion of the population may
be maintained in a state of unemployment.

Here in the United States we have already seen of what
immense value it has been to have work-people in large
numbers invest their savings in the great corporations to
which their work is given. The resultant feeling of ownership bridges the wide and sometimes ugly gulf between
employer and employed and leads on the part of the work-
people to genuine pleasure and satisfaction in the success
of the undertaking for which they labor and which they
in part own. Let this same principle of coöperation between employer and employed be carried a little farther.

Let each organized industry or series of industries plan ahead in systematic and scientific fashion for the welfare of their entire industry including the work-people, and a new spirit of contentment, of self-reliance and of a sense of justice would come into the life of the people. To be sure, there are many and various occupations which are beyond reach of a policy such as that just now described, and by them and for them different steps must be taken. The guiding principle, however, would appear to be always and everywhere the same, namely, that the industry, the locality, the family, should each accept its share of the burden of preventing unemployment, and thereby both distribute it so that it will not be impossible to bear and at the same time prevent the adoption of those purely sentimental and uneconomic measures of relief which can only demoralize and sap the moral vitality of a people.

SOCIAL INSURANCE

The word insurance has been mentioned, and this in one form or another is bound up with any sound system of relief from widespread and continuing unemployment. Insurance is essentially an accumulation of funds to meet uncertain losses. It is and can be scientific only when the losses in question have been accurately recorded over a sufficient time and throughout a wide enough area to provide an adequate basis for a mathematical study of the probabilities involved. Against death, disability, accident, or old age it is possible to provide insurance protection of one kind or another. In the case of unemployment, however, it is exceedingly difficult, and some wise men think it impossible, to build up a system of insurance on equally sound and scientific lines. However this may be, it is beginning to be clear, for both evidence and argument multiply to that effect, that something of this kind must be attempted. Let it be said at once that it would be a tragic blunder were we here in the United

States either to turn this matter over to the Federal Government or permit the Federal Government to control this field of public and private helpfulness. It is a matter which belongs to the several states and as to which they must face their responsibility, in coöperation, let it be hoped, with organized industry and with the full concurrence of both those who employ and those who are employed.

We are here dealing with a form of uncertainty which perplexes the wisest and the best-meaning of men. Several of the Swiss communes have adopted unemployment insurance of one sort or another, but without what may fairly be described as success. The reason appears to be that the insecurity of employment is a form of uncertainty with which it has thus far proved impossible for insurance on a scientific basis to deal.

Some very impressive and convincing statements of fact in this regard are contained in 'A First Report of the Royal Commission on Unemployment Insurance,' presented to Parliament in June last. This report traces in careful detail the development of unemployment insurance in Great Britain since action to this end was first taken in 1911. Before that time, unless a workman was a recipient of charity or was cared for under the provisions of the old Poor Law, there was nothing done for him by society as a whole. He was entirely dependent upon such provision as he might make for himself out of savings or, if he were a trade union member, upon the unemployment benefit to which he was entitled as a member of a union. Unemployment benefits of this latter kind have been established in Great Britain for nearly three quarters of a century. These benefits were, however, narrowly limited to workers in skilled occupations and extended by no means to all of these. It was the purpose of the trade union benefit to tide the individual worker over a short and casual period of unemployment and to forestall the necessity of trade union members having to accept work in emergency at less than the prevailing trade union rate of wage.

The unemployment insurance provision which was introduced in Great Britain in 1911 grew out of elaborate and most thorough inquiries, extending over four years, that were made by a Royal Commission. The system then introduced was confessedly an experiment and established compulsory state insurance against unemployment in a few selected trades which employed about two and one quarter million workers. This plan has been described as only a first line of defense against distress due to unemployment. Sir William Beveridge, who was as influential as any other single person in bringing this plan into existence, has said of it:

Compulsory Unemployment Insurance was introduced in 1911, primarily as a means of extending something like the Trade Union's system to unskilled and unorganized workmen. It was meant to provide a benefit, strictly limited in duration, to men whose eligibility for benefits could be determined by some simple automatic test, and under rules designed to interest work-people and employers alike in reducing unemployment and avoiding unnecessary claims. This last motive was, indeed, one of the main reasons for requiring contributions from employers; the contribution would vary from time to time with the rate of employment. The contribution from the State was justified partly as an expression of the interest of the State in reducing distress through unemployment, partly as a means of equalizing risks and contributions.[1]

Here we have presented a scheme which, with the changes in it since made, has been in existence twenty years. As originally conceived and adopted this scheme was in close accord with the argument made to the Reichstag by Prince Bismarck thirty years earlier. Both

[1] *A First Report of the Royal Commission on Unemployment Insurance* (London, 1931), 12.

experience and sound argument support the view that, if a scientific basis for a plan of unemployment insurance can be worked out, over and above that which can and should be provided by the highly organized trades and industries, it will involve a contribution by the insured workman, a contribution by his employer and at least a small contribution by the state to accompany the state's oversight and protection. The insurance policy, if written, should remain the property of the insured workman. He should be able to take it with him wherever he might go with his interest in it unimpaired and with the prospect that another employer would coöperate with him in keeping the policy alive.

Precisely this plan is in successful operation among teachers and administrative officers in American colleges and universities through the Teachers' Insurance and Annuity Association which was brought into existence thirteen years ago by the Carnegie Foundation for the Advancement of Teaching. A reserve fund that is built up by coöperation between the employer and the employed and that is supervised by the State is sound in principle and may with sufficient experience be made to work excellently in practice.

It never must be forgotten that a most important factor in the success of all these plans is the psychological one. It is the peace of mind which certainty instead of uncertainty, which expectation instead of fear, brings to the workman as years pass and as industrial conditions change, which matter most in his life and in the life of those who surround him and are dependent upon him.

The great danger in any such plan as that now under discussion is that it may become bankrupt through improper administration or that it be permitted to degenerate into a payment without proportionate contribution from the insured and under circumstances which transform it into a mere grant in aid at the cost of the public treasury. This is the deplorable and lamentable dole which, for every person that it genuinely relieves and assists, demoralizes ten others by giving them the impression that they may indefinitely receive from the public treasury a payment for unemployment. No man of human feeling would consciously permit any one of his fellow-men to suffer starvation or even deprivation of the necessities of life, but he will postpone until the last possible moment the acceptance and inauguration of any policy which will involve a payment from what has been properly described as a remote and impersonal source of relief. If in extreme cases a payment of this kind is to be made for a shorter or a longer period, then it should in every case be made by the locality in which the case of need arises or, at most, under our system of government, by the state. This is not a field which the Federal Government can enter without the gravest danger both to the morals of our people and to the foundations upon which our government itself now rests. Our experience with so-called veterans' pensions and allowances ought to be a warning to us.

When all has been said and done, when organized industry has recognized its obligation and accepted it, when the less well organized industries and those wholly unorganized have entered upon a soundly conceived scheme of unemployment insurance, there will yet remain a considerable margin of cases which are those of neither social derelicts nor social dependents. Might it not be possible for a considerable number of such cases to be taken care of by the locality in which they exist through the very simple device of having a family, a shop, an office, each take on one additional worker, one more than necessary under a strictly economical administration, to do the business in hand? By a simple process of local absorption such as this, distinct relief would be given, the cost would be widely distributed and in comparatively few cases would it be difficult to bear. Were one enlightened and far-sighted community to enter upon this course of action, it would find a thousand imitators, and before one knew it a great reduction would be made in the army of the unemployed at insignificant cost to anyone and without involving any charge upon the public treasury. Indeed, the net cost to any individual or establishment which participated in this process of local absorption might readily be less than the amount of the increased tax to be imposed in case long-continued unemployment of many individuals became in one form or another a public charge.

Still another important policy of similar kind is that persuasively presented by Mr. William Green, president of the American Federation of Labor. His proposal is to establish a five-day week and, eventually, a six-hour day. That this plan would have marked advantages both economic, psychological, and moral is highly probable, particularly if with its adoption went the removal of any restriction upon the amount of work which any skilled laborer could well do within the limit of time set by the six-hour or seven-hour day and the five-day week. If machinery is first of all to dispossess hand labor, there can be no good reason why it should not also give to hand labor the compensation of less onerous working conditions and more opportunity for leisure, refreshment, and the enjoyment of life. The shorter working week and what is known as adult education go hand in hand. The workman will then have some opportunity now denied him to read, to hear lectures and good music, and to participate in some of the exercises attendant upon the lighter side of life. He may also thereby widen and diversify his own skill and field of usefulness greatly to his own advantage. In a sense, the establishment of the five-day week and the six-hour or seven-hour day may be looked upon as part of the process of local absorption of the unemployed and the bringing about of better and sounder and more helpful conditions for many kinds of labor. No American who understands the fundamental principles of his country's social and political life will wish to deny these opportunities to any of his fellow-men.

It is worth noting how far we have already come in attempting to deal with these questions, although, thus far, our dealing has been piecemeal and bit by bit rather than in accordance with any carefully studied and generally understood plan. In the world as a whole there are nearly fifty million workers protected by some sort of insurance. Insurance against accident and illness has been still more widely adopted. In our own country every state but four has put upon its statute book a form of compulsory workmen's accident insurance, and a system of old age pensions and mothers' pensions is being generally and very rapidly adopted. All this has happened within some twenty-five years, and there is reason to hope that, since the urgency of this whole question is now so widely recognized, still more rapid progress will be made in the near future in lifting some of the heaviest and most grievous burdens which rest upon man.

What is always to be borne in mind, however, is the fact that so soon as any of these provisions for insurance become either openly or covertly a charge upon the public treasury, the tendency is for the amount drawn to grow rapidly and dangerously until the whole financial system of the country or state is in danger. There would probably not be money enough in all the world to provide general insurance for everybody on a non-contributory basis against all the changes and chances of this mortal life. It is only a few months ago that a public memorandum submitted by the treasury in Great Britain, referring to the Unemployment Insurance Fund in that country, stated that continued state borrowing on the present vast scale without adequate provision for repayment by the

Fund would quickly call in question the stability of the British financial system. The memorandum went on to point out that the Unemployment Insurance Fund is not only going deeper and deeper into debt, but that the rate of increase of this indebtedness is growing rapidly.

Obviously, a continuance of any such policy as this would be a blow to the nation's credit and quickly disrupt the whole system of international relations in trade and finance upon which Great Britain so completely depends for her prosperity and even for her existence. All this is quite apart from the demoralization which follows upon steady receipt from the public treasury of a definite income without any service being given in return. No matter by what name it be called, this policy, so long as it may continue, can only result in building up a nation of beggars. Should any such system be anywhere established or prolonged by the votes of those who are its direct beneficiaries, then there would come into existence not only a nation of beggars, but a nation of self-made beggars. It is clear-sighted and courageous recognition of all this which has played a large, perhaps a determining, part in the recent reorganization of the British Government.

THE CURRENCY QUESTION

There is one other aspect of this whole matter, mention of which may not be omitted. The present low value of silver, that precious metal which from time immemorial has been the measure of value and the principal store of wealth for vast populations spread over huge areas of the earth's surface, including particularly the peoples of India and of China, has fallen so low and so sharply during the past decade as gravely to limit, even in very large part to destroy, the purchasing power of hundreds of millions of human beings. It has been clearly shown that the cause for the great decline in the price of silver is not to be sought in its overproduction, but rather in national and international operations in the realm of finance consequent upon the demonetization and debasement of coinage in various lands. Since these processes are now substantially completed, there would appear to be opportunity, by international conference preferably at the instance of the League of Nations, to examine this question with a view to mapping out a course of constructive action. It is well understood that the rise in the value of gold, to say nothing of the excessive concentration of that basic metal in New York and in Paris, has complicated and disturbed a whole series of international relationships which were surely troubled and difficult enough already. Measured in terms of goods and services, international indebtedness that was incurred a few years ago must, if settled at the moment, be repaid on a scale about thirty-five per cent higher than that at which the indebtedness was entered upon.

It is just thirty-five years since William Jennings Bryan first startled, then alarmed, and finally convulsed the people of the United States by the financial policies which he advanced and advocated in his campaign for the Presidency. At that time and for some years thereafter he built up for himself much the largest purely personal following among the people gained by any American public man except Thomas Jefferson. His program and his policies were easily shown to be unsound and harmful, but, nevertheless, they appealed to millions upon millions of Americans for the reason that at bottom they rested upon and grew out of a situation which was instinctively felt, rather than clearly apprehended, throughout the nation; namely, that measured in terms of goods and services debtors were being called upon to pay much more than they had borrowed. As in 1896, so now. The existence of a condition such as this arouses first a feeling of injustice and resentment among debtors, whether governments or individuals, and also invites the bringing forward of every sort and kind of crude, unsound and unwise financial nostrum as a cure-all. For the present it is sufficient to point out that here, too, is a question of fundamental importance which requires prompt international study and prompt international action. If the hundreds of millions of men and women in India and China cannot buy the manufactured goods of Great Britain, of the United States, of France, of Germany, and of Japan, then the manufacturing industries in those lands cannot possibly flourish, they cannot possibly employ their proper share of labor, they cannot possibly pay profits or dividends to those who are their owners and managers.

THE CALL FOR ACTION

In short, the world is face to face with a grave and difficult situation with which it is not in the power of any nation adequately to deal, however large, however populous or however powerful it may be. International problems require international solutions. The necessary prelude to an international solution is international study, international consideration and international discussion. The sooner we Americans adjust ourselves to this necessary point of view and accept facts as they are, the quicker will our own domestic situation be relieved and the quicker will something approaching our customary prosperity be restored to us. To harp upon old and worn-out formulas, most of which were never wholly true at any time, and to continue to beat the tom-toms of a crude and vulgar national vanity, miscalled patriotism, are only to prolong the national agony and to make ourselves ridiculous.

Of all possible present situations in respect to human affairs there is just one which cannot be rationally maintained and that is the *status quo*. The easy-going habit of drifting which the lazy man loves, the convenient habit of waiting-to-see which the office-holder and office-seeker adore, and the holding-fast to what exists because this brings benefit and privilege to individuals or groups, are the three courses of action which simply must not be followed. Political wisdom consists largely in making such changes as are needed at the particular time that their necessity is shown. The political wisdom of today and tomorrow will rest in large part upon a quite new and changed point of view. The past has its constant and inspiring lessons to teach, and chief among these is that the past is neither the present nor the future.

Quite apart from the moral satisfaction and the economic gain of quickly and constructively dealing with what Ruskin called 'the vast question of the destinies of the unemployed workmen,' there is the vitally important end of increasing the security of the foundations upon which our political and social order rest, and which we believe to be the wisest and most just yet devised by man. If, as Junius wrote to the Duke of Bedford, we cannot be safe, we may at least cease to be ridiculous. It is nothing short of ridiculous that we should expose our fundamental principles to bitter and determined attack for the reason that in a time of plentiful production we cannot so adjust distribution as to satisfy the most elementary wants of men. It must be repeated over and over and over again that the ruling problem which confronts the world of today is none other than that of so organizing, integrating and developing the natural resources, the industries and the commerce of every land that there may be the greatest possible production and the quickest and most equitable distribution of everything which contributes to the health, the comfort and the satisfaction of the people of the whole world.

To this end those tariff barriers that have everywhere been built to prevent and harass trade throughout

. natural economic unities which pay no attention to
political boundaries, must be lowered in order that the
power to buy, to consume, may be restored and multiplied. It is quite futile to repeat that high tariffs assure
high wages when, with what is in many ways the highest
and most vexatious tariff that this country has ever
known, some six million men and women are without
any wages at all. Rates of pay may not have been materially altered, but wage-payments have been enormously reduced. A high wage-product requires a high
multiplier as well as a high multiplicand. We must be
able to manage these things, and quickly. Unless this
can be done, no political system is secure, no matter how
reasonable its principles, how deep-lying its foundations
or how splendid its achievements. Unsatisfied human
need will find ways and means to sweep all these away.

Bismarck, in that exceptionally important speech
which has already been described, used these words:

I do not think that our sons and grandsons will be entirely
free from this social question which has hovered before us for
fifty years. No political question ever comes to a full mathematical conclusion so that the books can be balanced. These
arise, have their day and finally disappear among the other
problems of history. That is the way of organic development.
I hold it to be my duty to take these problems into consideration without party bitterness and without temper.

These are truly wise words and the whole tenor of the
speech of which they are a part is to the effect that a
judicious and timely solution of any great social problem
is the surest safeguard against the success of unwise,
extreme and revolutionary policies. Just as the present
experience of the city of Vienna appears to show that a
constructive and well-ordered policy of municipal socialism erects the highest and strongest barrier against the
reactionary crudities and compulsions of communism, so

it will be found that true social-mindedness on the part of those who are privileged to live and work in the sphere of Liberty, with a government obedient to their will, is the surest prophylactic against the stiff and unbending formalities of Marxian socialism. The system of Liberty, despite its long and remarkable history, has never yet been fully and finally tested under the new economic, social, and political conditions which now prevail and which are steadily widening and deepening in character and importance. That system is now everywhere summoned to this full and final test, with able, shrewd, and powerful critics and opponents looking on and predicting failure. Intelligence and vision were never more in demand either among those who are chosen to exercise the power of government or among those who choose these governors. Intelligence is all-powerful. Vision is all-powerful. Intelligence and vision together will be found unconquerable. Remember that it is as true today as it was when the Wise Man of old wrote the words, 'Where there is no vision, the people perish.'

Chapter III

STABILIZATION OF INDUSTRY [1]

By Gerard Swope

In the situation that confronts us at the present, the most disturbing aspect is that men who are able to work, who are competent workers, who above all things desire to work, cannot find work to do. That this condition has ever been present in such periods detracts nothing from its wrongness. That industry must evolve and make effective those measures which will first ameliorate and ultimately eliminate these conditions, must be the reaction of everyone who gives thought to what is taking place. I say that industry must do this thing, because it will surely be done.

Benefits earned by a worker in one employment are wholly or in large measure lost by forced changes; or the right of choice of employment, which should be inalienable, is hampered. From the operation of individual life insurance and pension systems, however well conceived, has arisen the complaint of the 'forty-year deadline,' which, it is claimed, has seriously affected the ability of men exceeding that age to find new employment. Wide application is essential if benefits gained in one location are to follow the worker as necessity may indicate change of location, and this is a vital factor of any plan which will meet the need. If there were provided in the United States a system of benefits accruing through the life of the worker and following him where he might go, from shop to shop within a particular industry, or from branch to branch within industry as a whole, such provision

[1] An address delivered before the National Electrical Manufacturers Association at the Hotel Commodore, New York City, September 16, 1931.

would enlist, not merely interest on the part of the worker, but enthusiastic support.

Industry exists basically for serving the needs of the people, and therefore production and consumption must be coördinated. Consumption is by the mass of the population, not the few, and the great mass of the population is made up of wage earners and their dependents. That they may be able to buy and satisfy their needs, they must have not only adequate incomes, but must be sufficiently assured of the future to feel that they are safe in spending their money. The psychology of fear must be removed, and this cannot be done unless they have reasonable expectation of protection for their families in case of the bread-winner's death, protection for their old age, and protection against unemployment. By 'protection' I do not mean a protection that is given to them, but I mean protection that they themselves help to provide.

Shall we wait for society to act through its legislatures, or shall industry recognize its obligation to its employees and to the public and undertake the task? Coördination of production is impossible under our present laws, and it is vain to think of their amendment or repeal unless the public is assured of the constructive nature of the steps industry will take, and that the interests of the public will be adequately safeguarded.

The general principles underlying what I am going to say are as follows:

1. Every effort should be made to stabilize industry and thereby stabilize employment to give to the worker regularity and continuity of employment, and when this is impracticable, unemployment insurance should be provided.

2. Organized industry should take the lead, recognizing its responsibility to its employees, to the public, and to its stockholders — rather than that democratic society should act through its government. If the various states act, indus-

try will be confronted with different solutions, lacking uniformity and imposing varying burdens, making competition on a national scale difficult. If either the individual states or the Federal Government act, the power of taxation has no economic restraints.

3. There should be standardized forms of reports so that stockholders may be properly informed. As a result of the steady increase in number and size of corporations and number of shareholders, there has been much discussion of the uniformity, frequency, and regularity of reports of corporate activities, and considerable criticism of the form of these reports; some too conservative, some not sufficiently complete; while others are considered to be fair and complete; but even so there is a lack of uniformity among the different companies.

4. Production and consumption should be coördinated on a broader and more intelligent basis, thus tending to regularize employment and thereby removing fear from the minds of the workers as to continuity of employment; as to their surviving dependents in case of death; and as to old age. This should be done preferably by the joint participation and joint administration of management and employees. These things cannot be done by an individual unit — organized industry must do them.

5. If organized industry is to undertake this work, every effort should be made to preserve the benefits of individual originality, initiative, and enterprise, and to see that the public is assured that its interests will be protected, and this can be done most effectively by working through the agency of the Federal Government.

There is nothing new or original in what I am proposing. I am merely bringing together well-considered propositions that have found support, including some that have been put into actual practice.

The following plan is offered as a means to correlate into a comprehensive whole the at present undirected efforts of forward-looking business enterprises toward stabilization; for the further development of industry and commerce; for the protection of employees and stockholders; for the best service to the public and in general the best interests of society. Legislation will be required to make such a plan possible, including the probable modification of some existing laws.

An outline of the more important features follows:

1. All industrial and commercial companies (including subsidiaries) with fifty or more employees, and doing an interstate business, may form a trade association which shall be under the supervision of a federal body referred to later.

2. These trade associations may outline trade practices, business ethics, methods of standard accounting and cost practice, standard forms of balance sheet and earnings statement, etc., and may collect and distribute information on volume of business transacted, inventories of merchandise on hand, simplification and standardization of products, stabilization of prices, and all matters which may arise from time to time relating to the growth and development of industry and commerce in order to promote stabilization of employment and give the best service to the public. Much of this sort of exchange of information and data is already being carried on by trade associations now in existence. A great deal more valuable work of this character is possible.

3. The public interest shall be protected by the supervision of companies and trade associations by the Federal Trade Commission or by a bureau of the Department of Commerce or by some federal supervisory body specially constituted.

4. All companies within the scope of this plan shall be required to adopt standard accounting and cost systems and standardized forms of balance sheet and earnings statement. These systems and forms may differ for the different industries, but will follow a uniform plan for each industry as adopted by the trade association and approved by the federal supervisory body.

5. All companies with participants or stockholders numbering twenty-five or more, and living in more than one state, shall send to its participants or stockholders and to the supervisory body at least once each quarter a statement of their business and earnings in the prescribed form. At least once each

year they shall send to the participants or stockholders and to the supervisory body a complete balance sheet and earnings statement in the prescribed form. In this way the owners will be kept informed of the conditions of the business in such detail that there may be no criticism of irregularity or infrequency of statements or methods of presentation.

6. The federal supervisory body shall coöperate with the Internal Revenue Department and the trade associations in developing for each industry standardized forms of balance sheet and income statement, depending upon the character of the business, for the purpose of reconciling methods of reporting assets and income with the basis of values and income calculated for federal tax purposes.

7. All of the companies of the character described herein may immediately adopt the provisions of this plan but shall be required to do so within three years unless the time is extended by the federal supervisory body. Similar companies formed after the plan becomes effective may come in at once but shall be required to come in before the expiration of three years from the date of their organization unless the time is extended by the federal supervisory body.

8. For the protection of employees, the following plans shall be adopted by all of these companies:

(A) *A Workmen's Compensation Act*, which is part of the legislation necessary under this plan, shall, after careful study, be modeled after the best features of the laws which have been enacted by the several states.

(B) *Life and Disability Insurance.* All employees of companies included in this plan may, after two years of service with such companies, and shall, before the expiration of five years of service, be covered by life and disability insurance.

    I. The form of policy shall be determined by the association of which the company is a member and approved by the federal supervisory body. The policy will belong to the employee and may be retained by him and kept in full force when he changes his employment or otherwise discontinues particular service as outlined later.

    II. The face value of a policy shall be for an amount approximately equal to one year's pay, but not more than five thousand dollars, with the exception that the employee may, if he desires, increase at his own cost the amount of insurance carried, subject to the approval of the board of administrators, later defined.

III. The cost of this life and disability insurance shall be paid one half by the employee and one half by the company for which he works, with the following exception: The company's cost shall be determined on the basis of premiums at actual age of employees less than thirty-five years old and on the basis of thirty-five years of age for all employees thirty-five or over, and shall be a face value of approximately one half a year's pay, but limited to a maximum premium for twenty-five hundred dollars of insurance. An employee taking out insurance at age thirty-five or over will pay the excess premium over the amount based upon age thirty-five. This will remove the necessity for restriction against engaging employees or transferring them from one company to another because of advanced age, as it will place no undue burden of high premiums upon the company.

IV. The life and disability insurance may be carried by a life insurance company selected by the trade association and approved by the federal supervisory body or may be carried by a company organized by the trade association and approved by the federal supervisory body, or a single company may be formed to serve all associations.

V. The administration of the insurance plan for each company shall be under the direction of a board of administrators consisting of representatives, one half appointed by the management and one half elected by the employee members. The powers and duties of the board for each company will be to formulate general rules relating to eligibility of employees, etc., but such rules shall be in consonance with the general plan laid down by the general board of administration of the trade association of which the company is a member, and approved by the federal supervisory body.

VI. Provision for the continuation of a policy after an employee leaves one company and goes to another in the same association, or goes to a company in another trade association; continuance of the policy after retirement on pension; provisions with regard to beneficiaries; total or partial disability; method of payment of premiums by payroll deductions or otherwise, weekly, monthly, or annually, shall be embodied in the plan formulated by the trade association, with the approval of the federal supervisory body.

VII. If an employee leaves a company to go with one which is not a member of the trade association; if he engages in business for himself; or if he withdraws from industrial or commercial occupation, he may elect to retain the portion of the policy for which he has paid, in whole or in part, by the continued payment of the proportional full premium costs, or he may receive a paid-up policy, or be paid the cash surrender value for the part for which he has been paying the premiums. The cash surrender value of that portion of the policy paid for by the company will be paid to the company which paid the premiums.

(C) *Pensions.* All employees of companies included in this plan shall be covered by old-age pension plans which will be adopted by the trade associations and approved by the federal supervisory body. The principal provisions will be as follows:

I. All employees may, after two years of service with a company coming within the scope of this plan, and shall, before the expiration of five years of service, be covered by the old-age pension plan.

II. All employees after two years' service may, and after five years' service shall be required to, put aside a minimum of one per cent of earnings, but not more than fifty dollars per year, for the pension fund. The employee may, if he desires, put aside a larger amount, subject to the approval of the board of administrators.

III. The company shall be required to put aside an amount equal to the minimum stated above, namely, one per cent of earnings of employees, but not more than fifty dollars per year per employee.

IV. The above minimum percentage shall be the same for all

employees who are less than thirty-five years of age when payments begin and the minimum percentage for these employees shall remain the same thereafter. The percentage to be set aside by employees coming into the pension plan at thirty-five years of age or over shall be so determined that it will provide a retiring allowance at age seventy the same as though they had begun one per cent payments at the age of thirty-five. These provisions enable employees to go from one company to another in the same association or to different associations at any age with provision for retiring allowance which will be not less than the minimum rate of an employee who entered the pension plan at age thirty-five.

V. The amounts set aside by the employee and the company with interest compounded semi-annually at five per cent until retirement at age seventy, for a typical average employee, would provide an annuity of approximately one half pay.

VI. The administration of the pension plan for each company shall be under the direction of a board of administrators, consisting of representatives, one half appointed by the management and one half elected by the employee members. The powers and duties of the board for each company will be to formulate general rules relating to eligibility of employees, conditions of retirement, etc., but such rules shall be in consonance with the general plan laid down by the general board of administration of the trade association of which the company is a member, and approved by the federal supervisory body.

VII. The amounts collected from the employees and the companies shall be placed with a pension trust organized by the association, the management of which shall be under the direction of the general board of administration referred to hereafter. In no case shall such funds be left under the control of an individual company.

VIII. The pension trust shall invest all funds and place them to the credit of the individual employees, including the income earned by the trust. If an employee goes from one company to another in the same association, the funds accumulated to his credit shall be continued to his credit with proper record of transfer. If an employee goes to a company in another association, the funds accumulated to his credit shall be transferred to his credit in the pension trust of the association to which he goes. If an employee goes to a company which does not come under these provisions or which is not a member of a trade association; goes into business for himself; or withdraws from an industrial or commercial occupation, the amount of his payments plus the interest at the average rate earned by the funds shall be given to him. If an employee dies before reaching retirement age, his beneficiary will receive the amount of his payments plus interest at the average rate earned by the funds. When an employee reaches retirement age, the entire amount accumulated to his credit, including his own payments and those of the company, plus accumulated interest, will be given to him in the form of an annuity. If an employee goes to a company which does not come under these provisions or which is not a member of a trade association; goes into business for himself; or withdraws from industrial or commercial occupation, he may elect to let the amount to his credit (namely, his own payments plus those of the company and the accumulated interest) remain with the pension trust for transfer, if he should return to the employ of any company coming within the provisions of this plan. If he does not return to the employ of a company coming under these provisions, he may at any time thereafter withdraw the amount of his own payments plus interest at the average rate earned by the funds up to that time. Company contributions and accumulated interest credited to employees who die, or for reasons indicated above, receive or withdraw their own contributions and interest, shall be returned to the employer or employers who made the contributions.

IX. The rules governing the payments of pensions on retirement and all other rules governing its continuance shall be made by the trade association, approved by the federal supervisory body, and observed by the general board of administration and the boards of administration of the member companies.

(D) *Unemployment Insurance.* All employees on piece work, hourly work, daily, weekly, or monthly work, with normal pay of five thousand dollars per year or less (approximately $96.15 per week) shall be covered by unemployment insurance.

  I. All such employees may, after two years of service with a company coming within the provisions of this plan, and shall, after five years of service, be each required to put aside a minimum of one per cent of earnings, but not more than fifty dollars per year for an unemployment insurance fund.

  II. The company shall be required to put aside an amount equal to that put aside by the employees, as set forth above, namely, one per cent of the earnings of each employee, but not more than fifty dollars per year for each such employee.

  III. If a company regularizes and guarantees employment for at least fifty per cent of the normal wage paid each year to such employees, the company assessment for employees covered by such guarantee need not be made, but the employees will pay in a minimum of one per cent of earnings, but not more than fifty dollars per year, into a special fund for their own benefit.

    If such an employee leaves the company, dies, or retires on pension, the amount to his credit in the special fund plus interest at the average rate earned by the special fund, shall be given to him or to his beneficiaries or added to his pension.

  IV. If a company so plans its work that it is able to reduce unemployment, when the amount of such company's credit in the normal unemployment fund is equal to but not less than five per cent of the normal annual earnings of the employees covered, the company may cease making payment to the fund. Employees' payments will continue. The company will resume payments when its

credit in the normal unemployment fund falls below
five per cent of normal annual earnings of the employees
covered.

V. When the weekly payments made from the fund for
unemployment benefits amount to two per cent or more
of the average weekly earnings of participating employees, the company shall declare an unemployment
emergency, and normal payments by the employees and
the company shall cease. Thereafter *all* employees of
the company (including the highest officers) receiving
fifty per cent or more of their average full-time earnings
shall pay one per cent of their current earnings to the
unemployment fund. A similar amount shall be paid
into the fund by the company. The unemployment
emergency shall continue until normal conditions are
restored, which shall be determined by the board of
administrators of each company. Thereupon normal
payments will be resumed.

VI. The main provisions for the distribution of the funds
shall follow along these lines, unless modified by the
board of administrators as set forth in section D, para-
graph VII hereof. A certain small percentage of the
normal payments of the employees and the company
may be considered as available for helping participating
employees in need. A larger percentage of such normal
payments may be considered as available for loans to
participating employees in amounts not exceeding two
hundred dollars each, with or without interest as may
be determined by the board. The balance of the funds
shall be available for unemployment payments. Unemployment payments shall begin after the first two weeks
of unemployment and shall amount to approximately
fifty per cent of the participating employee's average
weekly or monthly earnings for full time, but in no case
more than twenty dollars per week. Such payments to
individual employees shall continue for no longer than
ten weeks in any twelve consecutive months unless extended by the board. When a participating employee is
working part-time because of lack of work and receiving

less than fifty per cent of his average weekly or monthly earnings for full time, he shall be eligible for payments to be made from the fund, amounting to the difference between the amount he is receiving as wages from the company and the maximum he may be entitled to as outlined above.

VII. The custody and investment of funds and administration of the unemployment insurance plan for each company shall be under the direction of a board of administrators consisting of representatives, one half appointed by the management and one half elected by the employee members. The powers and duties of the board shall be to formulate general rules relating to eligibility of employees, the waiting period before benefits are paid, amounts of benefits and how long they shall continue in any year, whether loans shall be made in time of unemployment or need, whether a portion of the funds shall be placed at the disposal of the board for relief from need arising from causes other than unemployment, etc., but such rules shall be in consonance with the general plan laid down by the general board of administration of the trade association of which the company is a member, and approved by the federal supervisory body.

VIII. If an employee leaves the company and goes to work for another company coming within the provisions of this plan, the proportionate amount remaining of his normal contributions, plus interest at the average rate earned by the funds, shall be transferred to such company and to his credit. If he leaves for other reasons, dies, or retires on pension, the proportionate amount remaining of his normal payment, plus interest at the average rate earned by the funds, shall be given to him, or to his beneficiary, or added to his pension. When such employee's credit is transferred to another company, or paid to the employee or to his beneficiary under this provision, an equal amount shall be paid to the coöperating company.

General Administration. Each trade association will form a general board of administration which shall consist of nine members, three to be elected or appointed by the association, three to be elected by the employees of the member companies, and three, representing the public, to be appointed by the federal supervisory body. The members of the general board, except employee representatives, shall serve without compensation. The employee representatives shall be paid their regular rates of pay for time devoted to board work, and all members shall be paid traveling expenses, all of which shall be borne by the trade association. The powers and duties of this general board shall be to interpret the life and disability insurance, pension and unemployment insurance plans adopted by the trade association and approved by the federal supervisory body, supervise the individual company boards of administration, form and direct a pension trust for the custody, investment, and disbursements of the pension funds, and in general supervise and direct all activities connected with life and disability insurance, pension and unemployment insurance plans.

Conclusion. The foregoing plan tends to put all domestic corporations of the class described on a parity for domestic business, thereby removing the inequalities of the different laws in the several states, provides for standard forms of financial reports and their periodical issuance for the information of stockholders, places on organized industry the obligation of coördinating production and consumption, and of a higher degree of stabilization. This will tend to assure more uniform and continuous employment for the worker and to remove fear from his mind, allowing him to devote himself whole-heartedly to his task. Cost of the product will include these items and will therefore be paid for by the users of the article or service and not in general by members of the community reached by the vicarious method of the imposition of a tax. Then organized industry will be in the position that it should rightly assume of serving the public, with public confidence and with the joint participation of workmen and management in the solution of these vital and far-reaching problems.

Addendum. The following provision is suggested to place domestic corporations of the sort described on a parity with foreign competition: Any company engaged in export business may, upon application to and approval by the federal supervisory body, deduct from its federal income tax the equivalent of x per cent of its export sales, this x per cent deemed to be the equivalent in selling price of the various provisions for the benefit of employees which the company must make under this plan and from which some foreign companies which the domestic companies have to meet in competition are free.

By this method American industry can discharge its obligation to its employees and, by holding its position in the markets of the world, bring additional work to America.

[About two months after the publication of his original plan, Mr. Swope elaborated certain aspects of his proposal in an address delivered before the Academy of Political Science, in New York City, November 13, 1931. Since the comments in the new document, entitled 'Discussion of "Stabilization of Industry,"' really form an integral part of the general scheme, the second paper is here reprinted in full as released to the press by the author.]

The greatest difference between this depression and those that have preceded it is the reaction of society. Never before has public conscience been so aroused to the responsibility of the community for the tragic consequences of unemployment. This has made for an eagerness to find a way out — a program by which progress toward a solution of this problem might be made. The widespread comment, discussion, and criticism of the paper on 'Stabilization of Industry' which I presented before the National Electrical Manufacturers' Association on September 16 is a reflection of this eagerness for a better way of doing things.

Some, of course, do not think the plan goes far enough, while others disagree with the means proposed. Some think that it would have serious consequences by dwarfing the efforts which have always characterized American industry — that it would bring more government regulation and management, instead of merely government supervision, in the protection of the public interest. Still others think that it would lead to price-fixing by agreement, instead of price-stabilization as referred to hereafter, and that it would result in curtailment of production, rather than, as at present, in stimulating increased production and lower costs and consequently lower selling prices to the public.

Some do not think that it is possible to stabilize industry, but think that it must be subject to the recurrent booms and depressions that we have always had. This, as Senator La Follette said, is the 'counsel of despair' and would be the negation of all effort toward progress. Had this been generally the conception of science and of industry, the remarkable progress that has been made would not have taken place. If we had accepted, as many did, that man could never fly, and that a heavier-than-air machine was impossible, and no effort had been made in that direction, the astounding developments in airplanes that have been made and are continuing, would not have enriched our lives.

No doubt the plan for stabilization of industry along lines that I have suggested would have to be modified as we have more experience, but such experience can be had only by trying one scheme or another to solve the problem, which, unsolved, leaves us with all the present chaotic, unhappy, and finally unendurable consequences.

I shall not repeat the plan here, but shall speak of some of its more important features and the points which have not been understood or have aroused criticisms, and shall endeavor to clarify, at all events, the expression of my own thought on each one.

1. There has been some criticism that the plan would include only companies with fifty or more employees, whereas in some industries it would be desirable to have companies with a smaller number of employees as mem-

bers of the trade association. Indeed, some industries which have a large number of small plants have already considered the plan and can see no objection to including companies with a smaller number of employees. Personally, I can see none either. I selected this number, as it would include the large companies, which might be more able and willing to try the experiment. Of course, if it is ever to be all-embracing, it should include the smaller companies; and also the benefits, especially to employees, should be extended in some form to companies doing only an intrastate business.

2. Some associations have outlined trade practices and business ethics, in conjunction with and encouraged by the Federal Trade Commission. This has been educational in showing what the elements of unfair competition are, and has led to a more general recognition by the member companies of what fair rules of conducting business among competitors should be. But recently this coöperation has been abandoned because some doubt has arisen as to the interpretation of how far the Federal Trade Commission might go in this work, and I understand there was a difference of opinion between the Federal Trade Commission and the Department of Justice regarding these activities. You will readily appreciate that if departments of the Government itself are doubtful as to the effect and interpretation of the Sherman laws, how much easier it is to understand this doubt on the part of men in business.

Methods of standard accounting and cost practice have been in effect for many years, especially in the electrical manufacturing industry. Some years ago the Uniform Accounting and Cost Manual of the Electrical Manufacturing Industry was approved by the Federal Trade Commission. This Manual has been used as a guide and standard in other industries and other countries. By the use of this Manual, the computations of costs are on a uniform basis and there cannot arise the great discrepancies in cost figures that often appear when various methods (or no method) of computing costs are used.

Simplification and standardization of products were much encouraged by, and industry followed the lead of, a former Secretary of Commerce. This resulted in fewer types of the same products, which meant lower costs and less risk of obsolescence, both being finally reflected in lower selling prices to the public.

Associations may collect and distribute information on volume of business transacted and inventories of merchandise on hand, which tends to stabilize prices. I know of no clearer statement of what trade associations may do in this direction, and of course no more authoritative statement, than that given by the Supreme Court in its decision on the Maple Flooring Case in 1925, from which I quote:

Mr. Justice Stone delivered the opinion of the Court, Justices Taft, Sanford, and McReynolds dissenting.

Coöperative advertising, standardization and improvement of product were not objected to by the Government, which, however, did object to

1. The computation and distribution of the average cost to all of the members of all dimensions and grades of flooring.

2. Computation and distribution of a booklet showing freight rates on flooring to many points of shipment in the United States.

3. Gathering from each of the members information as to the quantity and kind of flooring sold, prices received and stock on hand and consolidating and summarizing these reports and distributing the summary to members without revealing the identity of the members in connection with specific information obtained.

4. Meetings of representatives of members.

The Court pointed out that there was no agreement as to production, prices, or price maintenance and that each member conducted its business as it chose; that there was no proof that the prices were affected adversely to the consumer; that the proofs were that the prices were reasonable; though it was conceded that the information as to cost, production, and prices disseminated would tend to bring about greater uniformity in prices. It held that it did not cause any direct and undue restraint of competition, saying, *inter alia*:

It is not, we think, open to question that the dissemination of pertinent information concerning any trade or business tends to stabilize that trade or business and to produce uniformity of price and trade practice. Exchange of price quotations of market commodities tends to produce uniformity of prices in the markets of the world. Knowledge of the supplies of available merchandise tends to prevent over-production and to avoid the economic disturbances produced by business crises resulting from over-production. But the natural effect of the acquisition of wider and more scientific knowledge of business conditions, on the minds of the individuals engaged in commerce, and its consequent effect in stabilizing production and price, can hardly be deemed a restraint of commerce or if so it cannot, we think, be said to be an unreasonable restraint, or in any respect unlawful.

It is the consensus of opinion of economists and of many of the most important agencies of Government that the public interest is served by the gathering and dissemination, in the widest possible manner, of information with respect to the production and distribution, cost and prices in actual sales, of market commodities, because the making available of such information tends to stabilize trade and industry, to produce fairer price levels and to avoid the waste which inevitably attends the unintelligent conduct of economic enterprise. Free competition means a free and open market among both buyers and sellers for the sale and distribution of commodities. Competition does not become less free merely because the conduct of commercial operations becomes more intelligent through the free distribution of knowledge of all the essential factors entering into the commercial transaction. General knowledge that there is an accumulation of surplus of any market commodity would undoubtedly tend to diminish production, but the dissemination of that information cannot in itself be said to be restraint upon commerce in any legal sense. The manufacturer is free to produce, but prudence and business foresight based on that knowledge influence free choice in favor of more limited production. Restraint upon free competition begins when improper use is made of that information through any concerted action which operates to restrain the freedom of action of those who buy and sell.

One sentence of this decision is especially worth repeating:

But the natural effect of the acquisition of wider and more scientific knowledge of business conditions, on the minds of the individuals engaged in commerce, and its consequent effect in *stabilizing production and price*, can hardly be deemed a restraint of commerce, or if so it cannot, we think, be said to be an unreasonable restraint, or in any respect unlawful.

Some people fear, and have voiced the fear, that if trade associations take up these matters, they will curtail production, with consequent increase in price to the public. Personally I think industry — at all events American industry — has long since passed that point. We see the great advantages of standardization and mass production, with the consequent effect of lower costs and lower selling prices, thereby reaching a very much larger buying public. There are many instances where industry has been under no compulsion to decrease prices, but has done so because of a more intelligent grasp of the relation of prices to consumption and to production.

What the industry would endeavor to do would be to prevent *over*-production, and would regard as an unfair competitor any member of such trade association who, knowing the consuming power of the public and the stocks on hand in the possession of all members of the association, regardless of these facts built up a large inventory, which later must be sold at reduced prices, quite regardless of cost. Such practices are unfair to the competitors themselves and highly unfair to the labor employed; and such prices below cost for a brief period are of no lasting benefit to the consuming public.

In connection with limitation of production, there also arises another problem — that of the conservation of our natural resources. The practices of today are wasteful and are dissipating the heritage of the citizens of our country who are to follow us.

I said in my paper that much of the plan can be carried out without any additional legislation, and committees of different industries are now studying it to see how far they can go, but of course no one is sanguine enough to believe that by such voluntary action one hundred per cent of the industry will be enrolled. There will always be a minority who will not join in such a movement. In any event, it seems to me much better if we first have a thorough understanding of what such a plan commits us to, and by discussion, comment, and criticism find better ways of carrying it out — that we appeal to the understanding of the leaders of industry rather than exercise compulsion through the law.

As I have stated before some of the committees of the Senate, Congress could, if in sympathy with this program, pass legislation involving no fundamental change, which would greatly assist the program and encourage companies to join trade associations. Possibly the simplest way would be to modify the Sherman Law along the lines recommended by the American Bar Association, which would, first, remove the criminal aspects of the law, and, second, allow companies to make agreements and file them with the Federal Trade Commission and the Department of Justice. Then, if at the time of filing, or any time thereafter, either of these agencies should find that the agreements are contrary to the public interest, they may ask the companies to cease and desist. If there is a difference of opinion, the companies or the Government can still appeal to the courts. But the men in charge of the companies will not be subject to the penalty of going to jail for having committed a crime — a crime which today no one can clearly define and which indeed takes many years for the courts, and finally the Supreme Court, to define. Often such decision is by divided courts, below and above, which means a difference of opinion as to whether or not a crime has been committed.

A further inducement to join, which I believe would be preferable to compulsion, at least in the beginning, would be to make provision that such amounts as the companies contribute for the benefit of employees — for life insurance, old-age pensions, stabilization of employment, and unemployment insurance — will be deductible from their federal tax. These provisions do not make it compulsory to join a trade association, but they offer very great inducements to do so. If certain companies still do not join, *they* will suffer the handicap rather than those companies that are endeavoring to stabilize employment and assist their employees in the various ways mentioned. As a matter of fact, I think this method would result in a smaller cost to the Government than a direct contribution on the part of the Government, such as is the practice in some countries in Europe.

There is some doubt now in the minds of lawyers whether contributions made by employees for these various purposes are exempt from taxation and this doubt should be removed by making such employee contributions exempt from taxation.

3. We already have a federal supervisory body in the Federal Trade Commission. I am not suggesting, really,

an extension of their power, but maybe a clarification and interpretation of their power, for, as I have said before, there is today some doubt in their own minds and in the Department of Justice as to how far their activities may go. My thought for the federal supervisory body is not as a regulatory or managerial body. All through the plan I have suggested that the initiative be taken by the trade associations and not by the Government, that the government supervisory body shall act as a referee or umpire to interpret unfair competition and unfair trade practices as between members, or, if necessary, in the protection of the public interest, by its interpretation of agreements that may be filed with the Federal Trade Commission or as a result of its study of reports showing the trend of production and prices.

The public interest will be protected, it seems to me, because the federal supervisory body will receive reports periodically showing the volume of shipments and the amount of merchandise on hand. They will also know the price at which the merchandise has been sold at retail and they will have filed with them the income statements of members of the trade association prepared on a uniform basis. The volume of shipments will show whether production has been curtailed; the amount of merchandise on hand will show whether production is outrunning consumption, or vice versa; the retail price of the article will show the price trend; and the analysis of income statements, made on a uniform basis, will show whether the profits of the corporations engaging in this business have increased or decreased. These factors, it would seem to me, would give all the information necessary for a federal supervisory body to adequately protect the public interest.

4. To all who study balance sheets and income statements, the widely different practices and forms of statements, even in the same industry, must be apparent, and

uniformity in these respects would have a great effect upon the conduct of business, and in determining unfair competition.

5. The suggestion that regular, uniform reports be sent to stockholders has aroused no criticism or unfavorable comment, except on the part of smaller companies whose securities are not listed on the public exchanges. Some of them have felt that there should be no requirement as to the publicity of their reports. Nor do I suggest it. I do suggest that they follow the standard accounting methods and that they submit their reports to their own stockholders and to the supervisory body, but not necessarily to the public through the press.

The newspapers of October 28 stated that the President of the New York Stock Exchange had requested all companies whose securities are listed on the Exchange to make quarterly reports, which would be published. Heretofore the Exchange has required this from companies newly listed, but it has not been required from the companies listed on the Exchange before this became a requirement for listing. Of course this request will cover only those companies which are listed on the New York Stock Exchange. Some companies have objected to quarterly statements because of the seasonal variation in their business, and the suggestion has been made that each quarter they publish a report for the preceding twelve months, which would include the four seasons of the year and remove unfair and misleading comparisons.

6. You may recall that Congress passed a law making the amount of income taxes paid by corporations and individuals for 1924 and 1925 open to the public. A comparison was then possible of what the corporation reported to its stockholders and what it reported to the United States for tax purposes, and in many cases the two reports were very different. My suggestion simply means that the trade association, having agreed upon standard

accounting methods and fair rates of depreciation for its particular industry, should seek an agreement with the Internal Revenue Department and the federal supervisory body on these matters. There may be differences of opinion between industry and the Internal Revenue Department as to rates of depreciation as well as to methods of valuation of securities held by the companies and whether, for instance, more than the actual dividends and interest received should be included in income. If an agreement is impossible, a method might be found that would at all events make possible a reconcilement of the statements submitted to the stockholders and to the Government.

7. If, as already suggested, Congress, by modifying and clarifying the Sherman Law, encourages companies to join trade associations and offers inducements for such companies to stabilize employment, and these measures are approved and supported by public opinion, almost every company will join in this constructive endeavor and no compulsion will be necessary.

8. There have been few questions raised as to the life and disability insurance features and I think they are well understood. Plans of this kind have been adopted by many of the larger companies throughout the United States. This is also true of pensions. One point on which there may be a difference of opinion is whether the cost of these benefits should be shared between the employees and the companies. Personally I am convinced, from long experience, that the best reaction between men and management, and closest coöperation in working out such plans, can be had if contributions are made jointly by employees and the companies, and this is the only basis, it seems to me, for joint administration of the plans.

As stated in the plan, the most important feature is stabilization of employment, or really assurance of employment, and, if this fails, then unemployment insurance to reduce the shock and the tragic consequences of loss of work. Almost everyone wants to live as long as possible, but still we carry life insurance, because no one knows when life will end. Most of us want the house we own, and to which we are attached, to continue to exist, but nevertheless most of us carry fire insurance, so in case fire destroys our home we may have something with which to build a new one. So also with unemployment insurance. The most important matter is stabilization of employment, or assurance of employment, and if that cannot be accomplished, then unemployment insurance. The result of taxing industry for a portion of the cost will be to put a premium on industry's finding ways of stabilizing employment. The collateral effects, therefore, of unemployment insurance will be much more important to the employee, to industry, and to society than unemployment insurance itself.

Some have understood that the general board of administration (on which three members representing the public are appointed by the federal supervisory body) will manage industry. In my statement I think it is clear that 'the powers and duties of this general board shall be to interpret the life and disability insurance, pension, and unemployment insurance plans adopted by the trade association and approved by the federal supervisory body, supervise the individual company boards of administration, form and direct a pension trust for the custody, investment, and disbursements of the pension funds, and in general supervise and direct all activities connected with life and disability insurance, pension, and unemployment insurance plans.'

This plan seeks to place the same social burdens on companies competing in various parts of the United States. It puts their reports on a uniform and understandable basis. It places on organized industry the obligation of coördinating production and consumption and assuming greater responsibility for stabilizing employment. All of this should tend to a more intelligent management of industry, a higher degree of stabilization, and more uniform and continuous employment for the worker.

An important factor, which I think is basic, is that the cost of the product will include these items and will therefore be paid for by the users of the articles and not in general by members of the community through taxation.

I have endeavored to clear up a number of misconceptions of the plan as submitted and possibly to answer some of the criticisms that have been made. No doubt there are other features of the plan which will need further clarification and modification and other just criticisms can be made. The reaction of industry in general has been encouraging, and in the interest of developing better methods and better technique than we have today, it seems to me that the burden and responsibility of this forward march should be placed on organized industry. Organized industry should be encouraged to undertake these responsibilities. Even if industry falls short of an ideal accomplishment, there is no doubt in my mind that more progress will be made and it will be better done and cost less than if the Government, either state or federal, endeavors to do it.

CHAPTER IV

THE PUBLIC REACTION TO THE SWOPE PLAN

[THE presentation of Mr. Swope's plan struck fire immediately. American civilization is essentially urban and business in outlook. Its leaders of opinion have long been accustomed to hearken with alacrity to the pronouncements of great industrial administrators. Mr. Swope spoke as a man of affairs, as president of the General Electric Company. No academic taint condemned his utterance in advance; no suspicion of undue enthusiasm clouded his project. As priest-kings could lay down the law without question in primitive societies, so a captain of industry in the United States could propose a new thing without encountering the scoffs of the wise or the jeers of the practical.

Fortunately also for the advancement of Mr. Swope's cause, Mr. Owen D. Young addressed the National Electrical Manufacturers' Association on the same evening in support of the project. In an address which for brevity, penetration, and catholicity of view deserves to rank high among our state papers, Mr. Young discussed the scheme put forward by his colleague, explained its implications, and welcomed it as a definite contribution to the consideration of large economic planning. As a commentary on the Swope plan, as a document providing a wide economic setting for the discussion of the issues in hand, Mr. Young's address is here reprinted in full as it appeared in the *New York Times* of September 17, 1931.]

To the insistent calls for industrial leadership in these disorganized times, there has been a discouraging silence. To the demands for an industrial plan which would guard us in the future from repeating our present disaster, there has been little definite response. True, some have spoken publicly in general terms of what should be done. For the most part either these generalities have been so self-evidently true as not to need stating at all; or, they have been so indefinite as not to be practically useful. Some have put forth academic theses which, in varying degrees, stimulate our thinking, but are as far removed from practical application as researches in pure science. Some have had the courage to write definite plans on paper, but for one reason or another they have not received the support of operating concerns nor have they been submitted to the critical review of the public.

Tonight Gerard Swope, after previous conference with his associates in the electrical manufacturing industry, submits a plan for the organization of that industry which is definite in terms and which, if I am correctly informed, has received from many of you a testimonial of practicability. You and he have the courage to make that proposal public tonight. I congratulate you on that advance.

The plan is not free from criticism. Mr. Swope would be the first to admit that. There are grave questions both of public and of business policy lying at its very foundations. There are undoubtedly many improvements which could be made in detail. The significance of this event tonight does not lie in the possible criticisms of the plan, but in the fact that a responsible industrial manager and the members of a great industry are ready to put to the public an offer to assume voluntarily responsibilities of vast consequence, not only in the economic but in the social field. Here is a tender of social performance by an industry, definite in terms and measurable in effect. Its spirit is that of modern business. Its design recognizes obligations to employees and to general economic stability which have only been academically discussed before.

At this stage the plan is not only a definite proposition for debate but a proposal for action. It comes before the public with the willingness of an industry to adopt it, if public opinion supports it and the necessary authority can be had to institute it. So I congratulate you, Mr. President, and you, Mr. Swope, on this definite and daring step.

May I say, Mr. President, that economic planning will contribute to a standardized and so more stable prosperity, but in the same breath may I remind you that, like all other things in this world, it demands its price. A plan written on paper is of no service. A plan proposed for education is of some service, but it is likely to become obsolete before it becomes effective. A plan to be productive of quick results must be executed promptly. No one concern can make it effective. Coöperation is required by the great majority of the participants and the coercion of the rest may ultimately be necessary. I hate not only the term but the idea of coercion, and yet we are forced to recognize that every advance in social organization requires the voluntary surrender of a certain amount of individual freedom by the majority and the ultimate coercion of the minority. It is not the coercion of the recalcitrant minority, but the voluntary submission by the large majority which should impress us. Anyhow, the question is whether the people who are calling for economic planning really mean what they say. Are they willing to surrender their individual freedom to the extent necessary to execute a plan? It is fruitless to demand unified action by a large number of industrial units and by the individuals connected with them and expect to retain for each unit and each individual the same freedom and the same kind of initiative which existed before the plan was made. Too many people who speak of the matter seem to think that we can have an effective plan without paying anything for it. They are all for the advantages of the plan, but they refuse to pay the price.

Now I am not saying, Mr. President, that we should have an economic plan. All I am saying is that we should have something for discussion so as to see definitely what it costs. If the individual units of production are ready to surrender their liberty of action to the extent necessary to execute a plan, then the further question arises as to whether the public is ready to have them do so. We can retain in this country unorganized individual planning and operation, but if we do, its action will necessarily be at times chaotic, and we shall, as a result, pay the economic penalty of that disorder, such as we are paying now. We can in this country have organized economic planning with some curtailment of individual freedom which, if the plan be wise and properly executed, will tend to diminish economic disorder and the penalties which we pay.

Then, too, the question is to whom this individual freedom is to be surrendered? If the Government is to undertake the great obligations which Mr. Swope's plan visualizes, then the price must be in the form of a surrender to political government. If industry itself is to perform those obligations, as is here contemplated, then the surrender of the individual units is to be made to the organized group, of which the unit is a part. If results are to be obtained, they call for surrender somewhere. The question for the public is to say whether they wish the results, and if so, by what agency they are to be accomplished.

Therefore, I welcome the plan, not as a final answer to the problems with which it deals, but as a definitive proposal which will enable us to consider those problems intelligently. Other industries may develop similar plans, and if they do, then for the first time we should have organized units of the several branches of industry out of which we could build a National Industrial Council.

There are three courses open to us:

First. To do nothing. In that case, we should abandon

the cry for economic planning. We should accept the advantages and disadvantages of the present system — and it has both. It is a system of intensified individualism which, because of its disordered action, necessarily brings great peaks of prosperity and valleys of depression.

Second. To place upon industry itself the responsibility for the formulation and execution of a definite plan. This would pass the cost of protective insurances for employees to the public in the cost of the product in so far as it was not absorbed by better management. It would inevitably place on industry a high penalty for unbalanced economic conditions. Not only would capital in idleness have to be carried, but labor as well.

Third. To acquiesce in the Government providing the means for employee protection through the power of taxation. This carries only a political and not an economic check on such expenditures.

The tender which the electrical manufacturing industry makes to the country tonight requires every citizen to consider which of those three positions we should take or what compromise between them, if any, can be had. What is the answer? Which shall it be?

COMMENT BY OTHER LEADERS

On the day following the publication of Mr. Swope's plan by the newspapers, industrial leaders, editors, publicists, politicians, and professors began a torrent of comment and debate rarely, if ever, evoked by any economic propositions. On the whole the opinion was favorable. Mr. Samuel Vauclain, chairman of the board of the Baldwin Locomotive Works, remarked rather tartly: 'I don't care to comment on it — because I don't believe in it'; but his brethren in business enterprise generally took the opposite view. Judging by the weight of the returns, the verdict of American business was distinctly in support of Mr. Swope's project.

Speaking as president of the United States Chamber of Commerce, Mr. Silas Strawn pronounced Mr. Swope's plan 'an excellent one' and added that 'in fact it is entirely along the lines of one which the United States Chamber of Commerce has been working on.' About two weeks later, in the report on planning reprinted below (Chapter V), an important committee of the Chamber, while conceding that many of the details of the Swope plan might have to be changed, declared: 'It is most stimulating that the head of one of the country's greatest industrial companies recognizes the necessity for such forms of insurance.'

According to a dispatch to the *New York Times*, dated September 17, 1931, General W. W. Atterbury, president of the Pennsylvania Railroad, announced that he had called upon the employees of his company to join with the management in evolving a plan for stabilizing business and employment in the railroad industry — a plan which, he said, might be the first step toward national business planning to prevent a repetition of economic disruptions. General Atterbury also stated that legislation would be offered in the next Congress designed to place steamship, bus, and truck companies under the Interstate Commerce Commission with a view to eliminating unfair competition. 'Under the present anti-trust laws,' General Atterbury is quoted as saying, 'the country will never be able to control its production and distribution, and modification must come about before any plan for business stabilization can succeed.' Realizing the importance of foreign trade in our scheme of economy, General Atterbury suggested reductions in the tariff and a more conciliatory policy toward the countries of Latin America.

Although cautious in its judgment, the academic world was inclined to put its stamp of approval on the Swope plan. Dr. Leo Wolman, professor of economics at Columbia University, for example, found the project 'constructive' and thought that it contained 'the germs of something that was workable.' While reserving a final opinion until he could find time to study the text of the plan, Dr. John A. Ryan, director of the department of social action of the National Catholic Welfare Conference, stated that, in his opinion, the objects which Mr. Swope set out to accomplish were admirable, but added that the reports of the scheme which appeared in the press left some doubts in his mind. Taking up a few concrete issues, Dr. Ryan said:

In the matter, for instance, of the proposed equal contributions by employers and employees to funds for compulsory pensions, unemployment, disability and life insurance, and workmen's compensation — I'm not so sure about that, especially in the case of employees whose wages are so low as to make such contribution on their part a burden rather than a benefit, if not an economic impossibility.

Again, he recommends the compulsory formation, by law, of trade associations in every business and industry, and of course that would be necessary, for business men generally would not form such associations if not compelled by law to do so — they haven't sense enough; but I don't see how he is going to get it done by law under our Constitution.

It is suggested that these associations should control output and adjust production to consumption. But by what standard? It is always possible, of course, to adjust production to consumption by reducing production in any given industry, but that might mean the throwing-out of work of a great many employed in such an industry. Any reduction in output should include adjustment of hours of labor or danger of unemployment will not be minimized but increased.

In the matter of unemployment insurance, it would be very difficult, I fear, to raise enough money, whether by state or other agency.

Finally, it is suggested that exporters should be able to deduct from their federal income taxes certain amounts in proportion to their export sales. I am not at all in favor of that proposal. I see no need of stimulating our export trade by such means. In my judgment we should think less of exporting and more of consuming our goods at home.

Having already demonstrated his interest in economic planning and having made practical suggestions for procedure in that direction, Dr. Nicholas Murray Butler greeted the Swope plan as a decided step forward.

The plan in its essentials, it seems to me [said Dr. Butler] offers a very practical suggestion which ought to be followed up promptly. It fits in completely with the general line of thought which I developed in my Southampton address on unemployment on September 6.

Mr. Swope has plainly given prolonged study to this matter and has thereby placed us all under obligation to him. He offers what this country now most needs, namely, an example of constructive leadership.

In political circles the announcement of Mr. Swope's plan stirred up a confusion of voices. Some Democratic members of Congress flatly declared that they were against it because it involved a modification of the anti-trust laws. Others were more circumspect. Senator Hull, of Tennessee, former chairman of the Democratic National Committee, said that he intended to weigh the proposals and to give his opinion as to their practicability later. Senator Fess, chairman of the Republican National Committee, refrained from commenting on Mr. Swope's suggestion for government supervision of trade associations, but expressed the opinion that his general proposal was constructive in nature and would receive a careful study at the hands of government economists and industrial leaders. Senator Gore declared that great corporations which piled up surpluses in times of prosperity should take care of their employees in years of adversity and refused to approve any suggestions for government supervision over the operations of industrial concerns as to production and mergers.

Speaking for the agrarian interest which he has represented with such vigor, Senator Brookhart greeted Mr. Swope's plan with general approval, subject to certain qualifications, and added a counterblast:

If Mr. Swope proposes to organize a gigantic series of trusts and repeal the anti-trust laws I would go along with him, providing:

First, that in the enterprises to be formed each should have one vote, so that capital could not control the policies.

Second, that the earnings of capital be limited and capital be given a wage definite and fixed, just as is now given in wages, and the return on capital should be three per cent a year.

Third, that seventy-five per cent of the earnings of these enterprises above wages, capital return, and the ordinary expenses be distributed in proportion to the amount of business transacted by such enterprises, leaving twenty-five per cent of net earnings as surplus.

If Mr. Swope will modify his plan to this extent, I would be very glad to vote for repeal of the anti-trust laws. I am glad to see a great business manager conceding the collapse of the capitalistic system of our country.

Without going any deeper into the huge portfolio of press clippings which give the opinions of distinguished citizens in all parts of the country, there is warrant for concluding that Mr. Swope has made a pronouncement destined to force a crystallization of opinion in the United States on the subject of planning. Speaking with the authority of a man who knows the nature and possibilities of business management, he has put forward a project which is both practical and realistic. In the present stage of our economic evolution it appears to be the only alternative to the continuance of the historic system of ruthless competition which, by general admission, is one of the prime causes of the cycle of expansion, explosion, contraction, and disaster — a cycle that enriches and impoverishes, that periodically drives millions to the verge of starvation and endangers the orderly development of society. Inevitably, statesmen whose business it is to safeguard large national interests will have to choose a course: one leading in the direction of planned economy and the other backward to an outworn individualism.

CHAPTER V

PLANNING PROPOSALS OF THE COMMITTEE ON
CONTINUITY OF BUSINESS AND EMPLOY-
MENT OF THE UNITED STATES CHAMBER
OF COMMERCE [1]

*To the Board of Directors of the Chamber of Commerce of
the United States:*

The Chamber of Commerce of the United States
adopted the following resolution at its annual meeting
on May 1, 1931:

We commend and endorse the appointment of the special
committee of the Chamber of Commerce of the United States
for continued study of the possibilities of business and employment stabilization. This study should include means for relieving such unemployment distress as may unavoidably occur
from time to time, including a rational program of production
and distribution to be initiated by business itself.

In accordance with that resolution, your Committee
herewith submits its report.

ECONOMIC DEPRESSIONS

The United States of America, in common with most of
the economic world, is passing through a cyclical business
depression of great magnitude. Like all previous major
depressions, this period is accompanied by widespread
unemployment, a marked reduction in earning power
and, in general, economic disarrangement and distress.

In a time of great economic upheaval, it is natural to
emphasize its gloomiest aspects, and to believe that no

[1] Submitted to the membership in a referendum proposal to be acted
upon before December 15, 1931.

calamity of equal severity has ever before been experienced by our people. A study of our economic history, however, reveals the fallacy of this assumption.

The great depressions beginning in 1873 and 1893 undoubtedly entailed greater relative loss and suffering. To recall some of the phases of the depression of the seventies, with its prolonged and bitter strikes, the stoppage of railroad transportation, drastic reductions in wages, the bitter antagonism between employer and employee, and the necessity for calling out troops in many cities, should convince us that we have advanced far in our social relations and general welfare. A comparison between conditions during the panic of 1893 and our present situation would reveal an equally striking contrast.

The most significant difference between this depression and the previous ones is the better spirit which now exists between employer and employee. Today we find not a few but thousands of firms adopting work programs to rotate the available jobs among their workers. Instead of reducing the number of their employees and retaining a few while others are dismissed, employers today are dividing among the largest possible number of their employees the maximum of work they can provide. Our people have come to recognize their obligation to prevent suffering and distress. They appreciate that every man and woman should have an opportunity to work for fair wages, with every possible assurance of continuity of employment.

Encouraging as these considerations may be, nevertheless, your Committee does not minimize the seriousness of the present situation, and it approaches its task conscious of the duty which business owes to help in bringing about normal and stable conditions.

Your Committee feels that its task involves three principal considerations: *first*, the causes which have contributed to the intensity of the present depression; *second*, the long-time remedies which may be suggested to prevent its recurrence; and *third*, the measures which may be immediately applied to ameliorate present conditions.

PART I — CAUSES OF DEPRESSION

There have been twenty-two periods of business depression in the last seventy-five years. Of these, eleven have been of comparatively minor intensity and length; nine have been more severe, and two have been extreme and prolonged.

Men produce for the desire of profit. Possibilities of greater profit induce speculation and overproduction. These, in turn, bring about a surplus of goods, a corresponding lowering of prices, and finally the disruption of business, with resultant underconsumption. The surplus is later exhausted, production is resumed, and consumption is restored to normal, with the return of prosperity and employment; and thus the upward and downward swings are continued. While we cannot expect, with our present knowledge and experience, to prevent recurring depressions, let us hope that the depth of the valleys of the depressions may be reduced by avoiding the erection of high peaks in periods of undue activity.

So far we have not isolated the factors by which to determine the length of time a given business depression is likely to last. Wars and catastrophes, undue expansion such as occurred in railroad building in the eighties which was followed by financial collapse in the early nineties, and excessive speculation, may all be cited as causes affecting the character of succeeding business depressions.

We can say, however, that the intensity and duration of a major depression very largely corresponds to the intensity of the previous expansion or economic upward swing.

TECHNOLOGICAL ADVANCE

Many observers attribute our widespread unemployment to the rapid progress which industry and agriculture have made in the use of labor-saving machinery during the last twenty years. This unemployment they term 'technological.' We cannot accept the theory, however, that technological unemployment is largely responsible for our present economic state. Advances in the arts have reduced the price of commodities and have increased the sum total of human desires and the ability to satisfy them. It is an indisputable fact that, despite the replacement of working men and women by machinery, the proportion of our population gainfully employed in our factories and other activities was as high in 1929 as in 1899.

These are years for which the census of manufactures is available. During 1899 the average number of wage-earners in our manufacturing establishments was 4,713,-000, and they constituted six per cent of the entire population; in 1929 the number of wage-earners had risen to 8,742,000, and they were seven per cent of the population. That there was corresponding impetus to other fields appears, according to other Census reports, in the total number of persons with gainful occupations — 29,073,-000 in 1900, or 38.3 per cent of the population, and 48,832,-000 in 1930, or 39.8 per cent of the population. Such figures increase in their significance because during the thirty years there has been a large relative decrease in the persons with occupations in agriculture and there has in recent years been decrease in the number of younger workers.

Furthermore, while the number of men and women employed in gainful occupations has increased in substantially the same ratio as the population of the country between 1900 and 1930, it is also an arresting fact that during the same period the weekly hours of work in manufacturing establishments were substantially shortened — certainly by as much as one eighth and probably by as much as one sixth.

It has been demonstrated that reduction of hours may often be accompanied by an actual increase in productive capacity. This is particularly true where the hours of labor have been excessively long. With the reduction in hours of work during the last thirty years there has been a very material increase in production. Joined with other factors, this has brought about during this same period, according to a leading authority, an increase in real wages by more than a third.

Even if we could not accept, in its entirety, the theory that technological improvements are the primary cause of unemployment, no one will doubt that these improvements are a very serious factor in causing temporary unemployment, particularly if, as in the United States during the last decade, the technological advance has been extremely rapid. When men are displaced by machines, they should be retrained and assigned to other work wherever possible. This is a very important part of individual planning referred to later.

While it is right and proper that advances in civilization should be accompanied by a similar advance in productive capacity through new processes and improved machinery, nevertheless, such changes can come too rapidly and at a given time may affect more labor than can be readily absorbed by other industries. Again, production of a particular class of merchandise may outstrip the consuming power of the country for that product. It is proper that hours of labor should decrease, and that wages should increase, as the productive capacity of the nation grows.

SPECULATION

Speculation in its most reprehensible form has always accompanied periods of unusual prosperity. It has manifested itself by inflation of values in land, securities, commodities, or overexpansion of productive capacity and overextension of credit. This type of speculation is harmful both in its material and its moral effect upon individuals. No reference is here intended to legitimate activities carried on in our established commodity and security exchanges under intelligent supervision. Values of credit resources, the buying power of agriculture, and other producers, and business confidence generally, would improve directly from soundly steady prices. All exchanges should take constructive steps to prevent and control manipulative activities either upward or downward.

Among the suggestions to which your Committee has given consideration is that more stringent regulation should surround the granting of credit to the end that the temporary, prevailing prices of securities and other property, tangible or intangible, should not be the basis of credit extension by banks and other financial and loaning institutions. Credit extended on such a basis leads to inflation in prices and undue increase in debts. Debts invariably increase as prices rise. Prices remain high as long as there is no concerted effort to cash in on the high price. Whenever doubt regarding the stability of a given price level is reached, liquidation sets in and then the whole price structure collapses. This results in producing widespread maladjustment in debtor-creditor relationships, the wiping-out of equity holders and making unwilling owners out of creditors.

It is the belief of your Committee that the National Economic Council, to which reference is made later, can render a special service in sounding alarm signals in the earlier stages of great speculative activity.

WAR

It has been set forth in this report that studies of economic cycles demonstrate that all important wars of modern history have engendered disastrous business depressions. The World War brought about conditions which resulted in the aggravation of our present economic condition. It is our belief that another war would even be more terrible and destructive than that which ended nearly thirteen years ago. We believe that the security of modern civilization would be jeopardized by another calamity of such magnitude. We, therefore, urge that every possible step be taken toward a progressive world disarmament and that forces leading to international amity and good-will be carefully cultivated. At the disarmament conference soon to be held in Europe, we confidently hope that the United States will take a leading part in helping to achieve the apparent objects for which this conference is called.

AGRICULTURE

This country cannot be permanently prosperous until it has a reasonably prosperous agricultural population. Ten million workers and thirty million people are dependent upon the farm for their support. A large proportion, perhaps the majority, are receiving meager return for long and arduous labor. We are advised that the agricultural situation is being considered by the Chamber's Committee on Agriculture.

PART II — LONG-TIME MEASURES

Your Committee has received innumerable suggestions designed to forestall or cure the evils of depression. In one form or another, many of these suggestions contemplate the adoption of devices to establish a better balance between production and consumption.

PRODUCTION AND CONSUMPTION

In principle, your Committee is in accord with this point of view. Only through a proper coördination of production and consumption can a sane, orderly, and progressive economic life be developed. A freedom of action which might have been justified in the relatively simple life of the last century cannot be tolerated today, because the unwise action of one individual may adversely affect the lives of thousands. We have left the period of extreme individualism and are living in a period in which national economy must be recognized as the controlling factor.

Under our form of industry a large part of the national income is distributed through the instrumentality of industry and business, the distribution being in the form of wages, salaries, rents, interest, and dividends. If, then, as is to be desired, industry is to pay out high wages to people working a reasonable number of hours and is to set up reserves in time of prosperity for unemployment benefits and to provide means to care for accidents, sickness, and old age, business must be on a sound basis, and production must be balanced with consumption.

ANTI-TRUST LAWS

Many producers would prefer to gauge their output to the consuming capacity and divide the volume of such production among the different units of industry on an equitable basis. But they hesitate to attempt this today because of ever-present risk of incurring penalties under anti-trust laws which, suitable as they may have been for economic conditions of another day, are not entirely in consonance with the present-day needs of industry.

It is not suggested that the present anti-trust laws be

repealed, but it is suggested that they be amended to provide that

(a) Business concerns desiring to enter into contracts for the purpose of equalizing production to consumption and so carrying on business on a sound basis, may file such contracts with some governmental authority, the contracts to take effect and to remain effective unless the governmental authority having supervision finds on its own initiative or on complaint that such agreements are not in the public interest, in which event such agreements would be abrogated; and

(b) Business concerns that desire to combine may find out from some suitable governmental authority before the combination is made whether or not such combination is prohibited by the anti-trust laws.

We do not suggest the details of legislation, but we do feel that such agreements should be made, not only with the fullest publicity, but under supervision of some governmental authority which should, either upon its own initiative or upon complaint, have the right to review or annul such agreements. Business prosperity and employment will be best maintained by an intelligently planned business structure which affords a fair opportunity to make a reasonable profit through productive activities.

NATIONAL ECONOMIC COUNCIL

This Committee has considered carefully the feasibility of establishing a national economic council in the United States. It has reviewed the experience of European countries and it has sounded out the opinion of leading business men and economists, the majority of whom favored the idea. Our own studies have led to the same conclusion, and we are in good agreement with those consulted in regard to the functions and scope of such a council.

The Council should be an advisory body as its name

implies rather than an executive board with functions like those of the War Industries Board. The present depression is compelling evidence that our country is confronted with economic problems of the gravest importance. As yet there is not united or settled opinion as to how these problems should be met. An advisory council in dealing with them could perform a great national service, provided that it be so constituted that it would command respect by reason of the ability, integrity, and impartiality of its members, and so staffed that its recommendations could be based and supported with adequate analysis of conditions. A few illustrations will serve to indicate the range and character of the problems with which it might deal so as to help us decide what courses of action will best contribute to a sound economic life:

1. The tendency of productive capacity to outrun ability to buy — How can our enormous ability to produce wealth be controlled and directed so as to be of the most use instead of being as it now is a menace to prosperity?
2. The levels of wages — How should they be determined and maintained so as to contribute to prosperity?
3. Foreign trade, both export and import — The extent to which it should be encouraged and the methods by which international debts, resulting from this trade or otherwise, can best be dealt with.
4. In what way and by what agencies can authoritative information and statistics be gathered and published so as to be the most useful guides to industry?

Agriculture, transportation, credit, and finance, and curbing of harmful speculation are other subjects that call for consideration.

In order to speak with the authority desired, the council members must not only be of the highest ability and character, but they must also be representative of the country as a whole and not of any particular constituency, and they must be so appointed that they will be entirely beyond suspicion of control by any group. The council should be small, three, or at the most five, members.

It should be so financed that it can set up an ample staff of economists and statisticians, and it should call to its aid representative committees from various industries and professions. It should coöperate with government departments and with trade organizations, and encourage the latter to form strong economic councils of their own. It should be charged broadly with the responsibility of proposing policies and measures that will contribute to our economic well-being. It should be asked to make preliminary recommendations as promptly as possible, but it should be ensured ample time to demonstrate its usefulness.

We recommend that the officers of the Chamber of Commerce of the United States invite representatives of a sufficient range of industries and professions to coöperate with it in setting up a national economic council that shall be so chosen and established that it may have the ability and resources with which to meet these important responsibilities. After it has been established, the council should be independent in its deliberations and its judgments.

An appendix deals more fully with the reasons for appointing such a council, and proposes a method for setting it up. (See Appendix A.)

INDIVIDUAL PLANNING

Industrial planning to regularize production and employment is recognized by business management as an essential phase of successful business operation. Wholly aside from humanitarian considerations, the value of a carefully planned schedule for future production and sales, based on anticipated demand within the industry as well as on reliable forecasts of general business conditions, has repeatedly been demonstrated in a wide variety of industries.

While a study of several hundred company plans now in use reveals many differences in the methods of industrial planning, both for separate industries and for units within the same industry, these plans usually embrace one or more of the following features, namely, budgeting of production and sales, business forecasting, advance buying, timing of expansion of plant and equipment, manufacturing for stock, stimulating off-season sales, and establishing forward-looking personnel policies, including unemployment relief.

Your Committee is deeply impressed with the possibilities to be realized from a comprehensive expansion of far-sighted company planning, though we do not intend to imply that herein may be found a panacea for all industrial ailments. Experience demonstrates that regularization programs cannot be applied to all industries or to all types of products; but, within the limitations imposed by such factors as changing styles and excessive costs, individual planning offers very definite promise to many branches of industry as a means of eliminating waste, curtailing excess production, anticipating seasonal fluctuations and maintaining a scheduled rate of production throughout the year.

TRADE ASSOCIATIONS

There should be wide education as to the possibilities of company planning and we particularly recommend that trade associations study this subject for the benefit of their own industries. By constant emphasis and widespread publicity as to the type of company planning best adapted to their particular fields, these associations have abounding opportunities, not only to enhance the welfare of their own industries, but to contribute to the orderly and sustained progress of the nation.

Some trade associations have developed activities which materially assist concerns in their fields in their own planning for stability in operation and employment. Every trade association should undertake such activities, in order that the possibilities of planning may be utilized in each field in accordance with its conditions. These activities in the fields of production should include such relations with the fields of distribution that production may proceed with thorough understanding as to the requirements and preferences of ultimate consumers. Every producer needs for his own advantage the specialized suggestions and information distributors can give him as to markets and their extension.

RESERVES

Insurance in the form of accumulated reserves has been suggested as a protection against the consequences of unemployment, sickness, accident, and old age. In so far as such protection is based upon definite reserves previously established, it is to be most highly commended. Individual concerns have set up such benefit plans based either upon contributions by the company alone or upon joint contributions by the company and the employees. We commend particularly the purposes and general features of the so-called 'Rochester Plan' for unemployment benefits which, after 1932, will give partial aid against unemployment to over one third of the industrial workers of that city. A flexible plan, adaptable in large measure to general industrial application and largely modeled on this so-called 'Rochester Plan,' is described in an appendix to this report. (See Appendix B.) It is recommended for the thoughtful consideration of all employers.

EMPLOYMENT EXCHANGES

As the Committee points out in the appendix, a plan for unemployment benefits such as it presents should be supplemented and supported by efficient means to bring together persons who become unemployed and the opportunities for their employment. The Committee has accordingly added a short description of the unemployment center which has been set up in Rochester.

The plan which is proposed above, and outlined in an appendix, was prepared by a subcommittee after it had made thorough examination of compulsory unemployment insurance, both in principle and in practical application, and of experience with plans which employers, employees, or employers jointly with employees, have set up for themselves to provide benefits in the event of unemployment. The report of the subcommittee contains so much information that it has been considered an appropriate appendix to this report. (See Appendix C.)

COMPULSORY INSURANCE — THE DOLE

In this report, it will be noticed, the subcommittee has dwelt upon the nature of insurance which makes it intrinsically unsuitable for use to meet existing unemployment, for the reason that reserves have not already been set up. It concludes that unemployment is not, from an insurance point of view, a practical field for governmental intervention. Government compulsory insurance where it has so far been tried, in Europe, has proved inadequate through lack of sufficient reserves and has inevitably led to outright government payments, as in the English dole. It has thus engendered and encouraged unemployment.

Needed relief should be provided through private contributions and by state and local governments. There is every evidence that all requirements can in this manner be adequately met. Any proposals for federal appropriations for such purposes should therefore be opposed.

SWOPE PLAN

We also note with great interest the very thoughtful address of Mr. Gerard Swope, president of the General Electric Company, who has presented a most far-reaching plan for the creation of reserves, or insurance funds, for protection against unemployment, old age, sickness, and accident, together with a life-insurance policy equal to one year's wage. Many of the details of the plan may have to be changed, but it is most stimulating that the head of one of the country's greatest industrial companies recognizes the necessity for such forms of insurance.

Upon one feature of Mr. Swope's proposals the Committee desires to place special emphasis. Mr. Swope recommends that the plans for benefits he outlines should be adopted generally by each industry throughout the country. Obviously, representative trade associations are appropriate agencies to bring about such results and should be developed to perform this important function, in order that action in each instance may, in accordance with sound principle, be upon a voluntary basis.

WORKMEN'S COMPENSATION — PENSIONS

Upon some other features of Mr. Swope's proposals the United States Chamber has already taken action or will take action in the near future. For example, the Chamber has recorded its approval of the principle of workmen's compensation in legislation respecting industrial accidents. A representative committee will shortly submit to the Board of Directors recommendations of pension plans which employers should consider for their employees.

SHORTENING HOURS

Earlier in this report we have noted the gradual shortening of the hours of labor and the steady increase in real wages over a period of years. It is the belief of your Committee that this trend toward shorter hours for workers will continue in the future, and properly so. Our economic and agricultural organism, if properly coördinated, can undoubtedly provide the basis for a permanently high standard of living for our entire population, and at the same time permit a reasonable curtailment in working hours. But while we point out that such curtailment in general must come gradually, we recognize that it must come more rapidly at some periods and in some lines of industry than in others. We would sound a warning, however, that any extremely radical or abrupt change in the hours of labor may bring great economic harm.

PART III — IMMEDIATE MEASURES

Thus far our report has considered the causes of the depression and the long-time remedies to which we may look for tempering the severity of future depressions. What can be done to meet unemployment which now exists or may occur this winter?

It is not here a question about what can be done to stimulate business and proportionately decrease unemployment. The question is how to deal with the unemployment which arises by reason of business conditions, whether in amount it is decreasing or is increasing.

The answer is obvious. The task is to find work at which each unemployed person who needs wages may earn a livelihood for himself and his dependents. That means individualizing the unemployed. They necessarily have the greatest variety in training, experience, ability, and adaptability. Each one must have his capabilities determined.

LOCALIZATION

This can be done only locally. Its successful accomplishment can be assured through organization. Many cities already have organized for this purpose or they have made such progress that they can soon perfect their arrangements. Every chamber of commerce that is not already active in supporting a centralized organization of all the elements in its community, that can assist in bringing together jobs and men, should at once take the leadership in effecting such an organization for its city. In many of our large cities there may be opportunity to set up regional organizations. In an appendix the Committee describes in some detail the employment center which is being operated in Rochester. (See Appendix B.) Valuable suggestions can be obtained from this plan, whatever modifications in form may be found suitable to conditions elsewhere. It is the function and its effective performance that are of paramount importance.

There must be not only central registration of all individuals seeking work, but definite determination and record of the qualifications of each person in terms of his ability to perform various jobs. There should be added in each instance independent and sympathetic investigation, both to identify those who need work and to ascertain those who should have preferences by virtue of their conditions. There should be similar registration of the jobs to be done, and this registration must be in terms that will make for mutual satisfaction and understanding on the part of the applicant and of the prospective employer.

Thoughtful and persistent application of energy is essential to the greatest success of such an employment center. The activities must proceed to the stimulation of citizens, business concerns, and public authorities to provide and register employment opportunities, small as well as extensive. The possibilities of small opportunities have been demonstrated even in residential districts, where under a leader for a block it has been found possible to keep a man employed at the small jobs to be done around every house.

The stimulation of householders to identify work which can be done now to their advantage has large possibilities. Minor household repairs and maintenance, including painting, roofing, pointing-up masonry and chimneys, new shelves, cabinets, and partitions, remodeling rooms and porches, re-laying sidewalks, re-grading lawns and gardens, are but a few of the multitude of dormant work opportunities that may be mobilized into an impressive aggregate of work by an energetic campaign.

Such a campaign can be carried to every business concern, regardless of its field, with even greater results. Each business should be led to take stock of its work opportunities outside its regular activities, identifying all work it should now have done for its own advantage, and in accordance with its own situation. The jobs may be in rearrangement of stock, revision of records, reorganization of files, development of possibilities of sales, present or future, in new territory, repairs to buildings, installation of equipment needed to reduce operating costs, and preparation in other ways for demands and conditions which are foreseeable as certain to have to be met.

There should be close scrutiny, too, by each employer to ascertain if he is utilizing to the full his opportunities to rotate jobs, thus spreading the current employment among the largest possible number of employees in accordance with their needs. Industry has already done much to alleviate present conditions by this sensible practice of rotating employment instead of laying off a portion of the workers. We urge the extension of this principle to the utmost.

Public agencies should likewise be stimulated to proceed conservatively with needed public works and with such planning that will best support local employment. Public works are now giving employment to many thousands of men who are out of their usual occupations. This employment can be maintained and increased by appropriate planning and energetic attack upon the preliminaries which in each case have to be out of the way before construction can begin. The Federal Government can set an example for local and state authorities by speeding up its own program, which affects all parts of the country. All public agencies can be of material assistance in the general situation by proceeding with their normal purchasing of supplies and materials. Under modern conditions their volume of purchasing is so large that hesitation and delay upon their part may cause dislocation affecting employment.

Every local government should be stimulated, not only in its long-time planning and execution of public works but also in the identification and registration of all the work it can have done in the interest of health, safety, and comfort. In cleaning buildings, streets, and alleys, in removing litter from vacant lots, in improving drainage of streets and roads, in minor reconstruction at many points to improve the conditions of safety, a great amount of very useful work can be done.

ASSURANCES OF ACCOMPLISHMENT

When the number of businesses, the number of householders, and the number of public agencies in the United States are considered, it becomes evident that the problem of unemployment caused by the business depression can be met if everyone does his part. For accomplishment of the task, therefore, only organization is needed. That can be assured through the progress already made and through the leadership which existing local organizations can be counted upon to give. It will be understood in every locality, moreover, that the activities will continue throughout the winter. Their nature requires their continuance with unremitting energy. It will not be sufficient, for example, to obtain a large registration of work to be done. It will be necessary to conduct systematic surveys to find more work to be done, and later inspections to see it was actually carried out.

Such organization in each community as we recommend — and it is well tried and understood by business men — will demonstrate, we feel confident, the feasibility of meeting the local problem. Such a demonstration in itself will be valuable because of the added confidence it will bring to the community by reason of its knowledge that it is meeting its problems. This confidence will be reflected in readier response to requests for funds for relief purposes.

RELIEF FUNDS

Relief funds will be necessary, this winter as last, regardless of the success which is attained in placing unemployed men at work which needs doing. There are always many maladjustments in such a process; men who need work are not equipped to perform the work which is open for them; there is congestion of men of narrow occupation and adaptability in a region where the opportunity for their occupation has temporarily ceased; numbers of cases of distress of a kind suitable for charitable relief are brought to light in times of business depression and may be confused with unemployment distress. That the funds for adequate care for all such cases of distress will be forthcoming there is every assurance. The spontaneous generosity of our people has never failed, and it will be supplemented by city, county, and state funds on a larger scale this year than last. Preparations are under way to assist every city with suggestions. For that purpose, the President has set up a national committee, with distinguished personnel in its officers, its advisory board, and its committees. There will thus be a coördination of relief measures.

CONCLUSIONS

Both in finding work and in supplying relief, therefore, there are now before us tasks which are well within our abilities, without extraordinary measures of any kind, if we use the methods of organization with which as a people we are well acquainted. If we did not possess this experience with readiness of our people to participate in local organization for such purposes, we should need only to consider the tasks which have been before other countries, and the measures they have taken, to realize that our tasks are relatively much smaller and well within our resources if we use our well-tested American methods. Such a conclusion involves no minimizing of our situation. At the same time it implies recognition that we still have upwards of forty million persons employed in the occupations from which they obtain their livelihood, and that their continued welfare, too, deserves consideration. The volume of our existing employment is always to be recalled when attempts are made to estimate totals of national unemployment. However sincere and well-intended some of these attempts may be, their value for practical purposes could well be doubted even if the methods by which they are reached were not open to much criticism, tending to show material exaggeration as to the unemployment due to business conditions. Whatever the true national total might be at any given time it has little relevancy to the real task to be accomplished — through local effort finding work for those that need it and relieving distress where it exists through the efforts of those who can best understand the requirements and meet them sympathetically and adequately.

APPENDIX A — NATIONAL ECONOMIC COUNCIL

Under our economic system of private initiative and free competition, the United States has made greater progress than has ever been made before in the history of the world. Real wages and the standard of living have been raised substantially. But our progress is not even or regular. Both here and abroad there are periods of super-prosperity, followed by depressions that bring distress. There are recurrent dislocations of our economic machinery. This is a natural consequence of individual action, when no central coördinating influence is exerted over industry as a whole. Our problem is to retain the benefits of private initiative, and at the same time to supply, if possible, some degree of control or influence that will help to maintain a better balance and thus reduce the severity of business fluctuations.

The magnitude of our present depression is such that there is ground to doubt whether the measures so far considered will suffice either to pull us out now or prevent us from getting into another one like it. Planning by individual concerns, and even by whole industries, may not suffice to remedy such a severe lack of adjustment between production and consumption as we are experiencing. To an onlooker from some other world, our situation must seem as stupid and anomalous as it seems painful to us. We are in want because we have too much. People go hungry while our farmers cannot dispose of their surpluses of food; unemployed are anxious to work, while there is machinery idle with which they could make the things they need. Capital and labor, facilities for production and transportation, raw materials and food, all these essential things we have in seeming superabundance. We lack only the applied intelligence to bring them fruitfully into employment. This condition has led to a host of suggestions for national planning.

On first review of these conditions, it is not unreasonable to suppose that our maladjustments could be cleared by a planning board that had power to assemble the facts and then direct our people and resources into the various activities in which they would be most useful. This would call for a board that would function in some such way as the War Industries Board did. However, one's confidence in that suggestion is shaken when one considers the extreme complexity of our industrial organization, and realizes that such a board would have to take into its calculations the rapidly changing requirements of the immediate future, in addition to existing conditions. Indeed, when one thinks of a board rationing raw materials, assigning production to this and that factory, and handling the infinitude of detail that would come to it, or its subsidiaries, doubt of its advisability hardens into a conviction that even under the most favorable circumstances it could not be hoped that planning in that sense would be a satisfactory way out of our difficulties. Aside from these considerations, there is doubt of the constitutionality of such a planning board operating in peacetime.

There is another sense, however, in which planning on a national scale seems to be urgently needed. There are questions of fundamental importance in our national industrial policy on which we as yet have no united or settled opinion. To help us in dealing with these, some sort of a national economic council is needed. After careful consideration and after consulting leading business men and economists throughout the country, we are convinced that the time is ripe to set up such a body. We suggest that it be called National Economic Council rather than planning board, because of the implication of detailed plans with autocratic powers of control which the latter carries and which we oppose.

Foreign trade is one of these questions with which such

a council might deal. Many industries, with facilities which the purchasing power and perhaps even the physical needs of our own country cannot keep fully occupied, look to the vast needs of other countries for an outlet. It is a question whether we can long continue to export substantially more than we are willing to import, if we wish to get paid for our exports. Our foreign transactions have already attracted to us a seemingly useless superabundance of gold and embarrassed other countries with a shortage. What foreign-trade policy will give us the most wholesome conditions industrially and socially? This is a problem that calls for a thorough and dispassionate analysis of all of its many and intricate factors. It calls for the broadest and most statesmanlike attitude in the formulation of policies.

The level of wages is another subject on which opinion is divided. There is, on the one hand, distinguished and extensive judgment that wages should not be reduced below their pre-depression levels, and many voices on the other that wages must come down in terms of money, if not in purchasing power. There is an approach to unanimity of opinion that right wages and the sustained high purchasing power of the great mass of our working people are essential to our economic well-being. We still lack an authoritative discussion of this subject and the formulation of policies that will encourage such wage distribution as will contribute to sustained prosperity.

Still another situation, too little explored and discussed, which may lie at the very core of our difficulties, is the relation of our productive facilities to our needs. In the past, great areas of fertile and unused land, and a population growing rapidly by births and immigration, presented a condition which made it seem that real overproduction was well-nigh impossible. But it now appears that we have reached the point when many of our industries, such as soft coal, agricultural products, and shoes — to mention a few outstanding examples — can produce not only more than our people can buy, but — and this is the new element of the situation — more than they can actually use. Our use of power, our perfection of organization, and our exuberant technological developments have brought about this situation. The exhaustion of free land, the decline in the birth rate, and the limitation of immigration have sharply accentuated it. Here is a situation which calls loudly for exploration. If we are at the end of an era of unbounded opportunity for individual enterprise to make and sell the physical things which our people want, that is a fact of capital importance. We need to have more information as to whether or not this is the case, and if it is, we need the industrial statesmanship to face a new situation and tell us how to direct our great capacities for wealth-production into new and as yet unsatisfied channels of human need.

Agriculture, transportation, foreign debts, credit and finance, the curbing of harmful speculation, and the possible modification of our laws in regard to combinations are other subjects which might be similarly referred to without pretending that the list has been made all-inclusive. But this will suffice to indicate the range and gravity of the conditions on which we need to inform our national thinking.

The need for more accurate and authoritative information and statistics of a wide variety is another matter which might well claim the attention of such a council. As examples of these, the following may be mentioned: the best possible index of general business conditions, to supersede the indexes which we now have, not one of which is accepted as authoritative; adequate indexes of retail and wholesale prices and of unemployment; a national inventory of capital investment, plant capacity, and of export and domestic needs of industry and agriculture. The council might also recommend methods by

which industries could coöperate with each other and the
Government to secure stabilization. On all such questions its function would be to explore the needs and suggest the agencies, governmental or otherwise, by which
they could be met.

The problems outlined above demand early and intelligent action. Their importance is so painfully obvious
that we would be making a gesture of incompetence and
futility should we attempt to minimize them. They offer
an imperative challenge to the resourcefulness on which
our people pride themselves. With an abundance of
every resource, it is not conceivable that they are beyond our powers, if we firmly resolve to master them.

We suggest that in the methods by which industry
brings science and engineering to its aid in dealing with
physical problems, we have a clue to an appropriate procedure for dealing with economic problems. In its great
research establishments, industry has learned how to use
and control an effective tool for guiding its engineering
advance. It charges scientists with its problems, supports them with liberality, and acts with courage to make
their findings effective.

We recommend the appointment of a council, preferably of three members, five at the most, to be given the
responsibility of organizing a similar attack on our economic problems. The members must be men of the very
highest ability and integrity. They must have the experience and background which will enable them to understand sympathetically the circumstances of all the
essential elements of our industrial life, but they must
think and act for the country as a whole, and be without
obligation to any particular constituency.

We suggest that this council should be appointed by
a larger appointing board. The members of this board
should be invited to serve by the Chamber of Commerce
of the United States and should be representative of some

such group of interests as the following: The United States Department of Commerce, the Chamber of Commerce of the United States, labor, agriculture, manufacturing, banking, railroads, public utilities, distributive trades, the law, engineering, and professional economists. The appointments to the council should be made for a three-year term, at the end of which period an appointing board, constituted in the same way, should consider reappointments or changes.

The council should not represent any particular interests. In other words, it should be a body of impartial men of recognized ability and public leadership. The appointing board would have to recognize its great responsibility, and should be in practically unanimous agreement, as to the breadth, ability, and impartiality of its choices.

In several foreign countries there are national economic councils, which are relatively large bodies, made up of representatives of various interests, such as industry, labor, agriculture, etc. The delegates in such bodies are naturally expected to vote, or to use their influence, in behalf of the interests they represent. In order that these different interests may be adequately taken into consideration in the deliberations of the proposed council, the council would be expected to set up divers advisory committees made up of representatives from various industrial and other groups. The methods of appointing these committees, and of calling them to its assistance, should be left to the economic council itself.

The council would, of course, coöperate closely with existing trade associations, and it should encourage such trade associations to establish strong central committees or economic councils to study in detail the problems of coördination of production and consumption, stabilization of employment, etc., within their particular industries.

The members of the council should give their full time to the work, and they should be liberally paid. There should also be a permanent and adequate staff of able economists, statisticians, and men of affairs, to carry on the various studies that will be necessary. The work of the Government and of private individuals and research bureaus should be used to the greatest possible extent.

Financing the council is an important matter, but if there is sufficient agreement as to the importance of setting it up, it should be possible to find the ways and means. We suggest that the officials of the Chamber of Commerce of the United States explore the possibilities of raising sufficient funds, and ask the coöperation of the appointing board in this matter.

We believe that although the Chamber of Commerce of the United States should take the initiative in establishing the national economic council, the council, after it is appointed and in operation, should be entirely independent in its deliberations and its judgments.

The council should be charged with the immediate and continuing responsibility for suggesting policies and measures which will enable our country to direct its unprecedented powers of wealth-production into channels that will ensure our social and economic well-being. Time presses. We suffer much harm from our anomalous situation, and the council should, therefore, be asked for the earliest possible preliminary recommendations, but it should be assured the freedom and continuity which will give it ample time to prove its usefulness.

APPENDIX B

PLAN FOR UNEMPLOYMENT BENEFITS

The Committee, believing that employers are seeking a solution of problems relating to unemployment and believing that industry in the United States desires to solve this problem for itself, has undertaken to prepare and present what it believes to be a typical plan for the establishment of unemployment benefits, available for any employer or group of employers.

This plan is set forth in the accompanying document and has been adapted from the plan known as the Rochester Unemployment Benefit Plan, with modifications which experience and the judgment of the Committee have suggested. The Rochester Plan has been taken as typical because of the fact that it has already been put in force by a group of nineteen employers in the city of Rochester, New York — employers in various classes of business, and of size varying from a few employees up to one employer having thirteen thousand employees. This plan has received considerable attention and study on the part of those interested in the subject and has seemed to the Committee to be the most available plan to be used as a basis for that which is now presented.

In considering the plan now proposed, employers and other interested parties should understand that figures of percentage and of time are merely suggestions and that each employer's problem may have individual characteristics which require a change in these figures. A study of unemployment conditions in a given industry or in a given employment may dictate an increase or a decrease in the figures proposed in the typical plan.

The plan as presented permits establishment of a fund through appropriate bookkeeping entries on the part of the employer itself. It is the opinion of the Committee that the establishment of a trustee fund, outside the employer's own accounts, is worthy of most serious consideration. If such a fund is to be established, appropriate provisions for that purpose can be embodied in the plan as announced. Such an establishment would probably be through the medium of a trust company or of some other financial institution having charter power to manage the fund and distribute the benefits as provided in the plan.

It will also be noted that the plan submitted contemplates the establishment of the fund by the employer exclusively. Some employers and their employees may feel that it is wise to broaden the scope of the fund and possibly the extension of the period of benefit through the medium of contributions to be made on the part of the employees as well as of the employer. The Committee has not presented a plan embodying this feature, but the plan submitted may easily be adapted to that form by appropriate provisions as to the amounts of contributions on the part of employees and as to the segregation of the reserve created by such contributions and its separate distribution under the plan. In this case, in particular, it would seem wise to place the fund under the custody of a trustee.

In the final analysis, it is conceded on all sides that the most effective remedy for unemployment conditions lies in the direction of further stabilization of employment itself.

The important factor to keep in mind in considering unemployment benefit plans is the reduction of unemployment; the question of benefits is secondary. It is believed that the voluntary adoption of such a plan by a company will give incentive to stabilize and thereby reduce unemployment. In many cases the benefits to the employer resulting from the greater stabilization will outweigh the cost of the benefit plans. To the employee this plan gives greater security and will tide him over the earlier period of unemployment. At the same time because of the limited benefits, it should not result in less incentive on his part to save. The community in general will benefit because the money which will be paid out in benefits during a period of unemployment will maintain purchasing power to a certain degree. The payment of benefits will also reduce expenditures of charitable organizations and relief payments by municipalities.

The Committee believes that the general voluntary adoption of the proposed plan by American employers, together with its enthusiastic support, will result in great benefit to both industry and society at large.

The plan is as follows:

1. *Employees eligible.* Employees will be eligible to benefits under this plan provided they have been in the employ of the company for a continuous period of not less than one year and provided their earnings on a full time basis for the past three months have averaged less than $—— a week. (The amount to be inserted should be determined on the basis of local conditions.)

2. *Unemployment reserve fund.* An unemployment reserve fund will be created. The company will make an appropriation annually, beginning during the current year, of not less than 2 [1] per cent of the total payroll until five [1] annual appropriations shall have been made. The company may then suspend further appropriations when the reserves actually available in the fund are at least equal to the sum of the last five annual appropriations, but appropriations shall be resumed as soon as such reserves fall below that minimum, and continued until such minimum is restored. All income received from the investment of the fund will be added to the principal.

When after benefits become payable a prolonged period of unemployment occurs and, in the opinion of the management, the fund will be inadequate to take care of the benefits payable, the management may declare that an emergency exists. Upon this declaration of emergency, all officials and employees of the company who are not receiving unemployment benefits will be assessed one per

---

[1] The proper percentage and the number of annual appropriations will depend upon the company's unemployment experience and the degree of stabilization prevailing in the particular industry.

cent of their earnings. Deductions therefor will be made from the weekly or monthly pay, and such deductions will be added to the unemployment reserve fund. The company will appropriate into the fund an amount equal to these deductions in addition to the annual appropriations. The deductions will continue until the management declares that the emergency is over.

3. *Effective date of plan.* Benefits will become payable under the plan two years [1] after date of inauguration.

4. *Control and administration of the plan.* A committee will be appointed by the management to administer the plan and to define and interpret its terms and conditions. The decisions of this committee will be subject only to the general control and direction of the Board of directors of the company,

5. *Unemployment benefits.* The unemployment benefits shall be paid weekly at the rate of sixty [2] per cent of the average weekly earnings of the unemployed person, with a maximum of $——[2] a week. (The amount to be inserted should be determined on the basis of local conditions.) The last three months of full time employment exclusive of overtime will be the period for determining the average earnings.

6. *Waiting period.* No unemployment benefits shall be payable to eligible employees for the first two continuous weeks of unemployment.

7. *Maximum period during which benefits shall be paid.*[2] The maximum number of weekly benefits to be paid during twelve consecutive months or during any one continuous period of lay-off shall depend upon the employee's length of service prior to such lay-off, as follows:

[1] Benefits may be payable earlier provided sufficient reserves are available.

[2] Benefits and length of service, adopted in the Rochester Plan, after investigation of necessary requirements.

LENGTH OF SERVICE	BENEFITS
1 year to 1½ years	6 weeks
1½ years to 2 years	8 weeks
2 years to 3 years	10 weeks
3 years to 4 years	11 weeks
4 years to 5 years	12 weeks
5 years and over	13 weeks

8. *Unemployment benefit for part-time workers.* If, on account of slack work, an employee is receiving reduced pay due either to transfer or to part-time work, the deficit, if any, between his actual earnings and the amount he would receive in benefits, under the plan, were he wholly unemployed, shall be paid to him out of the Unemployment Reserve Fund. Such payment will cease when the employee has received an amount equal to the full unemployment benefits provided in paragraphs 5 and 7.

9. *Benefits to employees securing work outside.* If an employee receiving benefits secures permanent work outside and is no longer available for work with the company, the benefits shall cease. An employee securing temporary work outside will still be eligible for benefit, but in no case shall his weekly benefit exceed the deficit, if any, between his earnings on the temporary work and his average full time earnings on which his weekly benefits are based.

10. *Conditions for receiving unemployment benefit.* In order to receive the benefit, a laid-off employee shall report to the company as frequently as the company may require. A blank will be furnished on which he will be required to state what steps he has taken to secure employment. An employee making a false statement on this blank shall forfeit his benefits under the unemployment plan.

Note: If a suitable employment exchange is available in the community, add the following: The employee must also register at the employment exchange. When a job is available, the exchange will be asked to notify both the employee and the company, and if the employee refuses to accept work, which he can reasonably be expected to undertake, his benefits shall cease.

11. *Benefits not assignable.* Benefits under the plan shall not be assignable by the employee, nor subject to the claims of his creditors.

12. *Change or discontinuance of plan.* The company may, with three months' notice to employees, change or discontinue this plan at any time at its discretion, provided that such change or discontinuance will not affect the further payment of benefits to the extent provided by the fund available at the time of change or discontinuance.

The payment of benefits will cease if and when the Reserve Fund becomes exhausted.

13. *Reservations:*

(1) No unemployment benefits shall be paid to employees who have been employed for temporary work and were so notified when they were employed, unless they subsequently become regular employees.

(2) No benefits shall be paid for time off on account of the destruction of any part of the company's property by fire, lightning, earthquake, windstorm, or other accidents, but the company may at its discretion make payments to employees affected by such destruction.

(3) No benefits shall be paid to employees for unemployment due either directly or indirectly to strikes or other trade disputes in the company's plants or elsewhere.

(4) No benefits shall be paid to an employee laid off who fails to take such steps as may be required to secure employment or who fails to accept a transfer to a reasonable job either with the company or elsewhere.

(5) No benefits shall be paid to any employee who has been discharged for cause, or who voluntarily leaves the employ of the company, or who ceases to be employed for any reason other than lack of available work.

(6) No benefits shall be paid to employees receiving or entitled to receive sick benefits, accident compensation, disability benefits, or retirement annuities. Such employees shall be eligible for unemployment benefits only when sick benefits, accident compensation, or disability benefits have been exhausted and when they are capable of resuming work.

(7) Upon the death of an employee receiving benefits under this plan, benefits shall cease.

EMPLOYMENT CENTER

The Committee believes it is important to stress that the Rochester Plan of Unemployment Benefits is regarded by its participants as only *part* of a more widespread attack on the problem. In addition to the usual and extensive measures for the prevention of unemployment and stabilization of seasonal or fluctuating demands, all employers are pooling their employment activities through the 'Public Employment Center of Rochester,' and no employee is eligible to unemployment benefits unless registered therein, thus enabling the Center to place workers temporarily in any other available employment. Your Committee believes that the practicability and success of this employment-center activity warrants the careful consideration of other communities and offers the following brief description thereof:

In June, 1929, the Industrial Commissioner of New York State appointed a committee termed the Advisory Council on Employment Problems, to advise on methods of improving the state employment service and of contributing to a more effective organization of the labor market. Legislation was passed authorizing the Commissioner to accept private aid for research and experimentation, and according legal status to the Council. It was decided to set up an experimental public employment office which over a period of from three to five years should endeavor to work out standards for the conduct of the state employment service.

The Council selected Rochester as the site of the project and organization of the Public Employment Center was actually begun at the end of 1930 under direct supervision of the Committee on Demonstrations, a subcommittee of the Advisory Council. An annual budget of about seventy-five thousand dollars for a period of from three to five years was provided for by grants from the City of Rochester, the State of New York, the Spelman Fund, the Russell Sage Foundation, and the Rosenwald Foundation. After some months spent in locating a site, organizing the office and engaging the staff, the office was fully equipped and began to function in June of this year. Today it has its main branch in a large, modern office building with ample space for private interviews and waiting rooms. The Center is divided into five main divisions to serve all classes of employees: a Commercial and Professional Division in charge of the clerical group, stenographers, bookkeepers, salesmen, professional men and women; a Technical Division for the engineering group and the skilled trades and a Women's Division directed by a staff of women and composed of a Service Section for domestic service, waitresses, etc., and an Industrial Section for factory workers. The State Employment Service has been taken over by the Public Employment Center and now forms the Broad Street Division of the Center which accommodates the Labor and Farm Sections for both men and women. The fifth branch is the Junior Division which, for the present, is functioning as a separate unit.

The staff of the Center is composed of men and women of technical skill in placement and personnel work. Half the day is spent in interviewing applicants. In the afternoons the staff works in the field, acquainting themselves with the needs of the industries, and making contacts with employers. Records are kept of each registrant in the hope of building up a complete central file of all those seeking work in Rochester.

The Center has had the coöperation of many local groups. Even before the Center was considered, a group of employers in the city had after much study decided that Rochester industry needed such a service. With competent technical advice furnished by a Technical Advisory Committee, an adequate budget and a trained staff, the Center has achieved a significant success. Its purpose has been stated as follows:

1. To assist the employers of the area to secure suitable employees, and persons seeking work to secure suitable employment.
2. To assist in bringing about and maintaining a balance between the demand for employees in the various occupations and the supply of such employees in the area.
3. To determine for a comparable area the most practicable scope of a public employment office and the most effective and economical methods of operating it.
4. To serve as an authoritative source of information on employment in the area.
5. To assist in improving the operation of other local offices of the State Employment Service.

APPENDIX C — REPORT OF SUBCOMMITTEE

UNEMPLOYMENT INSURANCE

For the great majority of people, the necessities of life are to be derived mainly from income currently received as remuneration for labor. It is thus very desirable for both social and economic reasons that the maximum possible protection against loss of this income be made available. A large part of this loss of income is due to unemployment, and with respect to this portion of the loss two principal means of accomplishing the purpose are advocated. The first method, the inauguration of preventive measures leading to the reduction or elimination of unemployment, is quite generally accepted as the preferable mode of attack. But it is also agreed that, under industrial and economic conditions as thus far developed in this country, complete regularization of industry is an ideal to strive for, but not to anticipate attaining in the near future. It therefore becomes desirable to consider the practicability of supplementing the preventive measures with the second method of protecting the workers' income, namely unemployment benefits in one form or another.

There have been experiments in many different ways of providing protection for a worker against reduction of income because of his loss of employment due to no fault of his own. Different expressions are used to designate these plans, one of which is 'unemployment insurance.' For the purpose of this report, the term 'unemployment insurance' will be used as a broad classification, and hence will include those plans which are variously known as 'unemployment benefit,' 'unemployment reserve,' 'guaranteed employment,' 'dismissal wage,' etc., as well as specifically 'unemployment insurance.'

The European approach has generally been along the lines of state direction, if not compulsion. In the United States there has as yet been no organized state participation in such plans. These two methods of handling the problem will be analyzed and compared in subsequent sections.

DEFINITION AND ESSENTIALS OF INSURANCE

Many definitions of insurance have been undertaken, but, for the present purpose, the following may be a fair statement of what is generally meant by the term:

Insurance is that agency which protects an individual against loss by the payment, in the event of some definite occurrence resulting in a loss, of an agreed sum of money out of a systematically accumulated fund previously collected from or on account of a group of persons, of which such individual was a member. The contingency for which the individual is protected may be one which, so far as he is concerned, may never occur at all (such as fire or accident or even sickness), or may be one which is bound to occur at some time, but of which the time of occurrence is unknown (such as death).

A loss, to be covered by insurance, must be either a loss in property value or a loss in human value which can, in some measure, be evaluated in money. The latter class includes chiefly a loss arising out of temporary or permanent cessation of income, in whole or in part, resulting from death, ill health, or other disturbance to earning power. Employment has a value which is readily calculable in money, so that the risk of loss of employment, in so far as the monetary value of the loss is concerned, is a risk which comes within the foregoing definition.

One important factor in the definition of insurance is that benefits paid out on the occurrence of a loss must come from funds accumulated prior to the loss by collections from the individuals insured and / or from others. Hence, while insurance collects and distributes funds, it does not and cannot create funds. This point cannot be too much emphasized, for the reason that it is often assumed that the act of adopting an unemployment insurance plan will, in some manner, simultaneously *create* assets immediately available for the payment of benefits.

There is inherent in the definition of insurance another factor which is often overlooked. It is that there must be a *loss* and this necessarily implies that each individual to be insured is himself in employment and may normally be expected to be employed. Insurance, as such, may perhaps be able to take care of employable individuals when they lose income because of cessation of employment, but insurance can never afford protection to those who are not normally employable, without by that very circumstance, ceasing to be insurance. For individuals usually unemployable, the problem is not one of loss of income normally to be anticipated but utter absence of income. The problem of the unemployable is a problem to be solved only by charity or by poor relief in some form, and insurance, as such, is entirely unsuitable to such situations.

To be an insurable risk, the probability of the occurrence of the contingency must be predictable within reasonable limits; the fact that the event shall have actually occurred must be determinable with reasonable certainty; the contingency must be such that it is unlikely that it might happen simultaneously to all the insured, or to a relatively large group thereof, that is, it must be distributable; and the loss must be beyond the individual's control, as much as is possible.

THE INSURABILITY OF THE UNEMPLOYMENT RISK AS A WHOLE

The question to be considered is whether or not the risk of unemployment is insurable, according to the foregoing definition and requirements. Unfortunately, the correct answer as to a risk of this character is more difficult than in the case of such risks as death, accident, sickness, or old age. The rates of occurrence of all these latter are predictable with fair accuracy. The fact that death or old age has actually taken place is almost certainly determinable, and there is comparatively small question about sickness and accident. Each of these contingencies is largely beyond the individual's control, and with well-distributed risks the proportion of cases occurring at any one time is not large.

With unemployment insurance, however, the problem takes on a somewhat different aspect. In the first place, the unemployment risk is not in all its types predictable within reasonable limits, as is shown by the enormous degree to which the current number of unemployed in England and Germany exceeds the number expected by those who drafted the unemployment insurance laws in those countries. In this country the lack of success in making predictions has been too recent to require any comment.

With respect to the condition of verification of the occurrence of the contingency, the difficulty is not primarily in determining whether unemployment exists, but in determining whether the unemployment which has occurred is of a type for which it was intended to provide insurance. An effective solution is primarily a matter of arriving at an acceptable definition of unemployment for insurance purposes which shall determine the right to receive benefits, and of setting up a proper claim machinery, so as to eliminate illegitimate claims without imposing an undue handicap on legitimate claimants. The experience to date, while hardly satisfactory as yet, justifies the expectation that with respect to this condition, an effective solution is likely to be found.

With respect to the further test that insurance is unsuitable to cases where the loss may occur to a considerable number of the members of the insured group simultaneously, it is hardly necessary to point out that the risk of unemployment is much less a satisfactory subject for insurance than the usual type of risk for which insurance is generally used.

THE INSURABILITY OF SPECIFIC TYPES OF UNEMPLOYMENT

The risk of unemployment viewed as a whole being apparently not a suitable subject for insurance, the next consideration is to analyze unemployment as regards its various causes and to consider them separately. The major causes have been classified as follows:

(1) Cyclical — resulting from business fluctuations and trade depressions.
(2) Seasonal — occurring regularly during certain periods of the year in a specific industry subject to such variations; e.g., in the building and clothing industries.
(3) Technological — resulting from basic changes in production methods, overexpansion in an industry, changed fashions, or loss of markets in which the product was formerly distributed.
(4) Industrial disputes, such as strikes and lockouts.
(5) Causes of a personal nature, such as inaptitude, poor training or placement, or limited physical, mental, or moral qualifications.

It is generally conceded that the last two classes of unemployment — that caused by industrial disputes and by the personal disqualification of the employee — must be excluded from any intelligent program attempting to provide protection by insurance. Further discussion will be limited to the first three classes, but one of the difficult problems in administration is found to be the detecting of any claims really belonging to type four or five, or by those voluntarily idle, who may prefer unemployment benefits to a steady wage.

With respect to such first three classes, study of the experience to date, as outlined in subsequent sections of this report, has led to no final conclusions, but it has indicated certain limitations which further experience may show to be the utmost extent of any insurance program from which results may be expected. Experience has so far indicated that insurance might properly be used in the case of persons who are normally in employment, for protection against loss from certain seasonal unemployments, and, for a limited period, from cyclical and technological unemployment. Insurance has not been able and probably never will be able to provide against loss from long protracted unemployment due to continued depression, without becoming, at least in part, relief or charity instead of insurance. At best, insurance benefits paid during unemployment occasioned by fundamental changes in industry and other forms of technological unemployment are but temporary assistance, while, on the other hand, the availability of such benefits, through insurance, may actually become an obstacle to improvement, since the relief so afforded may well have a tendency to suppress the desire or necessity of the recipient to fit himself for other work.

Experience has also shown that unemployment insurance, if it is to be on a sound insurance basis, even for the limited field within which it may perhaps be practiced, will require, as in the case of old age protection, that a substantial portion of the benefits payable to an insured, shall, in the last analysis, come out of contributions to the fund made by that insured or on his account. This situation results primarily from the fact that one of our basic conditions for insurance, that the contingency shall not occur simultaneously to all members of the insured group, is not satisfactorily met in such cases.

A brief résumé of European and American experience with unemployment insurance will indicate to what extent the above considerations are realized in actual practice.

EXPERIENCE WITH GOVERNMENTAL UNEMPLOYMENT INSURANCE

GREAT BRITAIN

The first national compulsory unemployment insurance act ever introduced by any government was adopted in Great Britain in 1911. The original law included only a few industries, covering about two and a quarter million workers. After a few minor enlargements, the scope was greatly expanded in 1920, so as to include almost the entire working population, with the exception of agricultural laborers and those engaged in domestic service. At the present time over twelve million workers are insured under the scheme.

When the plan was inaugurated, employers and adult employees each contributed five cents a week, and the State paid three and one third cents, or one quarter of the total. At that time the benefit payable was $1.70 a week for adults, and was limited to a maximum of fifteen weeks in any insurance year, or one week's benefit for every five weeks' contributions paid, whichever was the less. As a result of the increased cost of living and political pressure, these benefits have been increased repeatedly, up to the present figure of $4.14 a week for adult males, graded down for women and children. At the same time, the rule limiting benefits to a fixed proportion of contributions paid has been abolished; and there is no maximum duration of benefits, subject to the condition that thirty contributions have been paid in the preceding two years. These increases in benefits have not always been accompanied by a corresponding increase in contributions, so that, while the original scheme of 1911 was able to build up a surplus of over $100,000,000 by 1920, these increased benefits, together with the increased unemployment brought on by the economic depression, soon turned this surplus into a deficit. In spite of a temporary respite in 1924–25, this deficit has grown almost constantly, until now it stands at over $400,000,-000. At the present rate of expenditure, the total contributions required to balance the cost would be seventy-nine cents weekly, instead of the actual rate of forty-five cents, this even omitting the cost of the transitional benefits, amounting to forty-one cents additional.

The history of the plan through the decade since 1921, during the time this tremendous debt was accumulating, is interesting as showing how extraneous influences can alter the form of an initially sound insurance plan and turn it into a hopelessly insolvent government subsidy and a major political issue. In addition to increasing benefits, additional payments for dependents were added, without appropriate increase in contributions. The original rule was that a person claiming benefit had to prove that he was capable of working but unable to obtain suitable employment. The amendment of 1930, however, transferred the burden of proof from the employee to the State, which now must present evidence that the applicant has rejected a suitable offer of employment. Immediately after this change became effective, there was a great increase in the number of persons claiming and receiving benefit.

In the original plan, there were two provisions designed to encourage and reward the stabilization of employment. When a worker attained the age of sixty, any excess of his personal contributions paid over the benefits he had received, was refunded, with interest at two and one half per cent. There was also a refund arrangement for employers with good employment experience in the preceding year. These two essential features were never greatly stressed, and, when the fund began to run into debt, they were abolished, as a supposed economy. Thus, at the present time, there is no incentive for either employer or employee to try to protect the solvency of the fund, and many abuses have arisen, most of which are quite legal within a strict interpretation of the law.

To provide for workers whose claims to benefits had run out, or whose contributions were insufficient to entitle them to any benefit at all, the 'Uncovenanted' or 'Extended' benefit was introduced in 1921. This emergency measure has been renewed several times and is now called the 'Transitional Benefit' whose purpose is to tide these workers over the present abnormal industrial depression. It provided that a person normally employed in an insurable trade might receive unemployment benefit, in spite of having insufficient contributions to his credit, if the public interest made this seem expedient to the Minister of Labor. In August, 1924, the discretionary powers of the Minister were revoked and the benefit was made payable as a 'right.' This act of a Labor Government was reversed in 1925 by a Conservative Government, which restored the Minister's discretionary power. Another Labor Government in 1929 once more made this benefit a right, and this is its status today. All that is required is the payment of eight contributions in the preceding two years, or thirty at any time. The Act of 1930 placed the cost of these extra payments entirely on the State, and since late in 1930 these benefits have cost the Treasury a great deal more than have its contributions to the regular fund. The cost of this is not included in the $400,000,000 deficit mentioned above. This is the feature that has given the whole system the name of 'dole.' The regular insurance scheme might be made solvent by increasing contributions or restricting the benefits, but this provision is entirely separate, and is purely a government subsidy of poor relief.

The only feature of the plan remaining substantially unchanged is the administration. Although this was transferred in 1917 from the supervision of the Board of Trade to the Ministry of Labor, the system is substantially the same, and, under both of these bodies, the Labor Exchanges have handled the greater part of the work. These exchanges are an essential feature of any unemployment insurance plan. It is here that workmen register and lodge their claims. Their inability to obtain suitable employment is tested substantially by whether or not the exchange can offer them jobs. The function of finding jobs for men and men for jobs has been rather submerged by the vastness of the exchanges' task of handling claims for benefit.

GERMANY

There are two fundamental differences between the unemployment insurance plans of Great Britain and Germany. In England, the flat-rate system of contributions and benefits prevails. That is, they are based on a few broad age and sex classifications, without regard to salary. In Germany, however, both benefits and contributions are a percentage of the workers' wages or salary. Thus, when compulsory insurance was started in 1927, the contributions were placed at three per cent of the payroll, divided equally between employer and employee, and benefits were graded according to salary class, ranging from seventy-five per cent of wages in the lowest class to thirty-five per cent in the highest, with additional benefits for dependents.

The history of the contribution rate illustrates the second major difference from English custom. This difference is the part played by the National Government. Whereas, in Great Britain, the Treasury makes a regular contribution about equal to that of each of the other two parties, and lends money freely when the contributions do not suffice, in Germany, the Reich makes no contribution normally, and a different procedure is adopted when the fund runs into debt. Instead of increasing benefits and liberalizing the restrictions to help the workers during the period of stress, the German plan looks to the solvency of the fund, and raises contributions, tightens the restrictions for benefit, and, unlike the British practice of *lending*, subsidizes the fund, but only up to half its deficit, specifying that the remainder must be raised by increasing contributions, decreasing benefits, or some other such measure. Thus the contributions were raised by successive stages to 6.5 per cent in October, 1930, and for that year the excess of expenditures over the contributions of employers and employees was $176,-

000,000. Corresponding to the Transitional Benefit in England, Germany provides 'Crisis Benefits' for those whose claims to standard benefits have run out. However, contrary to British practice, these benefits are smaller in amount than the standard benefits, both as to qualifications and duration of benefits, and are payable only at the discretion of the Minister of Labor. As in England, these benefits are financed entirely by the Government, but in Germany, the local governments must relieve the federal of one fifth of these expenditures. This different approach may be attributable to the credit standings of the two nations, but the net result is that the fund is closer to balancing in Germany, despite a proportionately greater number of unemployed. However, the plan is much younger, and comparisons may be misleading.

The general eligibility requirements are similar in the two systems, but the management is in different hands. In England, Parliament directs the work, the Minister of Labor being directly responsible to it; but in Germany, a separate corporation manages the work comparatively free from political dickerings.

FINDINGS OF GOVERNMENTAL COMMISSIONS
CONCERNING BRITISH AND GERMAN PLANS

In both England and Germany, commissions have recently been sitting to study the serious problems which have arisen. In the past there have been several other committees appointed for the same purpose, the major changes in legislation being the results of these committees' reports. The final report of the Royal Commission in England is not due until fall, but it has issued an interim report suggesting (1) an increase in contributions, (2) a decrease in benefits, (3) general tightening of restrictions, especially for the transitional benefits and for some particular classes of people, such as casual workers

and married women. The only recommendation acted
upon favorably by Parliament was the third, which was
made partially effective by giving the Minister of Labor
certain discretionary rights in dealing with some of the
'anomalies' or 'abuses' included in the Commission's
report. The first and second recommendations were
ignored, and instead, Parliament raised the borrowing
power from £90,000,000 to £115,000,000 and extended
the transitional period a further six months. Hence,
instead of reducing the deficit from about £40,000,000
to about £8,000,000 a year, as was estimated in the Commission's report, and also saving £10,000,000 in transitional benefits, the deficit will continue its present rate
of increase of approximately £1,000,000 weekly, unless
further steps are taken, as the changes adopted will save
at most £5,500,000 yearly, in all. Similar recommendations were made in the report of Sir George May's National Economy Committee, appointed with the broader
task of balancing Great Britain's general budget, except
that this committee suggested still more drastic economies, estimating a total saving to the Treasury from the
unemployment benefits of about £66,000,000. It was this
report that precipitated Prime Minister Ramsay Mac-
Donald's resignation as Labor Prime Minister, and the
formation of the new National Government. This temporary government is pledged to economies, including
a cut in the unemployment insurance benefits, which has
resulted in a complete break with the Trades Union
Council, which controls one hundred and sixty seats in
Parliament and has been the backbone of the Labor
Party.[1]

In Germany, the Braun Committee, set up for the same
general purposes as was the Royal Commission in Eng-

---

[1] The English election in the autumn of 1931 altered the political situation and there has been a reduction in the burden carried by the State.
(*Editor.*)

land, recommended a temporary reduction of some of the benefits and increased restrictions. These recommendations have been substantially adopted, and may help to hold down the deficit.

GENERAL CONCLUSIONS

The history of these two plans illustrates how state compulsory unemployment insurance has worked out in practice. Although both plans were worked out 'as nearly as possible' on an actuarial basis, subsequent events have vitiated all estimates of the amount of unemployment to be expected. Incidentally, in the United States there would be even a much less satisfactory basis for forecasting rates than these two countries had. It would seem that the requirement that, to be insurable, the rate of occurrence of a contingency must be reasonably predictable, is not met by these examples of national compulsory unemployment insurance. It seems especially evident that insurance cannot give protection against the effects of continued long-term depression, or technological unemployment, such as has been troubling England particularly during the last decade.

The difficulties of the Umpire (the final authority in determining claims for benefit in England) in deciding cases, the ultra-fine legal points that arise from the infinite variety of occupations and circumstances, and the existence of the so-called 'anomalies' in the British plan, indicate that the existence of unemployment as defined in the acts is difficult to determine.

While Great Britain and Germany typify the compulsory type of unemployment insurance abroad, there is a different type of plan in certain other countries, such as Belgium, Denmark, Norway, and Switzerland. In these countries, unemployment insurance is of a voluntary nature, and government participation is usually limited to subsidizing private funds that meet certain requirements. The private nature of these funds assures the interest and coöperation of all members, and the comparative freedom from political controversy makes them adaptable to the exigencies of the situation, rather than the whim of any group of people. Even so, the pressure of the present depression has caused considerable agitation for an increasing amount of governmental participation and control, and the voluntary nature of the plans is threatened.

PRIVATE PLANS IN THE UNITED STATES

There has been little development in actual unemployment insurance schemes in the United States. Those in operation have been initiated by the employer and/or the employee, with no action by the state, and hence may be called voluntary, as contrasted with the British or German compulsory schemes.

There was a rather active interest in unemployment insurance and kindred subjects during the period shortly after the depression of 1920–21, and several of the plans adopted were doubtless prompted by that interest. The interest subsequently subsided until last year, when it was revived by the conditions then current.

The plans in operation may be divided into three groups: (1) plans established by employers, (2) plans established jointly by employers and trade unions, (3) plans established by trade unions.

Excluding plans providing only dismissal wages or indirect benefits in the form of loans or savings available for withdrawal, estimates varying from 100,000 to 250,000 have been made for the number of wage-earners covered. This variation is caused primarily by the widely different interpretations of what constitutes an unemployment insurance plan. Using a moderately strict interpretation, a fair estimate would be not more than 200,000, and probably less than 175,000. This limited scope is comparable to the voluntary plans in Europe, and indicates one possible disadvantage of leaving the subject to private initiative. However, with proper encouragement, along the lines indicated in the concluding section of this report, there is reason to believe that there would be a considerably larger participation in this country. It must also be remembered that probably a considerable number of employees are being kept on the payroll, although there is not sufficient production to need them, because employers are loathe to discharge a man with a family. It is possible that, in a number of cases, the workers would be laid off if there were an insurance plan to maintain them. Thus, the estimate given for the coverage in this country is probably considerably too small, as compared with conditions under compulsory plans.

An interesting type of private initiative in this country is found in the joint union-employer plans, whereby an agreement is entered into by the manufacturers and the unions to pay unemployment benefits to union members. In some cases both employers and employees contribute to the fund out of which benefits are to come; in others the employers alone support the fund. Most of these arrangements are found in the various branches of the garment trades, the plan of the men's clothing industry alone including about 60,000 of the total of approximately 65,000 workers so covered.

AMALGAMATED CLOTHING WORKERS OF AMERICA

The agreement between the Amalgamated Clothing Workers of America (men's clothing industry) and the firms in the Chicago market was started in May, 1923. Similar arrangements were made by manufacturers and unions in Rochester and in New York during the year 1928. Under the original Chicago agreement, employers and employees each contributed 1.5 per cent of payroll, but, in 1928, the employer's contribution was raised to three per cent, the employee's contribution remaining as before. Under the current agreements between the employers and the trade union, the maximum scale of benefits is forty per cent of wages, with a maximum of twenty dollars a week, for not more than seven and a half weeks in a single year. The actual scale of benefits has been varied in accordance with experience and prospective conditions, so that, at the present time, the benefit consists of thirty per cent of full-time earnings up to fifteen dollars a week. To simplify bookkeeping, the beneficiary receives two checks a year, one in April and one in November. From May, 1924, when benefits were first paid in Chicago, to May, 1931, over six million dollars has been distributed and there was a balance in the combined fund of about three quarters of a million dollars in May, 1931. Instead of having one common fund for the entire industry, there are six separate funds — one for the contractors, one for each of the three largest companies in the industry, one for the rest of the inside manufacturers, and the last for non-association inside shops.

The number of clothing workers in Chicago has steadily declined during the years the plan has been in operation, owing to the reorganization of the industry. For example, one firm now uses a machine which has made possible a substantial reduction in its cutting force. Other improvements in production have also resulted in the employment of a smaller working force. As a consequence, after negotiations with the union, 'a dismissal wage' of five hundred dollars each was offered to two hundred and fifty cutters who agreed not to seek work again in Chicago in the men's clothing industry. The firm which made this offer supplied half of the amount required; the remainder came from cutters who were retained and who agreed to forfeit their unemployment benefits for two seasons.

The Clothing Workers' Agreement in Rochester closely follows the Chicago plan, though benefits are lower, being only twenty-five per cent of full-time earnings, and are paid for a shorter period (five weeks benefits a year is the maximum allowed). Contributions are also lower, being limited to 1.5 per cent of the payroll. The employers' contributions began on May 1, 1928, and, according to the original agreement, employees' contributions were not to start until May 1, 1929. But these terms were later revised and payments by employees have been waived during the period of the present agreement.

The New York plan is much less definite than either the Chicago or Rochester agreements. There is but one fund and the employers alone contribute to it. Benefits are paid from time to time as the condition of the fund warrants. No formal rules cover eligibility, the rate of benefit scale, or other similar matters. Eight months after contributions began a depression in the market brought about a period of severe unemployment, and although it had been planned to allow the fund a longer period of accumulation and to formulate rules and regulations before beginning the payment of benefits, the board of trustees decided, as an emergency measure, to vote a sum of money to aid members most seriously affected through lack of work. Under this arrangement, the individual beneficiaries were designated by the officials of their several local unions, and payments were made in discretionary amounts, based on the merits of each case. The same conditions have arisen periodically since the first disbursement was made, and further sums have been paid out, but the trustees have not yet provided formal rules covering eligibility, benefit scale and other similar matters.

The New York market differs from those in Chicago and Rochester in that a much larger percentage of the work is done in contract shops, and seasonal unemployment is considerably higher in New York than in either of the other markets. These differences in market conditions and the absence of formal provisions of operation in the New York plan preclude any comparisons with the functioning of the Chicago plan, which is much older, or with the Rochester plan, which made its first payments on a formal basis as recently as May, 1930.

The success of the Clothing Workers' plan, especially in Chicago, where it has been in operation for eight years, in one of the most unstable and hardest hit of all American industries, is eloquent testimony to what can be done by private initiative in a coöperative spirit. It is understood that the occupation is seasonal, and no attempt is made to pay benefits in the off season. The plan covers only loss of employment occurring within the usual full-time employment periods.

GUARANTEED EMPLOYMENT PLANS

The system of guaranteed employment is another approach to the unemployment problem. One of the largest of the companies having this type of plan is Procter and Gamble, in Cincinnati, Ohio. This company adopted an employment guarantee plan on August 1, 1923. While all the factories of the company are not covered, over three quarters of the employees are included. No special fund is set aside to cover salary payments during periods when there is no work, the entire cost of living up to the terms of the guarantee being charged to production.

Employees, to be eligible for benefit from the plan, must have a service record of at least six months and earn less than two thousand dollars a year. They also have to buy stock in the company equal in market value to a year's wages. Such employees are guaranteed full pay for forty-eight weeks in each calendar year. No payments are made, however, while the plants are closed for cleaning, overhauling, and inventory, or during holidays or vacation times. In the period of four weeks for which there is no guarantee, half pay is given if the person reports for work, though this is not stipulated in the agreement. The company has the right to transfer an employee to work other than his usual job, but it must pay him at his regular hourly rate of wages.

Guaranteed employment plans, while possibly suitable in a few specific cases as above, would not be practicable for industry in general. If a company's employment is already stable, so that its employees have regular employment anyway, the guarantee of employment is merely a gesture, giving the worker no more security than he had in the first place. If employment is not steady, and no reserves are built up, then, unless a margin of ineligible employees is maintained, any considerable fluctuation in normal employment would soon bankrupt the company, as, besides full wages, all the materials and machinery for an unwanted surplus of products must be furnished. On the other hand, if a reserve is set up, out of which full or partial wages are paid when employment cannot be provided, then the plan is not really 'guaranteed employment,' but actually the usual 'unemployment reserve' plan.

GENERAL ELECTRIC COMPANY

Recently the total number of employees covered by individual company plans was more than doubled when the General Electric Company adopted a plan. This company announced its unemployment insurance plan on June 16, 1930, to take effect in any of their plants where sixty per cent of the employees approved of it. This is the first private company plan to which employees contribute, and it is also the largest company plan in existence. The participation of the employee is voluntary. Approximately 35,000 employees have been contributing to the plan and, up to December 1, 1930, they had paid in $350,000. Contributions are one per cent of actual weekly or monthly earnings and must be paid as long as wages do not fall below fifty per cent of average full-time earnings. When enough contributing employees are temporarily laid off, or forced to go on part-time work so that payments from the fund amount to two per cent or more of the average aggregate earnings of contributing employees, the usual procedure is stopped, and all employees, whether eligible for benefits or not, earning fifty per cent or more of their average full-time wages, must contribute one per cent of their earnings. This rule includes even the highest officers of the company. The company contributes an amount equal to the employees' contributions. It has created a trust for the money and has guaranteed an annual interest rate of five per cent. Unemployment is to be defined by the administrators of the plan. No payments will be made for the first two weeks of unemployment. After that, the employee is to receive approximately fifty per cent of his average earnings, but in no case is the benefit to go above twenty dollars per week. Such payment shall continue as long as the administrators approve, but not longer than ten weeks in twelve consecutive months.

The original plan required that contributions were to be made for six months before benefits would be paid. On November 25, 1930, the company announced that, because of the business depression, a substantial number of contributing employees had been laid off. Under the rules, these workers were not entitled to assistance. Nevertheless, it was decided to start payments at once, but to limit these to a maximum of fifteen dollars per week. Every employee earning fifty per cent or more of his full-time rate began contributing one per cent of his earnings on December 1, 1930.

Besides this plan of actual payments for loss of work, the General Electric Company has a very definite and elaborate stabilization policy which includes overtime at rush periods; shortening the hours in dull periods; manufacturing for stock in those departments in which it is

possible; increasing the force as slowly as possible; transferring workers to especially busy departments; and,
when it becomes necessary to dismiss workers, dropping
new employees, single persons with no dependents, and
those who are most easily spared, first — always with at
least one week's notice. The normal working week is
five and one half days, but at the present time practically
all the factories are on a five-day schedule, with many
departments working much less.

ROCHESTER UNEMPLOYMENT BENEFIT PLAN

Another way of handling the problem by private initiative is to have a group of companies in one locality
band together in an attempt to stabilize employment
and indemnify workers when such employment cannot
be offered. The most recent illustration of this type is
the plan known as the Rochester Unemployment Benefit
Plan.

An important part of the Rochester plan is the coöperation of both business and civic interests. Rochester was
selected by New York State as the location for a demonstration central employment bureau. Legislation has
been passed permitting the State Department of Labor to
accept funds from private sources for conducting such a
demonstration. Several foundations in New York City,
working through the Industrial Relations Counselors,
Inc., have provided a fund, supplemented by a subscrip-
tion among the larger concerns in Rochester, the total
sum being about seventy-five thousand dollars a year,
which will be used to finance the demonstration. This
bureau was organized in the spring of this year, and a
high-grade man has been obtained to manage it. In order
to be eligible for payments under the unemployment
benefit plan, an unemployed worker must register at this
public exchange. There is also a permanent committee
in Rochester, studying the unemployment problem. This

committee has a secretary who can devote his full time
to the work of the organization. In this way coördination and efficiency are achieved, and public interest is
maintained.

The unemployment benefit plan itself was adopted
in February, 1931, by fourteen manufacturing establishments in Rochester, New York, which employ a total of
twenty-six thousand persons, approximately one third
of the industrial employees of that city. Since that time
four additional employers have signified their intention
of joining in the movement to protect their employees
by an out-of-work benefit system. It is likely that additional employers will join the movement and it is hoped
by the interested parties that ultimately practically all
employers in Rochester will set up machinery such as is
provided under the plan to protect workers in times of
unemployment.

As worked out, the terms of the plan allow considerable
latitude to individual employers, as to the amount to be
set aside, method of administration, etc., the aim in having a city-wide plan being to give to employers subscrib-
ing to it a working basis upon which they may build systems suited to the peculiar conditions of their respective
establishments and to the degree of stabilization they
have achieved. Methods of stabilization have been
practiced for some time. The companies vary in size
from one of forty-five employees to the Eastman Kodak
Company which has thirteen thousand employees in
Rochester. The companies originally represented are:
Eastman Kodak Company, Bausch & Lomb Optical
Company, Stromberg Carlson Telephone Manufacturing
Company, Rochester Telephone Corporation, the Glea-
son Works, Taylor Instrument Company, Consolidated
Machine Tool Corporation, the Todd Company, the
Pfaudler Company, Vogt Manufacturing Company,
Yawman and Erbe Manufacturing Company, Sargent

and Greenleaf (Inc.), Davenport Machine Tool Company, and Cochrane Bly Company.

Of the companies coming under the plan, one is a public utility and the others are manufacturing concerns, their principal product being photographic goods, optical goods and instruments, telephones, radios, thermometers and other recording instruments, machinery, check protectors and signers, gear-cutting machines, auto trimmings, office furniture and filing systems, and locks.

Besides effective methods of stabilization, this plan includes unemployment benefits along the broad lines of the General Electric plan, financed entirely by the employers in normal times, with provision for an emergency assessment of one per cent on all employees and officials, to be matched by the companies in times of unemployment emergencies. The companies are normally to contribute to a reserve fund annually up to two per cent of their payrolls, the exact percentage to be estimated by each employer so as to cover his expected claims. For example, the Eastman Kodak Company examined its employment records for the past thirty years to determine the amount of annual contributions to be made by the company.

FOND DU LAC, WISCONSIN, PLAN

A somewhat older plan, but on a smaller scale, is that of the group of five companies in Fond du Lac, Wisconsin. These five companies (the Demountable Typewriter Company, Inc., the Sanitary Refrigerator Company, the Northern Casket Company, the Standard Refrigerator Company, and the American Lock and Hinge Company) entered into a joint agreement which became effective on September 1, 1930. Each company signing this contract undertakes to hire workers laid off by any of the other parties to the arrangement, whenever this is possible. If no work is available in any of these companies, the employee laid off is to be paid sixty-five per cent of his average wage for not more than one hundred working days by his own employer. Only employees with two years' service are covered by the plan. There is a fifteen-day waiting period before benefits start. Each company pays its own claims from a fund raised as it sees fit. In cases of dispute, the State Industrial Commission is to act as referee. The agreement is to run for five years, but a company can withdraw at the end of any year if the experiment is not working satisfactorily. This is the first attempt that has been made to shift employees from one company to another.

COMPARISON OF COMPULSORY STATE PLANS WITH PRIVATE PLANS

The above descriptions of the actual workings of European government-controlled unemployment insurance plans and private plans of America show that the interest and coöperation engendered by individual operation can largely overcome the objections, from an insurance point of view, to state plans. One great difference is in the coverage. The private plans cover only workers who are actually gainfully employed, with reasonable chances of continuing in employment; while compulsory government plans, in their endeavor to insure the entire industrial population (subject to certain exceptions), find it practically impossible to exclude workers who are not normally actually employed. This results from the attempt to protect many persons against the loss of a continuity of employment that they never had, which was shown above to be contrary to the principles of true insurance. Private plans pay benefits only for a limited period, or as long as funds are available, and when this limit is reached the unemployed must seek elsewhere for relief. Even compulsory plans, however, pay insurance benefits for only a small part of the country's unemployment. Out of approximately five million workers registered as unemployed at the employment exchanges in Germany, only about half are receiving regular insurance benefits, the remainder receiving relief through 'crisis benefits' welfare work, or not at all. So that even with an unemployment insurance system, a large part of the cost must be met by straight poor relief. Both England and Germany are temporarily trying to meet the situation by providing 'transitional' or 'crisis' benefits, and still enormous expenditures are found necessary as pure additional poor relief.

Experience also indicates that a compulsory plan has reduced the incentive of many employers to stabilize employment in their enterprises, thus actually increasing the evil for which a remedy is sought. This is primarilv due to the fact that improvement of employment conditions in an employer's own establishment does not bring a decrease in his insurance charge, but rather increases it, as he must pay a larger number of contributions. On the other hand, in a privately operated plan, where an employer bears a large portion of the burden of the unemployment in *his own plant*, there is a direct financial incentive to keep employment as steady as possible, and unemployment at a minimum. This is in direct contrast to the effect of compulsory governmental plans, which often tend to stabilize *un*employment, and keep some workers content to rest on their benefits rather than work for their wages. Even the employers may be affected in this way, as it has been found that several employers consciously arrange their lay-offs, in coöperation with their employees, so as to entitle the employees to the largest unemployment benefit possible.

One of the most important precepts to be gleaned from experience is that the State that feels it can rest on its oars after adopting an insurance system will be rudely shocked, and the social welfare workers who think that all their difficult cases will be taken care of by the insurance scheme are doomed to disappointment.

Considering the three requirements of an insurable risk already discussed, it appears that the risk of unemployment is at best only very roughly predictable, under either private or state plans, but as for being determinable and beyond the control of the individuals insured, the private plans have been far more successful. An important requirement of any plan is the necessity for keeping the benefits paid down to a figure considerably under the normal wage, so as to reduce to a minimum any tendency towards malingering.

CONCLUSION

The conclusion to be drawn from the foregoing comparison, then, is that unemployment is not, from an insurance point of view, a practical field for government compulsory insurance. When developed by private initiative, with proper foresight and safeguards, it might be found practicable, after careful and cautious experimentation, to provide limited benefits for a reasonable period in the event of cyclical and seasonal unemployment. There is considerable question as to insurability of technological unemployment, and all cases where a man has really permanently left the industry. These cases must be differently handled, for example, by payment of a dismissal wage. In any type of plan, an efficient system of employment exchanges, with which both employers and employees willingly coöperate, extensive vocational guidance, provisions for the mobility and transportation of labor, and, above all, a spirit of coöperation and enthusiasm for the plan on the part of all parties concerned, are essential to any lasting success.

The fundamental conclusion that we draw from our study is that we would not desire to see so-called 'unemployment insurance' schemes based upon the English

or the German models adopted in the United States. But
we do not favor a policy of mere negation. The existing
system of dependence primarily upon charity we regard
as unsatisfactory. Some methods involving much more
extensive coverage must be sought. In the last ten years
practically the primary approach to the problem by industry has been in preventive attempts through stabilization and similar methods, presumably in the expectation
that their success would make benefit plans unnecessary.
Accordingly, there has been only a very limited development during that period of unemployment reserve plans.
As a matter of fact only a very small percentage of our
normally employed workers have been furnished protection through the operation of definitely organized
unemployment reserve plans. We believe that an active
interest in such plans exists among employers as never
before. We believe that many more will experiment by
working out plans suited to the situation of the particular
industry. This tendency should be encouraged and
actively pushed by every possible means, for it may be
that out of such experimentation, sound plans of wider
application will emerge.

But we should not be content to rely solely upon the
unstimulated evolution of voluntary plans. To us, therefore, both the methods used abroad and in this country
seem to be deficient. At the moment we have no better
substitute to suggest.

Whatever improved methods may ultimately be developed, should, we feel, be of such a character as to
involve four fundamental features, as follows:

1. Coverage eventually of at least a majority of our wage-
   earners.
2. Liability definitely limited to the reserves accumulated.
3. Pressure on individual businesses and industries in the
   direction of stabilization of employment.
4. The maximum practicable administration by elements in

industry and the minimum possible share in administration by political agencies.

We believe that the energies of American business should be earnestly and intensively devoted to the development of better methods along such lines. We do not think American business should content itself with a merely negative attitude which was satisfied to consider only the defects of European systems.

SUGGESTIONS FOR PRESENT ACTION

With regard to present action on the part of state or federal governments in this country, there is much constructive work that only these governments can accomplish. Of course there is no way by which any government, or any other agency, can give protection or assistance through insurance of any nature to those people now actually unemployed. That is basic in the nature of insurance — for insurance is not appropriate to cover a loss after that loss has occurred. If this were possible there would be an astonishing number of applications for fire insurance on burnt homes. Relief to those at present unemployed can only be given as pure relief, and legislation which proposes to provide relief for the unemployed through state aid should be clearly and distinctly classified as relief legislation. In no way, directly, should it be possible to construe such legislation as unemployment insurance. Any such attempt would only hinder the progress of any sound plan that might subsequently be proposed. Also, at least until the experimental stage is passed, any compulsory insurance scheme is inadvisable, because such plans are difficult to amend properly when experience shows that some change is necessary. They are too liable to amendment for the purpose of relieving the unemployed, rather than safeguarding the insurance principles. In England especially, serious considerations towards placing their unemployment insurance on a more sound basis have come about only when financial disaster has threatened the nation. Also it must not be supposed that any plans for future insurance benefits will completely eliminate the present need for poor relief, as that method is always necessary in cases where the loss is not covered by the insurance plan.

However, there is much the State can do to improve the situation. Education and information and guidance in these fields are needed. The State can be of great assistance in coöperating with employers in their attempts to find solutions, and in preventing the adoption of plans which, obviously, can result only in failure. The State might encourage the formation of an organization of employers, whose main purpose and function would be to encourage the adoption of such plans, and to be well acquainted with the practical problems involved, so that it may act as a clearing-house for information, and give competent advice when legislation is proposed. Such an organization should be either an entirely new group, or should be affiliated with some existing nation-wide organization, but with sufficient freedom in the affiliation to allow it to function as a full-time unit without other interests to distract it.

This organization should encourage in every way further experiments by private concerns. Apparently there is a considerable latent willingness on the part of employers to make such experiments. They lack only the necessary information or a little encouragement. Such an agency could do much to influence employers to set up unemployment benefit schemes of their own volition. An important function of this agency would be to encourage and coöperate with communities in experiments such as that initiated at Rochester. Such an agency would emphasize the advantages of this type of plan to the companies, the employees, and to the community in general. With the additional incentive provided by the adoption of an unemployment benefit plan, employers will undoubtedly strive to find additional means to reduce fluctuation in employment. Greater effort will be made to stagger production, to seek new marketing methods, and to find new products which might be added so that fluctuation in production could be reduced. Foremen and superintendents will know the cost which lay-offs in their department cause, and it will bring home to them the advantages of stabilizing. It is also felt that such a plan will result in reduced turnover, and that there will be better morale among the employees.

To the employee such a plan brings greater security and would help tide him over a period of unemployment. At the same time because of the limited benefits it should not result in less incentive on his part to save. The community in general will benefit because the money which will be paid out for benefits during the period of unemployment will enter into circulation and maintain purchasing power to a certain degree. It will also reduce the expenditures of the charitable organizations and the payment of doles by the municipalities. The general adoption of company unemployment benefit plans would be an important factor in minimizing the effects of depressions.

An adequate measure of government financial assistance for the establishment and maintenance of satisfactory employment exchanges might be a desirable feature. This plan, to be successful, must also include means of encouraging employers and employees voluntarily to avail themselves of the services of these exchanges. Without such voluntary enthusiasm, a system of public employment exchanges is almost certainly foredoomed to failure.

Experience has clearly shown that the best time, as far as the possibility of successful results are concerned, for laying plans for any movement toward employment stabilization or unemployment relief is during times of depression, such as the present, when everyone is fully alive to the hardships which result from unemployment. From the distress of the moment may arise a movement ending ultimately in greatly improved conditions, furnishing effective weapons for combating any future recurrences of the present industrial depression. Delay means only the cooling-off of ardor and the dulling of memories that would induce people to accept, possibly, a small present sacrifice in order to assure greater future stability. However, in the enthusiasm of the moment practical common sense should not suffer at the hands of haste. No benefits can be paid until a sufficient reserve has been accumulated, and no laws should be enacted except those which will insure, as far as possible, that these private undertakings are being administered on a basis consistent with sound principles. The function of the State should be to point the way rather than to undertake itself, the actual administration of unemployment reserve plans.

And above all, it must not be forgotten that in times of depression it has always proved necessary to follow up and supplement the regular insurance benefits with poor relief, in one form or another. Any action that is taken in regard to the relief of distress due to unemployment, whether it be insurance or relief, should not be allowed to cloud the real issue of prevention. Industry and State must maintain their efforts to reduce unemployment to as small a figure as is at all possible, thus pushing the problem of mitigating its effects more and more into the field of the unnecessary.

The subcommittee submits this report, conceiving its function to be that of investigating and reporting on the question of insurance. It has not undertaken to express

its opinion or to make concrete suggestions as to alternatives for insurance, as such, assuming it to be the intention of the Committee itself to canvass plans for relieving
the immediate emergency, and, if in agreement with the
subcommittee as to the impracticability of insurance,
to indicate what alternative or alternatives might be
usefully adopted against the possibility of a future
emergency.

CHAPTER VI

THE AMERICAN FEDERATION OF LABOR LOOKS FORWARD TO PLANNING

IN OCTOBER, 1931, the executive council of the American Federation of Labor laid before the annual convention of that association at Vancouver a report on the present economic situation which contained, among other things, the following passages dealing with methods designed to prevent or at least mitigate the evils of industrial depressions:

UNEMPLOYMENT PREVENTION BY COÖRDINATING ECONOMIC DEVELOPMENT

National Planning. Business depression is a very costly experience. No economic group escapes heavy losses. The social wastes to the nation and the economic wastes to industry amount to enormous totals of tangible and intangible values. It is quite obvious the technical ability to produce has far outstripped our understanding of our economic structure. Our distribution of the returns from production are not balanced. Increased profits have been monopolized by the few so that incomes of the masses — wage-earners — have not increased sufficiently to provide buyers proportionate to the capacity of industry to produce. Instead of shortening the work-day as output per worker increased, industries have taken away jobs of some workers and compelled the rest to work the standard which was adjusted to an older technical equipment.

It is obvious that business has been following the wrong principles. Each group, each industry, each company, has been advancing its interest against the other, often at the expense of the others. To control our business machine so that it will function regularly, we must learn how different parts work together so that we shall have a balance of forces and a balance in progress. Team-work is what we need and leadership for team-work. Team-work comes from organized intelligence and coördinated activity.

When industries were organized on a more limited scale with a smaller output, their dependence on wage-earner buying was not so obvious. Mass production, however, must be accompanied by mass buying. The principles of balance in industry are the key to sustained progress. Single companies or even industries cannot work out the principles of balance. Fact-finding and plans must be national in scope. While we have some vague information on the forces involved in balancing consumption, production, and distribution, we have not the facts necessary for control.

Balance is not a result that can be maintained by arbitrary decision; it comes through working with laws in the light of knowledge of the facts. The first step toward getting balance in our economic machine, is a coördinating group through which information of all elements and groups in production shall bring together the necessary information to reveal the interplay between economic forces and thus the facts that should guide all groups in their individual planning as well as in the development of policies for concerted action. To give all groups an understanding of how the national mechanism works so that each may understand how it fits into the whole operation is the first step in developing team-work. Nothing more definite should be imposed upon any national economic council that might be created by our Federal Government. We do not yet know enough to plan the agencies or chart the functions of economic control. We do, however, know that national economic conferences will disclose the way. We have, therefore, repeatedly urged upon the President of the United States that he call a national economic conference to find a way forward. Such a conference would be a step toward planning on a national scale. We have everywhere throughout industry very successful attempts at planning by industrial undertakings, by industries, by unions, by communities, by states, and by geographic sections. But this is not adequate — there must be comprehensive planning by all the groups that affect each other. No one industry can prevent business depression — nor even all industries, unless they work together.

The interchange of information through reports, documents and conferences is basic in developing balance.

Public Accounting. The interrelation between the interests of all groups and industries and the necessity for coördinated efforts to prevent excessive boom periods and business recessions, make very plain that the facts of all business enterprises should be public property. The idea that private ownership entitles the owners to secrecy in methods and decisions is out of keeping with the fact that these factors directly affect results for other groups. Private ownership may entitle owners to make decisions, but full reporting of all the facts should make the information available to all concerned.

The conduct of industry is a matter of so much consequence to all employed in the industry, to investors, to the communities, to the maintenance of markets, to our national economic balance, that we must work toward full and open records by prescribed forms of cost and production accounting. Any employer or groups of investors who have the privilege of operating gainful industry in any community ought to be required to make regular and prescribed reports. Public accounting according to prescribed methods is an obligation which accompanies the privileges to operate a business undertaking which affects the community as well as those who supply the credit and those employed by the undertaking. In a very definite way, interrelation of economic activities is increasing the degree of public interest in all business undertakings. This means that there should be public accounting on the facts of business which should be filed with the Federal Government and compiled there. The records should be open to responsible organizations.

Federal Labor Board. In addition to collecting industrial information, the Federal Government should provide for the coördination of data bearing on wage-earner progress. There should be such basic data as man-hours, length of work-week, productivity, employment opportunities, unemployment, wage-earner incomes, technological displacement, etc. There should be indexes that would disclose mounting unemployment, trends in distribution of income, inadequate buying power as balanced against production, so that the need for shorter work-hours and higher wage-rates might be realized in advance of the cumulation of forces making for business depression. Such a federal labor bureau would warn labor and business of unbalance due to inadequate returns to wage-earners so that something could be done to prevent disaster for such causes. It need have only the authority to make facts public in order to render service and have effective influence. It should also study the problems of labor and suggest constructive policies. It should be representative in character and provided with a technical staff.

Nothing but approval and support is given merchants, industrialists, and farmers who organize to manage their businesses efficiently and to increase their incomes. Such groups are given the benefit of doubt when practices are under question.

On its record of social and industrial service, labor asks the same privilege to organize to control their interests and to increase their incomes. Such a federal labor board would give labor federal assistance and service comparable to what is given farmers and industry. We ask for equality of opportunity. If we are to have balanced progress, labor must be in a position to keep pace.

Organization of Workers in Trade Unions. Such a bureau as proposed above could be really constructive when supplemented by effective organizations of workers to advance their interests in proportion to the progress of industry and society.

To prevent progress from being badly balanced by too much income going into capital goods and too little into the pockets of wage-earners; to make sure that work-hours are decreased in proportion to productivity increases instead of letting machines produce unemployment; to make sure that production experience is put to service in eliminating wastes; to make sure there is available producing workers competent, resourceful, and skilled, are union functions.

Only a union has the independence, the power, and the authority to assume responsibility for keeping wage-earners' progress abreast social and economic progress.

Employers who have been fighting trade unions, who have refused their employees the right to organize, who have refused to meet effective representatives of their workers in order to negotiate terms and conditions of work, who have opposed the shorter work-day, and the five-day week, who have resisted wage increase, have stood squarely against the road to progress and have opposed their own best interests.

The union is an instrumentality of progress. It manages the business interests of wage-earners so that they can make progress. Sustained progress does not come from trusting to chance; it comes from thought, planning, and organization to put plans into effect.

Organization of workers in unions under their own control is essential to planning on a broader basis and to planning for related groups where interests are interdependent. In fact, unless labor participates in the councils, national planning and balanced progress are impossible. Unorganized, labor cannot participate in a representative group.

Organization of workers in trade unions is a highly commendable and essential movement which should be accepted as public policy.

Employment Service. Unless the work of directing the unemployed to employment opportunities is effectively organized, there will be delays in connecting workers with jobs at hand. When a job means such essential and constructive relief, every effort should be made to conserve its utilization.

Every industrial community ought to have a public employment agency so efficient as to command the respect of employers and employees. This office should have its contacts with industries and all employing groups and have at hand that specialized information of job requirements necessary to render satisfactory service.

In addition to conserving all available jobs, the local employment service can extend its usefulness by helping to make the public conscious of responsibility to provide all work possible, such as repairs, cleaning, building, service positions. The director of an employment service has a creative as well as an administrative responsibility.

Effective organization of the labor market and every possible vigilance to increase the number of jobs available is essential economically in order to provide the consumer buying power upon which production depends. Those industrialists who are efficient managers have widened the scope of their planning to include the full cycle of forces that affect their production. Every industrialist must buy, sell, and plan production over a period of years. He must understand and work with the principle of in-

dustrial balance. The employment service is a fundamental tool in maintaining consumer buying which is the
ultimate balance for all production.

Vocational Counsel and Retraining. If assistance in
knowing the jobs available is supplemented by help in
adapting work skill and experience to various industries,
an element in flexibility is introduced that will help in
meeting the problem of technological unemployment.

The unprecedented rate of technical change in the past
decade has made it plain that vocational education
should provide opportunities for adults. Services for
adults will be most practical when coördinated with the
work of the employment service. The employment service accumulates information on the kinds of work for
which wage-earners will be hired and the relative number
of employees needed. The vocational counsellor should
know what industries make use of similar skills so that
courses of retraining can be worked out.

Our educational agencies should consider this problem
of vocational education for adults and make provisions to
meet it. Experience in this field will in turn be recipro-
cally helpful in keeping vocational education for boys and
girls practical and adapted to industrial and worker
needs.

*Balance Worktime and Wages Against Increase in Pro-
ductivity.* Economic equilibrium depends on keeping a
balanced relationship between economic forces. For instance, consuming power must keep pace with producing
power, income from trade and industry must be so distributed that it will increase the capacity to buy in proportion as it increases the capacity to produce. When
these factors are thrown out of balance, trade and industry can no longer function normally, and we are plunged
into business depression.

It is the task of trade unions to see that the worker's
side of the balance is kept up, and that workers advance

proportionately with other groups. Wage-earners and small salaried workers with their families, form eighty-three per cent of the nation's population and receive fifty-four per cent of the national income. Almost the entire amount of this income is spent to buy industry's products and services or to pay rent, for there is little margin for savings. In recent years workers have received about $32,000,000,000 a year. The immensity of this sum and its huge influence as an economic force make it essential that workers' income advance proportionately with industry's producing power. Industry depends on workers' buying; it is a severe handicap when workers' incomes do not keep pace. The graph below shows thirty years' development in three essential economic forces:

1. *Productivity.* The solid line shows producing power per hour for the average worker in manufacturing industry or 'productivity.' There have been striking increases in productivity in other industries, as mining, transportation, agriculture, but manufacturing is taken to show the trend, since more complete figures exist. Productivity in manufacturing increased twenty-six per cent from 1899 to 1919; fifty-four per cent from 1919 to 1929. The rapid rise of the line after 1919 shows the speed of these advances in the least decade. The increase in industry's producing power has been enormous.

2. *Real Wages.* The line for real wages shows the advance in wage-rates per hour in all industry in terms of the goods they will buy. Real wage-rates advanced 4.2 per cent from 1899 to 1919, compared to the twenty-six per cent advance in productivity, and thirty-six per cent from 1919 to 1929, compared to the fifty-four per cent advance in productivity. It is clear from the graph that the line for real wages advances much more slowly than the line for productivity.

3. *Leisure.* The line for leisure represents the increase in workers' leisure in all industry through the shortening

of work-hours. It rises very gradually. The gain in leisure from 1899 to 1919 was seven hours a week (from a
fifty-eight hour week average in 1899 to a fifty-one hour
week in 1919), the gains were most rapid from 1915 to
1919. But since 1919, gains in leisure have been practically at a standstill, until the five-day week drive started
in 1926.

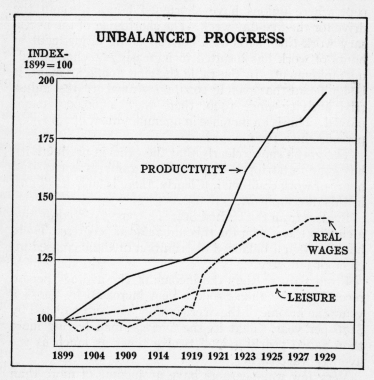

Because of the increase in productivity in manufacturing industry, work which took the average man a fifty-
nine-hour week in 1899 could be done in forty-seven
hours in 1919, but the work-week in manufacturing was
actually shortened only from fifty-nine to fifty-two

hours. In 1929, work which took the average man a fifty-two-hour week in 1919 could be done in thirty-four hours, but the work-week in manufacturing was actually shortened only to fifty hours. That is, an eighteen-hour decrease in necessary work-time was compensated by only a two-hour decrease in actual work-hours. This development in manufacturing is typical of other industries except where unions have shortened hours through the drive for the five-day week. The shortening of the necessary work-time without a corresponding adjustment in hours of work has resulted in increasing 'technological' unemployment. In the table showing unemployment, it is significant that even in 1929, the year of greatest industrial activity since 1920, there were 2,400,000 unemployed. This is an increase in unemployment of 1,000,000 persons since 1920.

The graph shows clearly that the gains in productivity have far outstripped the workers' gains in wages and hours of work combined. Clearly, there is lack of balance in this development.

Figures from the United States income tax records give a clue to the reason for this unbalanced progress. There has not been a balanced distribution of the increased income of industry.

From 1919 to 1927 the income of the average person receiving more than $5000 a year increased by $2151 a year; the income of the average wage-earner increased by $176 per year. That is, the average man having more than $5000 yearly gained twelve times as much as the average wage-earner.

Very few wage-earners have an income of more than $5000 a year. We may take this group, then, as representing income receivers outside the wage-earner and the small salaried group.

In 1927, the proportion of wage-earners to those with higher incomes was approximately as thirty to one. The federal income tax statements report a little over 900,000 returns which show an income of $5000 a year or more; their average income was $15,388. There were over 27,000,000 wage-earners whose average income was $1205. Would it not be possible to balance the gain of this lower income group and at the same time increase the total? In the eight years from 1919 to 1927, total wages paid in the United States increased by $9,855,000,000 a year, while total income paid to those with more than $5000 increased by $5,354,000,000 a year.

This unequal distribution of the nation's income throws the industrial mechanism out of balance. A large proportion of the income of the rich is reinvested and goes to increase the capacity of industry to produce. When the distribution of wealth is unbalanced, industry's producing capacity soon outstrips the buying power of the public. In June, 1929, at the very peak of our recent industrial boom, when industry reached the highest production in its history, our mills and factories were so much overbuilt that even then they were nowhere near producing up to capacity. The rates of operation in a number of different industries for which we have figures are given below. If figures for other products were available they would show that this same condition ran throughout industry: Cotton finishing, sixty per cent of capacity; silk spinning, sixty-three per cent; steel castings, eighty per cent; steel barrels, sixty-two per cent; oil refining, eighty-three per cent; paper box board, seventy-seven per cent; Portland cement, eighty-one per cent; glassware for lights, forty-six per cent; glass containers, eighty-two per cent.

There was another period when the incomes of the rich increased enormously. This was in the years of high war and after war profits. After both these periods of unbalanced distribution, the nation was plunged into serious business depression.

A central fact-finding agency is needed which will measure progress, and balance gains in producing power against gains in buying power, and the shortening of necessary work-time against actual shortening of the work-week. Science is to help human beings gain control of their environment with increasing ease and sureness. Unless technical progress means greater control through leisure for workers, there is a lack of balance in human factors.

Job Security. Trade unions have made some headway in securing recognition of the fact that wage-earners are partners in production. Production is a joint undertaking. One group supplies capital; another credit; another group does the buying; another plans production; another does the fabrication or work necessary to give plans tangible form; another sells the product. All functions are necessary and interrelated. All make either tangible or intangible investments in the production undertaking and are dependent upon its success for their incomes.

Wage-earners invest their special skills, their creative capacity, their judgment based on work experience, their ability to use materials, tools, and time economically; they organize their lives around their specific jobs. They practically invest their lives and their capacities in their work. They have a very real claim to ownership of their jobs.

In view of these investments, workers have a right to returns in the way of job security. Rules covering employment, jointly negotiated, should specify the period of time for which workers are employed. Workers who prove their capacity and demonstrate their ability should constitute a staff of permanent employees, secure in employment under prescribed conditions.

Security of job means assurance of income which makes it possible for the wage-earner and his family to plan their living over a definite period of time, and budget expenditures to their best advantage.

Wage-earners who are daily or weekly in fear of loss of job cannot plan their living or use their minds most effectively. Fear is not the force that stimulates greatest productivity. Industry, through the coöperation of management and labor, could develop methods appealing to incentives more fundamental for production purposes.

HIGH WAGE PHILOSOPHY

In the 1925 convention the Federation first pointed out the importance of increasing workers' buying power to create a market for industry's growing product. This high wage principle has gradually gained following. Industrial leaders could not fail to see the economic power of workers' buying and its importance as a force for progress.

The test has come in this depression. To liquidate wages is to destroy the home market, cut down the demand for American products and services, and consequently reduce production more drastically than is necessary to liquidate the stocks on hand. Impaired worker buying power deepens and prolongs depression. Considerable reduction of buying power has resulted from unemployment and part-time work, but realization of the pernicious effect of wage reductions has prevented a widespread liquidation of wages such as we had in the depression of 1921. Growing adherence to the high wage principle over the last few years, strengthened by the President's stand against wage cuts, has brought effective support from the leading industrialists of the country. Reports from the Bureau of Labor Statistics, although they cover only a small sample of American firms, enable us to make a comparison between the policy of 1921 and that of 1930. In the full year of 1921, there were ninety-two wage cuts per one hundred firms reporting to the Bureau, while in 1930 (full year) there were only seven cuts per one hundred firms reporting. Although wage cuts have increased in 1931, there has still been no widespread tendency toward a 'liquidation of wages' such as we experienced in 1921. In the first seven months of 1931, the number of cuts reported per one hundred firms was twelve, compared to fifty-four in 1921. This means that once business starts upward, recovery will be more rapid and business will be able to reach higher levels in a shorter space of time. For unemployment and part-time work arising from depression make only temporary reductions of workers' buying power which are quickly remedied as business improves; while reductions of wage-rates lower workers' living standards and reduce their buying for a period of years. It may be eight or nine years before wage-rates recover after a liquidation such as that of 1921, and progress in industrial production is hampered by this long-time reduction of buying power.

BANKERS AND WAGES

Through their control over credit, banks have control over industrial policies. Reports have been frequent and well confirmed that conditions of credit from banks have included specifically wage reductions. As a part of their general efforts toward contraction and liquidation, a number of outstanding bankers have urged wage reductions paralleling price declines.

The following statements were made by prominent bankers:

It is not true that high wages make prosperity. Instead, prosperity makes high wages. When wages are kept higher than the market situation justifies, employment and the buying power of labor fall off. American business has proved its goodwill in dealing with labor in this point in the past year, and in many industries may reasonably ask labor to accept a moderate reduction of wages designed to reduce costs and to increase both employment and the buying power of labor. Our restricted immigration, coupled with our relative abundance of capital and natural resources, is sufficient safeguard for American wages.

.   .   .   .

If there is one point upon which we all agree it is that the American standard of living must be maintained. However, we must not confuse the standard of living with the cost of living, and we must not confuse an arbitrary fixed wage in dollars and cents with a real wage in its purchasing power.

Employers must be as quick to recognize the real wage in a rising market as labor must be to recognize the real wage in a falling market, if there is to be any stability in prosperity and employment hereafter. Business cannot prosper if costs eliminate profit; and labor cannot work as fully as it should if capital is denied a proper return.

.   .   .   .

Anyone who gives the matter the slightest serious thought knows that wage levels are controlled by impersonal economic principles.... Wages are paid out of the earned incomes of industry. If general economic conditions so affect such incomes that internal economics are necessary, certainly no one is personally to blame for that.

I am not saying that wage reductions should be made, but if any industry discovers that conditions call for an adjustment in costs of operations, including wages, it would be a very questionable act of stewardship in respect to the responsibilities resting upon its management, if it attempted to keep wages or other costs at an arbitrary level at the expense of the capital funds of the business.

.   .   .   .

It may be pointed out that the wages of money have already been markedly reduced, as can be seen by a comparison of interest rates on bank loans and investments received today as compared with a year and a half ago.

Bankers have argued that the decline in the costs of living meant that a wage cut would not lower standards of living. Their understanding of the situation was based upon a fundamental hypothesis that labor should be kept within certain definite limits that would keep it always dependent — a modern version of the master and servant philosophy that has curbed labor's efforts and ambitions for progress.

Labor believes that it has a right to something more than its present share in returns on the output of industries — that it is a partner in production and should have status accordingly.

Labor also points to the fact that wages constitute a very large portion of the buying power upon which retail sales depend to form a market for our products.

Wages are not just the price of labor in the market governed by the law of supply and demand. They are advance credit paid in advance of the product which the worker helped to create. Higher wages are necessary to maintain an economic machine geared to high production.

Labor further points out that wage-rates and labor costs are not the same thing and that high wage-rates usually resulted in low labor costs per unit production.

Furthermore, the maintenance of wage-rates is a dynamic factor in sustaining our economic machine and in supporting confidence. The sturdy common-sense of American wage-earners has been one of the most constructive stabilizing forces in this business depression. To cut his already inadequate wages in addition to reducing him to part-time work would be a most sorry expression of appreciation.

We look to American bankers for assistance in getting money out of the banks into circulation and to supply business undertakings with the necessary credit. We believe that bankers could perform their functions more wisely if they had regular and intimate contacts with production technicians and representatives of wage-earners.

Bankers like every other group must take into account their need to promote the welfare of the workers as well as all other economic groups. We look to bankers to help level up the incomes of wage-earners and all the under-privileged.

We look to the bankers to be concerned to increase the amount of money put to buying uses and no group spends its income more freely than wage-earners.

Chapter VII

A DEMAND FOR STATE ACTION ON
A SECURITY WAGE [1]

By John T. Flynn

I propose, as a source of income for working-people out of employment, that we adopt the principle of the security wage.

By the security wage I mean a small margin of current earnings not paid to the workers, but reserved for periods of idleness. It is that part of the worker's whole wage which he now earns but does not get. If he did get it, he could not administer it for the purposes of security, chiefly because it would be absorbed rapidly and inevitably into his current expenditures to cover the deficits in the so-called living wage.

This security wage would be something apart from the living wage. The latter is the sum which is now paid to the worker, though in most instances it is not yet actually a living wage. The security wage would be a sum — a certain proportion of the actually paid wage — which would be credited to the worker, but would not be given to him. It would be turned over instead to a government created and controlled corporation which would administer the wage in his interest and in the interest of society. It would provide him with a limited income in times of unemployment and with a reasonable annuity in old age. It is, of course, in essence a form of unemployment and old-age insurance, but it is distinguished from most other proposals by certain differences of basic principle which I have tried to characterize by calling it the security

[1] *The Forum*, October, 1931.

wage. I shall try to set out here the underlying principles of the proposals.

There is no use talking about unemployment relief in this depression. The handling of that is in the hands of time and charity. We are dealing with it by the method we so much denounce, that is, by the dole, for which credit must be given to those who are so much opposed to doles. In Detroit forty-five thousand families get ten dollars a week from funds supplied by taxpayers. That is a dole. Help is being given to as many more from funds raised by the Mayor's Committee from private sources. That is a dole, though it goes by another name. The same thing has been done in one way or another everywhere. Nothing else will be done during this depression until natural laws, unassisted by our business leaders, mend the matter. But it is quite time we set about doing something about employment, not in the next depression, but in the next prosperity. For do not forget that when the boom comes back to us, we will still have from 1,500,000 to 2,000,000 people unemployed.

In this immense population of ours we have always a large army of unemployed people. In the merriest boom periods there are still dislocations here and there — bad spots on the brilliant field of prosperity. The motor industry, the building industry, the electrical industry soar aloft over the gleaming peaks of the business cycle; but others, perhaps the textile industry, the soft-coal industry, the wheat farmers, still linger in the sterile valleys of the cycle. We speak of *this* depression. It is only a collection of depressions, noticeable, horribly obvious, profoundly disturbing because there are so many of them all at one time and in one place. The depression will pass — *the* depression — but many depressions will remain, lost among the mounting number of prosperities, just as a few prosperities are now lost among the multitude of depressions.

A couple of million people out of work does not disturb us. But each man out of work is a kind of economic menace. He is, in fact, a walking depression. There is a kind of contagion in the man, not merely because he evokes gloom, but because he is an actual condition of depressive weight to the force which threw him out of employment. At the very crest of the boom these human depressions were scattered everywhere. In one house lives a salesman rejoicing in the good days of the automobile business. His nextdoor neighbor is an unemployed victim of the depression in the cotton business. There is a continual warfare between these two forces — these prosperities and depressions. Not infrequently it happens that the depression of the man in the silk business, sending its influence out through devious ways, travels around the world, to smite, after a while, the prosperous automobile salesman next door.

THE RESPONSIBILITY OF BUSINESS

One of the most amazing features of our current journey through the wilderness is, first, the almost universal recognition that we ought to do something about unemployment relief in future crises; and second, that practically nothing *has* been done about it. This year, by a curious chance, marks the one hundredth anniversary of the first unemployment fund set up by the printers in New York. They provided three dollars a week, which, considering the state of wages then, is somewhat better than most of our present plans. So the subject is not new. Ten years ago, Mr. Hoover, as Secretary of Commerce, named a committee to study the problem. It surveyed, researched, and recommended. Before anyone could get excited about it, prosperity flooded over the land and drowned the feeble interest in the report.

Now we are in the midst of another depression. We have been hobbling about on the floor of this depression for about two years. A few unemployment insurance bills, without leadership, have been introduced in some legislatures. About four states have named commissions to study the subject. A few business men in Rochester and Fond du Lac have organized a kind of group unemployment fund. The General Electric Corporation has established a plan. There is a good deal of talk, of course. I do not quarrel that nothing has been done. That is quite natural. My criticism is that no plan, backed by any influential leadership, has ever been proposed.

Why is this? I ask the question because I think there is an explanation of this sterility of leadership. At least I venture to suggest one. It is an apparently rooted conviction that this problem of providing for unemployment belongs to business; that business has the right to deal with it and, given time, will ultimately do so. Jobs are the fruit of business. It is the function of business to furnish the jobs. If jobs are to be made more secure, if means for providing unemployment insurance are to be worked out, why then, of course, should not business do it?

Business men and their critics seem to be at one on this. The former think the problem is theirs by right. The latter think business has the duty of solving the problem as a kind of price which it must pay for the privilege of operating.

The idea is worse than false. It has stood completely in the way of anything being done at all. First of all, when we say the matter must be handled by business, we are handing the problem over to something which does not exist. There is no such thing as business, in the sense in which the word is used here. Men have a way of speaking of business as if it were a separate, recognizable, autonomous entity endowed with the means of functioning as an intelligent unit.

A business can act for itself. The Standard Oil Company of New Jersey, within the limits of the law, can rule itself because it is a definite, highly organized body provided with all the utensils of management. But the oil business, of which the Standard Oil Company is a part, certainly cannot rule itself. What is the oil business? It includes a great number of corporations, some producing crude oil, some refining it into gasoline, others transporting it in pipes, others manufacturing drilling and refining machinery. There are still others engaged as wholesale distributors, thousands operating as retail distributors. The oil business includes all these concerns, their managers, their workmen, and — we might add — the millions who buy the total product and furnish all the money. It constitutes not a group of coherent units, but many groups of hostile units, perpetually at war and all appealing continually for the interference of the State against some special group. If this is a fair picture of the oil business, how much more is all this true of business taken as a whole.

This, it seems to me, is the crux of the whole matter. What do we mean when we say the problem is one which must be handled by business? Do we mean that individual business units will each deal with the matter as it affects their employees? Or do we mean that business as a whole will, through some organized form, take the matter in hand?

Obviously, if we mean the latter we are committing this profoundly important subject to an agency which has no actual existence. If the former, then we are merely quieting our minds in some such way as the man who would advocate in this day that the problem of fire insurance should be handled by each business corporation for itself.

Individual business units cannot deal successfully with the problem. The factors to be controlled are too numerous. Moreover, individual business units large enough to act continuously fail to reach vast areas of the working population. They cannot reach the construction industry, the millions of employees of small independent shops and stores — these are examples of employees which will never get anything from individual private unemployment insurance. If the job cannot be done by business as a whole and if business as a whole has no functional existence; if, in fact, there is no such thing, then we shall have to be content to permit the problem to languish or entrust it to other hands.

THE STATE AND UNEMPLOYMENT

But business men are not willing to have the subject withdrawn from the hands of business, for that means handing it over to the State. And they are afraid of the State. That way, they fear, lies socialism or, worse, communism. They cannot possibly contrive any method for putting the problem intelligently into the hands of business as a whole. Hence their minds refuse to function beyond that *impasse*. No plan for dealing with this important subject has been proposed because no plan for handling it through business can be achieved by human ingenuity.

Business as a whole is nothing more or less than the community as a whole engaged in the job of making a living. It is the total of producers, distributors, and consumers looked at in their ordinary daily activities of producing, distributing, and buying. No machine has ever been devised for these people to get together in their producing and distributing and consuming capacities and act as a unit. Separate groups do form at times to act against some other group or against the whole. However, the very people who compose the entire business population happen to have in another grouping a machine for unit action. And this we call the citizenry and the government. It is the only organization which comprises all the elements in business. It is the only one which is capable of adequate action.

Individual business corporations, dealing with their own payrolls and their own employees, have attempted something in the way of unemployment insurance. But the whole episode of individual corporate action has been pitifully limited in point of numbers and pitifully feeble in point of efficiency.

First of all, almost all the plans have collapsed under the weight of the present severe test. Fifteen such plans have come to my attention. Three of these have been only recently formed and hence have had no opportunity to reveal their weaknesses. Of the remaining twelve, two went quickly out of existence and the others have crumpled under the pressure of the current depression.

Some of them afforded very inadequate relief — nine dollars a week in one case. One of them attempted full pay for a full year of unemployment. But of course that could not stand up. Most of the others provided half pay, with a fixed minimum, but for only a very limited period. Only one or two made any provision for workers let out for any purpose. The relief was limited to lay-offs. In the case of the Rockland Finishing Company, the unemployment insurance was put into effect in 1920 and had to be abandoned after the 1920–21 depression had practically devoured it. A more important case, that of the Dennison Company, started in 1916, was severely taxed by the 1921 depression. I understand the present depression has nearly exhausted the fund. The General Electric plan, announced only a short time ago, provides a maximum unemployment payment for ten weeks and no weekly payments in excess of two hundred dollars and is limited to lay-offs.

It would, of course, be unfair to say that these plans do no good. But one can see how futile they are against the immense field of the problem at which they are aimed.

In Rochester fourteen corporations have gone into a group plan in which all of their twenty-six thousand employees are insured. Half of these are in the Eastman Kodak works. They propose to pay, beginning in 1933, as high as sixty per cent of the regular wage of a laid-off employee for from six to thirteen weeks, depending on the length of service.

There is in all these plans a confession of their inability to cope with prolonged unemployment. All of them disclaim any capacity to provide any insurance for the dismissed man. What is more, up to 1930 the number of workers covered by these plans was only 8830. Now the number is about eighty thousand — eighty thousand out of a total of forty-five million.

Workers themselves, organized in unions, have attempted something. There are about thirty-five local arrangements providing for pitifully small and inadequate relief. Of union attempts on a national scale there have been thirteen plans. Of these nine failed before 1930, even before any very serious strain had been put on them. All these union plans covered less than thirty-five thousand workers.

More ambitious and more important were the plans in which the workers, organized in their unions, and the employers, organized in their trade associations, collaborated in joint schemes of guaranteed employment and unemployment funds. These plans cover less than one hundred thousand workers, almost all of them in the garment industries. In these plans, however, the greatest stress has been placed upon guaranteed employment and in most instances the firms have been able to furnish the full amount of employment. But even here only a small percentage of the people in the garment industry have been affected. Yet the very effort to provide the guaranteed forty weeks of employment to the factory workers has helped to intensify the unemployment situation among the so-called outside workers. All the insurance plans combined do not reach three hundred thousand workers.

LOOKING OUT FOR THE WORKER

All this can hardly be called dealing with unemployment insurance. The attempts we see have reached less than one per cent of the workers, counting all those that failed and including those new plans which have not yet had a trial and which, upon their very face, carry utterly inadequate relief.

There are other reasons which suggest themselves against the efficacy of privately worked-out schemes. First of all, the corporation back of the plan is one which, we have to concede, in the light of business history has little claim to immortality. The worker ought to have some reasonable expectation that, after many years spent with an employer, the unemployment benefit will not fail him when he needs it because his guarantor has ceased to exist. It would be easy to name a score of large corporations whose guarantees ten years ago would have been considered as good as gold, which either no longer exist or have ceased to be considered sound. The fund to protect the worker ought to be in hands which will continue to exist regardless of the fate of the business enterprise from which the accumulated funds are drawn. The right of the worker to the unemployment benefit should be an absolute one which attaches to his status as a workingman and not to his status as the employee of any particular concern. Failure of individual concerns is frequently the cause of unemployment and so the benefit in such cases would lapse at the very moment when it is needed.

Furthermore, we will never get unemployment insurance through private arrangement save for those workers regularly employed by very large corporations. Small corporations have not enough employees to be able to handle the purely actuarial problem of risk. When a single plant closes down, the whole risk-bearing foundation of the plan is unemployed — corporation and employees. However, in the nation as a whole, even in so serious a depression as the present one, where six million people may be out of work, there remain forty million who are employed. The risk of unemployment can be distributed over a whole population. It cannot be scientifically distributed over a single plant or even a single industry.

There will be no unemployment insurance in this country worth talking about until the job is undertaken by the State. Mr. Gerard Swope, a far-seeing and socially minded executive, warns his fellow industrialists that they had better set about the job or the State will do it. Now there is good reason for this fear of the State by those business men who are terrified by the word socialism. But after all there are certain well-defined areas of human control which, if they are to be acted upon at all, must be acted upon by the State. And this business of unemployment insurance is one of them. It will most certainly never be dealt with by business.

When we come to the puzzling question of state unemployment insurance, there are many delicate questions to be answered. Shall it be done by the states or by the Federal Government? Shall it be handled by the Government directly, or through a government-owned corporation or through private corporations under state or federal laws like compensation insurance? Where shall the necessary funds be drawn from — the employers, the employees, the State, or from all or any two of them? What shall be the measure and extent of relief?

It is in an attempt to answer these questions that we arrive at the principle of the security wage. Here there are certain definite facts which seem to stand out beyond question:

First, unemployment, while it may be greatly mitigated by business men in the more intelligent administration of the business, cannot, certainly not for many years, be wholly done away with.

Second, unemployment is the almost inevitable lot of men past a certain age under our present system.

Third, the wages paid the vast majority of our working people, while better than in any other country in the world, are not sufficient to enable them to provide against extended periods of unemployment.

Fourth, the average workingman cannot save a sum large enough to afford him a living in his old age. Even the thriftiest do not succeed in saving more than a few thousand dollars. The interest on that would not avert starvation for more than a few weeks. The principal itself would be exhausted with harrowing speed.

Fifth, in the absence of unemployment insurance of some kind the man out of work must depend upon charity, given either by private individuals or by the State.

Sixth, if the money for unemployment insurance and old-age pensions is supplied by the State the relief is still charity.

Seventh, if it is supplied from funds paid wholly by the employers, the relief is still touched by the character of charity.

All this being true, we must now recognize that the income to be provided during unemployment should belong to the worker as a matter of right. The funds from which the whole insurance fund is raised should be drawn from money which can be ear-marked as the property of the worker himself.

I propose, therefore, that the insurance fund shall be created through payments made by the employers for the account of the worker. The actual paying of the whole sum shall be by the employer. This sum shall be, not a percentage of the wage deducted from the wage actually

agreed on, but a percentage of the wage in addition to
that actually paid the worker. Some such provision as
the following will cover my meaning:

The employer shall pay to the employee, in addition to the
wages paid him on a weekly or monthly basis, an additional
sum, which shall not be deducted from the agreed wage, but
which shall be —— per cent of the agreed sum, but in addition
to it. This wage shall be considered a part of the regular payroll of the employer and shall be paid regularly for the account
of such employee, to (the corporation charged by the State
with the administration of the fund).

This, it may be objected, is merely a fiction to disguise
the payment made by the employer. It is something
more than a fiction. It insists on classifying the payment
properly. It marks it, identifies it at the outset as a sum
earned by the employee and not handed over to him out
of the kindness of his boss. The great insurance fund
created would be the property of the workers who are
benefited. The payments they would receive would be,
not relief, not doles, not charity, but sums created by
their own earnings, coming back to them like any other
form of insurance.

On the score of cost the answer is that now we are compelled to suffer a large part of the cost through public and
private charitable funds created in a hurry and administered in a ramshackle fashion. The City of New York
will this year pay out seven million dollars in old-age pensions to men over seventy, every one of whom earned in
his lifetime enough to have provided his own annuity if
the saving had been made possible by some such plan as
I have outlined. As it is, the employers of most of these
men have retained those sums for themselves and now
New York taxpayers must make the sum up *de novo* each
year to take care of that neglected duty.

The problem involves many difficulties. There are

many details which would have to be settled. I have contented myself here with laying down the belief that we
can and will get no unemployment insurance from business; that the initiative will have to be taken by the State
and that the State should move to take the whole matter
definitely out of the hands of charity and create the necessary fund from the wages of the workers, paid by the employers through the medium of the security wage.

CHAPTER VIII

THE MONETARY FACTOR IN BUSINESS DEPRESSIONS

By WILLIAM C. EWING

[THE present crisis has produced the usual crop of proposals for avoiding the heights and valleys of industrial depression by currency stabilization and the adjustment of credits to the requirements of steady business. There are some economists who apparently think that the rise and fall of prices as measured in money or the fluctuations in the dollar as measured in commodities are responsible for the expansion and contraction of business; and hence they reason that some simple currency and credit expedient can be found to prevent radical price variations and thus maintain industry on a fairly even keel without resorting to the complicated operations of planning.

If such a clever device could really be found, it ought to be hailed as the great Morrison Pill for the Cyclical Disease, but there is ground for thinking that most expedients of this character put the cart before the horse. Perhaps it is the absence of planning that makes price fluctuations and perhaps also finance is a function of industry rather than a prime cause of its movements. Certainly panics have occurred under every kind of currency and banking system the wit of man has yet established and just as certainly industry has often risen out of the valley of depression without resort to currency inflation. Yet beyond question there is an intimate connection between currency and credit institutions on the one side and industrial operations on the other. It may be that they are in truth parts of the same thing and that centralized control over banking, credit, and currency will become a phase of efficient industrial planning. Any other alternative seems to be impossible.

As a rule those who consider the problems of large-scale planning give little consideration to the currency and credit aspects of the subject and those who deal with these aspects of economy assume the permanence of the kind of industrial anarchy which characterized early capitalism. But any effort to think our way through the whole complex involves an examination of both sides of the shield. That any simple currency expedient can alone prevent business cycles or automatically keep industry on a stable base is highly doubtful. It is equally doubtful whether planned economy can proceed in industry without strong control over currency and credit facilities and operations. A rationalization of production in a monetary chaos is inconceivable, and certainly price inflation and deflation contribute to the violence of the upswings and collapses. It follows, therefore, that a reconsideration of the monetary factor must accompany all discussions of measures designed to maintain a fair balance between production and distribution. For this reason the review of the subject by William C. Ewing, of the Stable Money Association, deserves the most careful examination.]

The people of America have been concerned during the past winter, as never before in this generation, about the social suffering which has resulted from the world-wide industrial recession. From suicides among the supposedly wealthy, to bread-lines for the poor, the past year has been phenomenal. In several countries, conditions similar to those in America have resulted in political revolutions. In our own country, instead of taking violent action we have been indulging in reflections regarding the soundness of an industrial system which has ever been accompanied by recurring periods of depression, starvation, and bankruptcies. The experiences of the past year have resulted in a great deal of thought concerning the desirability of radical changes in our industrial system. People in various walks of life are expressing the opinion that, if our present system cannot be made to work more smoothly, we must adopt a better. Outstanding industrial leaders consider that this situation presents the greatest challenge to the capitalistic system. That staunch supporter of capitalism, Daniel Willard, president of the Baltimore and Ohio Railroad, recently said: 'A system under which it is possible for five or six millions of willing and able-bodied men to be out of work and unable to secure work for months at a time, and with no other source of income, cannot be said to be perfect or even satisfactory.... We have all come to see more clearly than ever before that the mere existence of the problem presents a serious challenge to our entire economic system.'

The most encouraging factor in the present situation is the fact that so many able men and women are realizing that palliatives are not sufficient. Some of those who have been most active in efforts to assuage social suffering during the past year are insisting that their treating of symptoms must not be allowed to take the place of curing the disease. Colonel Arthur Woods, chairman of the President's Emergency Committee for Employment, says: 'We must be fundamental enough in our thinking to realize the necessity of trying to find out what started this economic typhoon. Collectively we must seek the reasons.'

CAUSES OF INDUSTRIAL FLUCTUATIONS

Many concomitant causes are responsible for industrial upheavals. Weather conditions affect the farmers; developments in the moving-picture business throw musicians out of work; new inventions affect the stability of employment of wage-earners; changes in the tariff may make or break manufacturers. But each one of these classes, and every individual in the land, is affected by one constantly active factor — that of our unstable monetary system. If a farmer contracted to deliver wheat at a fixed price per bushel, and discovered when the time for delivery arrived that the bushel was three times as large as when he made his contract, no one would marvel at the fact that the prosperity of farmers fluctuated. If the ton or the yard were subject to variations of two hundred per cent, merchants would readily understand the reason for fluctuations in their profits. But we are so accustomed to variations in our unit of value that, until quite recently, scarcely anybody gave consideration to the subject, though such variations have greatly exceeded two hundred per cent.

It would be interesting, were it possible, to determine the relative importance of the various factors which occasion our industrial upheavals. There are no authoritative studies to quote, but only opinions held by careful students of the subject. Summarizing these opinions, it is fair to say that the greatest single cause affecting all classes and all occupations is the instability of our unit of value. An estimate made by the editor of an influential farm journal in the Middle West will serve as an illustration. Scientists or mathematicians will understand the carefulness of this editor from the fact that in his work in developing new species of corn and of chickens he adjusts his observations by the method of least squares. A year ago (that is, before the recent drought) he estimated the recent misfortunes of the farmers to be due forty per cent to variations in the purchasing power of money and sixty per cent to all other causes combined — weather, bad judgment, vegetable and livestock diseases, etc.

One other cause for business instability should be given special attention because it is so much misunderstood and has been so much overrated as to tend to lead us astray and waste our energies on what is for the most part an effect rather than a cause of variations in business prosperity. I refer to overproduction. There are two kinds of overproduction: the actual but rare production of goods beyond the possibility of consumption, and the production of goods beyond the ability of consumers to purchase, even though the need for consumption equals or exceeds the production. The former type of overproduction, sometimes encouraged by legislation in an endeavor to secure certain national objectives, has occurred in sugar and coffee and perhaps in copper and a few other products. Of the second kind of overproduction, innumerable examples could be cited, such as the overproduction of foodstuffs and clothing while thousands of people are going hungry and in tatters. Professor G. F. Warren, of Cornell University, points out that during the years 1919 to 1929 'food and feed crops could decrease one per cent and population increase sixteen per cent, and still we could have a disastrous depression due to overproduction.' As a matter of fact it was not a period of overproduction, but one of poor distribution, as is the present.

The careful studies of Mr. Carl Snyder, statistician of the Federal Reserve Bank of New York, show clearly that neither in foodstuffs nor in commodities as a whole has world production since the war exceeded the previous rate of increase. The logical conclusion to be drawn from his work is that we cannot reasonably hold that overproduction in industry has caused the present business depression.

EFFECTS OF *INCREASE* IN THE VALUE OF MONEY

When, for any reason, the amount of money in relation to the needs of business becomes less, each dollar will buy more of the goods in which we trade, just as a shortage in the cotton crop tends to make each pound of cotton more valuable. Variations in the value of money are measured by changes in the level of prices — not in the price of any single commodity which may be specially affected by local conditions of weather, strikes, increase in manufacturing efficiency, etc. — but in the prices of all commodities: in what is called 'the general price-level.' Indexes of the general price-level are issued regularly by various authorities, including the Federal Reserve Banks, Professor Irving Fisher, and the Federal Bureau of Labor Statistics, this last being based on the prices of more than five hundred commodities. Let us now see what is the effect on business and social conditions when money increases in value; that is to say, when prices persistently fall.

When prices are falling, prudent people delay their buying as long as possible. If a grocer needs a new delivery truck, and if the price of delivery trucks has been falling during the past year and gives promise of continuing to fall, he will not only wait until next month to buy a new truck, he will wait until his old truck falls to pieces. And he will be quite right, for by such methods he may be able to pull through hard times instead of going to the wall as so many of his competitors are doing. This is equally true of every other merchant, of manufacturers, of railroads, and even of ultimate consumers except when they are buying immediate necessities. A printer of Christmas cards, with plants in various parts of the country, told me a year ago that he had sent out his agents in the spring as usual to get orders for the 1930 Christmas trade, but that they had returned without the expected orders because all the dealers had decided to wait before placing their orders, to see how the market was going and how largely people would probably buy. Of course that meant shutting down his plants and throwing his employees out of work. And what his customers were doing to him he was undoubtedly doing to the manufacturers from whom he purchased his raw materials; for he certainly would not be foolish enough to place a year's order for paper on a falling market.

This attitude is equally characteristic of the retail merchants. They organize 'buy now' campaigns, but they themselves do not 'buy now.' Store managers in various parts of the country tell me that it has become a fixed policy to keep in stock only what can be sold immediately. Some are ordering each week goods which they formerly bought in monthly or larger lots. 'Buy now' campaigns, on a falling market, can appeal only to the improvident or to persons who are so wealthy that they can afford to be uneconomical. No prudent person will buy today what he knows he can get cheaper next month, unless the goods purchased are immediate necessities.

This unwillingness to buy on a falling market may begin with the ultimate consumer; but it very quickly brings about the same attitude on the part of the retail and wholesale merchants, the manufacturers and the producers of raw materials. All along the line it means unemployment, part-time work or cuts in wages; and this, in turn, lessens the buying power of the community and thus further depresses business. It must be apparent that *the only way to break this vicious circle is to stop the downward trend of prices*. If our grocer learns that the price of trucks is going up next month, he will place his order immediately; if he could be assured that prices would move neither up nor down, he would buy reasonably whenever the needs of his business required. Incidentally, he would be saved the necessity of gambling on whether future prices would move up or down — a subject to which every merchant must now give the most careful thought. The effect on farmers of the fall of prices since the war is well illustrated by one class of cases out of several which might be cited, that of enlargement of farms. Ten years ago farmers were encouraged to increase their production. Many of them purchased additional land at the going prices of that day. Today they are trying to pay off their mortgages with money which is worth forty per cent more than it was when they borrowed it. The result is very serious for the farmers and for all who are dependent upon them. One indication of their disaster may be seen in the statistics of bank failures in the farming districts.

EFFECTS OF *DECREASE* IN THE VALUE OF MONEY

From the facts already considered, it follows, *per contra*, that industry and trade will be stimulated by a continuous rise in the general price-level; everyone will then rush to buy for future, as well as for present, needs, knowing that delay will result in having to pay higher prices.

By increasing the available amount of money in proportion to the needs of business, the general level of prices can be forced up, and the stimulation of business and the reëmployment of the unemployed will result. But such a rise in the price-level brings with it evils which are not less serious than those resulting from falling prices. Even in the day of its prosperity, industry experiences difficulties due to the necessity of increasing wages and salaries to meet the increased cost of living. Within a twelvemonth period of rising prices the United States has suffered from four thousand strikes.

But the greatest burden of rising prices falls upon others than manufacturers and merchants. It falls chiefly upon people who have fixed incomes. To a certain extent this class includes wage-earners, since an increase in wages always lags behind the increase in the cost of living. This lag is much greater in the case of salaried employees; in fact, there are certain classes of salaried people with whom this lag is so great as to be tragic. Many will remember poignantly the economic condition of salaried professional people at the close of the war, when a dollar was worth less than half of what it was five years before.

Endowed institutions, including most of our colleges, are very hard hit by the lessening of the value of money, since their income is fixed not in value but in the number of dollars. Staffs of endowed institutions often accept relatively small salaries because of retirement pensions and exceptional permanence; but permanence is a doubtful asset when the salary is only half the cost of living. I know of one college which sold some of its investments and used this capital for running expenses; the more usual occurrence, however, was to hold those members of the staff whose circumstances necessitated their remaining, while losing many others to industry.

Another class of persons who lose by the decrease in the value of money is those who have laid away money, as such. A person who deposited one thousand dollars in a savings bank in 1915 and withdrew it in 1920 would have found that one thousand dollars plus interest was worth less than half what it was when he left it with the bank. Similarly, a person who took out adequate life insurance in 1915 and died in 1920 would have left his family dependent instead of independent, as he had planned. There may not be any great public sympathy for the idle rich who live on the income of investments made by their parents, yet there has been many a tragedy in the lives of crippled orphans, of elderly ladies untrained for labor, and of other worthy people whose futures have been planned by those responsible for their welfare — a welfare which is jeopardized by rising prices.

Allowance for increased efficiency in industry and other detailed points are worthy of careful study; but it is quite safe to say in general that the social welfare of our country demands absolutely that our unit of value shall not fluctuate. We do not know whether this ideal can ever be fully attained; we do know that it can be closely approached, that to a great extent monetary fluctuation can be eliminated. Those fluctuations have indeed already been modified to a considerable extent by one alone of the several methods which are under consideration. It is appropriate that we should now examine the outstanding plans which have been suggested for stabilizing the value of money.

SUGGESTED PLANS FOR STABILIZATION

Before examining detailed plans for stabilization, let us note certain general considerations which must influence us in forming judgments. We should realize that the problem of unstable currency is an international problem; if there was ever a time when we might have solved this problem for ourselves, that time is now definitely past. International exchange would wreck any plan that might be designed on a purely national basis. Also, if we may judge by past experience we must realize that any plan is imperfect which relies largely upon the judgment of men who may, even honestly, favor the interests of some particular class or be subject to political influence. My own belief is that the automatic — the gyroscopic — working of any plan is essential to its perfection; we should never think of permitting any group of men to determine when a pound should equal fifteen ounces and when it should be changed to seventeen; it is far more important that the unit of value should be independent of human frailties than that the unit of weight should be thus independent.

There are four types of stabilization plans which are being given serious consideration:

The Central Bank Plan. All the progress which has been made up to this time in stabilizing monetary units has been made by this plan. Many of the world's leading bankers are endeavoring to secure national stability through their central banks and are hoping that the Bank for International Settlements, at Basle, will be a powerful agency for bringing about international stability. In our own country, the Federal Reserve System has exerted such a stabilizing influence that most observers believe that but for its salutary influence we should have suffered a far worse *débâcle* than we have experienced during the past year. The Federal Reserve officials do not make any exorbitant claims along this line; they realize that certain notable successes in stabilizing the value of the dollar may be matched by failures, due sometimes to the newness of the system and sometimes to pressure by the Treasury Department. They oppose legislation requiring them to keep the general price-level stable, partly because they are not sure that they could always obtain that result and partly because they do not dare to experiment very much with such a powerful engine.

The great inflation of 1919–20, from whose reaction we are now suffering, was due to action which was forced upon the Federal Reserve System by the national administration, under emergency war legislation. If Congress could make such action possible in time of war, it can do so at other times if there is sufficient pressure from interested classes. The present personnel of the Federal Reserve System is greatly interested in securing stability of the dollar; but this is not their first duty as prescribed by Congress. Moreover, this personnel is determined by a combination of presidential appointment and election by commercial banks. It is conceivable that at some future time this combination might replace the present Federal Reserve officials with men concerned only with the interests of some particular class.

Whatever we may think of the dangers of requiring the Federal Reserve System to stabilize the dollar or of leaving it to the judgment of its officers, as is now the practice, it must be admitted that at the present time the Federal Reserve System and similar central banks in other countries are our sole reliance in preventing violent fluctuations in the purchasing power of money. What progress we have made has been made exclusively through their agency and the interest of many of their officers in further stabilization holds promise of continued progress.

The Fiat Money Plan. A generation ago it was the 'long-haired, wild-eyed' agitator who suggested doing away with a metallic base for our currency. Today we find serious economists citing the fact that since the war we have reduced our legal gold reserve ratio to forty per cent and have left in the hands of officials the determination of the amount of money to be issued. They ask why we should not carry this scheme to its logical conclusion by reducing the gold reserve to zero, since the value of money is dependent upon its amount rather than upon our ability to exchange it for gold. The objection to this plan is the same as the objection to our Federal Reserve legislation: the question whether such powers should be left to any group of officials, and whether, in time of emergency, Congress will not require these officials to inflate the currency. If it is true that history repeats itself, this is a dangerous plan. But perhaps we have become so wise that we can avoid repeating the mistakes of the past.

The Compensated Dollar Plan. This is the most fundamental plan yet proposed. Instead of increasing or decreasing the amount of available money, as in the central bank plan, it determines by definition that a dollar shall be that number of ounces of gold which shall be necessary to purchase a fixed quantity of goods, as determined by the index number of the general price-level. Theoretically this would seem to give a unit of value which would be unchanging; but in practice it would be necessary to adjust the weight of the dollar at fixed intervals, as weekly or monthly, or at whatever time is necessary to keep the fluctuations of value within fixed bounds. This, however, could be relied upon to keep the purchasing power within very narrow limits, while our lack of plan in the past has resulted in variations of nearly three hundred per cent. As at present developed, the weakness of this plan is in the field of international exchange; unless the principal countries adopted this plan at the same time, all the gold might be drained out of the country which alone adopted it, or all the world's gold might be attracted to that country.

From a scientific point of view this plan is interesting because it attacks the root of instability. For our unit of length we have the invariable distance between two marks on a bar in the Bureau of Standards; for our unit of capacity we have a definite number of cubic inches; for our unit of weight we have the weight of a particular piece of metal in the Bureau of Standards; but for our unit of value we have, not a specific value, but a certain number of grains of gold. This plan proposes to substitute for this weight unit a value unit.

The Mine Control Plan. Professor Lehfeldt, of South Africa, proposed, in view of the threatened shortage in the supply of gold in the near future, that those nations which produce the world's gold should take over the mines within their boundaries and, by joint action, control their output as well as the proportion of that output which should be allowed to flow into commercial use. This would make it possible for the gold base of the various national currencies to be kept at such amounts as might be necessary in order to stabilize the units of value of each nation. Aside from the difficulty of securing such united action, this plan has the defect of dealing only with the gold base. Since most of our transactions are by the medium of paper money and bank checks, we should still have to control the purchasing power of our money through the central bank or other method.

Bimetallism is another plan by which it has been proposed to accomplish much the same purpose as that at which the Lehfeldt plan aims. Under the bimetallic plan, the dwindling gold supply would be supplemented by the use of silver at such ratio as would keep the two metals at parity as a basis for the credit structure. Economists are practically united in the opinion that bimetallism would be ineffective on a national basis. International bimetallism would have, in addition to the difficulties of the Lehfeldt plan, the added problem of adjusting the ratio between two metals as their production varied, independently of each other.

CONCLUSION

It is by no means impossible that the ultimate solution will be a combination of two or more of the proposed plans. The problem of stabilization has its complications, though they seem not to be insuperable. So long as we hold to the gold standard in its present form, we must consider the subject as made up of two elements: the gold base and the superstructure of credit. Concerning the gold base, the Harvard Economic Society has said: 'If the decline in gold production now in prospect after 1935 is followed by a serious decline of commodity prices, this result will be due not to inescapable economic law, but to causes wholly within the control of human volition.' Most authorities agree that we can similarly control our credit structure if we put our minds to it.

After the Civil War inflation, we suffered for thirty years from declining prices, unemployment, bad business, and social misery, mitigated only by occasional brief periods of relief due to business cycles. Since the World War we have gone through the first ten years of deflation. Shall we stand quietly by during the next twenty years until we again reach the low level of 1896? There are those who would like to have us do so; and some of them are powerful. They claim that these violent fluctuations drive out of business the weaklings and encourage efficiency; and as they themselves are numbered among the strong ones, they welcome such a development.

Monetary stabilization is not a panacea. It will not cure all of our social and industrial ills. It will, however, greatly mitigate them. It will relieve the business man of most of his present necessity for gambling on the future of prices; it will make possible the regularization of general business and of employment; it will relieve most of the social distress which results from irregular employment outside of the strictly seasonal trades. It will remove the greatest single cause of fear from both the wage-earner and his employer. It will give security to the investor as distinguished from the speculator; it will encourage thrift by ensuring a return of real values from savings bank and life-insurance investments.

Whether we shall have a stabilized purchasing power for our money depends upon two factors: the working-out of technical methods by the economists and an intelligent demand on the part of the general public. In one or the other of these ways every leader of thought can exert a constructive influence. The traditional American spirit of adventure is appealed to by the statement of Sir Charles Addis that 'It is simply intolerable that we should continue to sit with folded hands while industry and trade throughout the world are becoming the sport of our ineffectual monetary systems. We must be masters in our own house, the rulers, and not the slaves of money.' From his earliest school-days, the American child is led to revere the spirit of our pioneer fathers which led them to create ordered progress in the wilderness and to attack fearlessly conditions which were almost beyond the power of men to control. And shall we, their children, admit that we are unable to control our own invention, that in our monetary system we have created a Frankenstein which periodically makes life difficult for most of us and

intolerable for some? Or shall we unitedly determine that
the monetary machine which we have created we can
and will perfect so that it shall never again prove a
menace to our business and social life?

Chapter IX

THE ADVANCE OF LARGE-SCALE AGRICULTURE

By Walter B. Pitkin

[The system of agriculture on which Thomas Jefferson founded his faith in the future of the American Republic was entirely different from that prevailing now in the age of machinery, specialized crops, and dependence on world markets. The ideal of that system, largely realized in practice for a time, was the small farm tilled by the owner and his family with simple tools. The farm unit was mainly self-sufficing, for the family produced its own food, most of its clothing, and sold only a small portion of the produce to secure 'cash' for taxes and incidental expenses.

That this scheme of agriculture has long been in distress and in peril of dissolution is well known. The pressure of large-scale production with the aid of machinery and the difficulties of finding markets for the increasing output have raised a question whether historic agriculture can be preserved. Some of our statesmen have long been seeking a program for restoring it to its former vigor and preserving it against dissolution, but in recent years there has arisen a whole school of critics who insist that all such efforts are futile, that the way out of the agrarian depression, which is world-wide in its scope, lies in the abandonment of old methods and the adoption of new plans, far-reaching in economic implications and almost revolutionary in character. The general philosophy of the new school is trenchantly stated by Professor Walter B. Pitkin, in the following article, entitled 'The Great

Dirt Conspiracy,' published in *The Forum* for August, 1931.[1]]

A vast conspiracy is on foot to prevent the United States from progressing apace with the rest of the world. It is a reactionary movement of the first magnitude, backed by immense wealth and influence. Several of our mightiest multi-millionaires are enrolled under its banner. So are many owners of magazines and newspapers, hundreds of merchants, and millions of farmers. And, of course, away up in front march the army of thirty-cent statesmen, waving the Stars and Stripes and belching pæans in praise of the good old American Farm Home, its quarter-section, and its half-wits.

For this is a conspiracy to preserve the ancient American farm system against the ravages of the Industrial Revolution, which is just reaching the plowlands. The Industrial Revolution is symbolized by fifty-cent wheat. And the Old Order is perfectly represented by the thirty-cent statesmen who crave dollar wheat and its equivalent in all branches of agriculture. For dollar wheat means the protection of quarter-sections and half-wits. Quarter-sections and half-wits are the foundation stones of the Old Order. They must and shall be preserved, shout the thirty-cent statesmen.

Twenty-seven million farmers want to be saved. They dislike radical changes quite as keenly as you and I. They would like to save their homes and firesides — and who wouldn't? It's silly to berate them on that score. But facts are facts; we must face them and adjust ourselves to them somehow. And the greatest of all facts which have boiled up to the surface since the World War are those which reveal the Old Order as hopelessly out of

[1] It is proper to say that Professor Pitkin's article called forth vigorous dissent from many friends of agriculture. See *The Forum* for September, 1931.

step in the world's mighty onward march toward civilization. They disclose the quarter-section as a slave pen,
and the little farmer against society.

Hundreds of economists and agronomists now know,
past all doubt, that mass production in farming must
follow mass production in the city mills and factories.
They know that, in most basic lines of agriculture, it is
feasible now. They know that it will cut the cost of
production far below the best figures obtainable on small
farms, no matter how well equipped these may be.
Hence, in open competition the super-farm will ex-
terminate the Old Order. Here's how it works out in
wheat.

The Tennessee hill-billy spends $2.40 to grow a bushel
of wheat, and his brother in other poor wheat regions
spends $2. The fairly skilled farmer on good wheat
land spends between $1 and $1.10. He'll tell you, of
course, that he doesn't; and he'll show you his cash records to prove it. But, like all quarter-section half-wits,
he fails to count his own time on a fair wage basis, and
usually he makes no normal allowance for overhead. So
he kids himself into thinking that he grows wheat for
from sixty-five cents to ninety cents. But he can't fool
the Industrial Revolution!

In the Texas Panhandle, Hickman Price, the first
industrialist to perfect super-farm methods, grows wheat
at a true cost of forty cents and less, according to land and
season. To do it he drives the largest tractors day and
night, trains his crews precisely as the great factories do,
and analyzes every step in all operations. Up in Kansas,
the great chain of farms organized by J. S. Bird achieves
like results. And anybody else who has the money and
brains to handle tens of thousands of acres as a food factory can grow wheat around the same figure.

Now it costs between twenty cents and forty cents to
haul wheat by train from various sections of the wheat

regions to Chicago. So when wheat sells in Chicago at seventy-five cents, the small grower loses twenty-five cents on each bushel before he has put it on board the cars; and another twenty cents if that sum happens to be his freight bill on the bushel. So he is in the red to the tune of forty-five cents a bushel. On the same basis, though, the super-farmer of the New Order shows a net profit of fifteen cents a bushel.

Out in Montana, Professor M. L. Wilson has demonstrated that production costs drop as acreage units increase in size. The quarter-section half-wit simply isn't in the running. The man who tills eight hundred acres makes a fair showing; he can operate an acre of wheat for $7.77. But he who operates three thousand acres in a unit with the proper machinery cuts the cost to $3.82 an acre. As Wilson analyzes his results, the cash operating cost of a bushel of wheat on an eight-hundred-acre tract is forty-three cents, and on a three-thousand-acre tract it drops to twenty-one cents. This is not the true cost, but simply the cash outlay; yet it indicates clearly the trend.

Those of us who have been studying the matter for many years know that even the three-thousand-acre unit cannot cut costs to the level of the ten-thousand-acre unit. How many farmers own ten-thousand-acre units? Or can buy the necessary machines to operate such units on lease? Very few. Even in the wheat belt, where farms run large, the average falls far below those dimensions: in Montana it is six hundred and ninety-eight acres, in South Dakota it is four hundred and three. So, you see, the farmer is clean out of the picture. He will never be able to supply us with wheat or any other staple at prices even approximately those reached by the super-farm. Only large capital can get the results. And the farmer is, as the income tax statistics show, our lowest income class.

RUSSIAN COMPETITION

Enter Russia. The drama cannot proceed further without its favorite villain.

Russia must work along for three or four more years before the twenty-five million acres managed by the Grain Trust are thoroughly modernized. Already she has cut wheat-growing costs to seventy-five cents a bushel. (The claim that in 1930 the Giant Farm near Salsk produced 3,300,000 bushels at a true cost of fifty cents per bushel needs to be scrutinized with care.) Nobody who understands the situation doubts that, before 1936, the Soviet experts will be exporting at least two hundred million bushels of wheat whose cost at the railway siding will be under fifty cents. And that will fix the world market price.

Thoughtful farmers, and business men who deal with farmers, begin to see that America can hold its own in the great tomorrow only by matching Russia's fifty-cent wheat with Kansas fifty-cent wheat. Prices of everything that can be produced with tractors far more powerful than the largest now in service, and through organization methods analogous to those of the finest factories, will decline during the next generation. Along with wheat we shall behold all field crops become cheaper year after year, until a level is reached which, in the eyes of the quarter-section half-wit, will spell ruin and chaos.

In all these field crops, the average American yield can easily be doubled while the cost per unit produced declines. For the larger the corporation farm, the cheaper become fertilizers, cultivation, and harvesting. About eighty per cent of the gross bulk and value of farm crops may be thus handled. Thus with all grains save rice in Russia and Siberia, where *five times* as many first-grade acres as we Americans possess await the Soviet plows. Thus with cotton in the Sudan, where the British already grow the fiber far below American production costs. Thus with sugar beets, which even now can be raised in a glut at bankruptcy prices.

In the face of such a situation, the American farmer has only two courses open, as a matter of straightforward economic practice. He may go the way of the coolie, or the way of the corporation. By the first route he competes against fifty-cent wheat by drudging fourteen hours a day, eating boiled potatoes and cold beans, driving his family into his fields along with his mules, and dying of overwork at forty. By the second route he exchanges his farm for stock and bonds issued by the Consolidated Golden Acres, Inc., which concern rips out all his fences, burns his old sheds, sells his tiny tractor and implements as junk, and at one bold sweep tills ten townships.

Everybody opposes the first course. But only the small farmer and his political and business parasites oppose the second. Scientists, economists, and financiers alike now agree that the way of the corporation is our only road to prosperity. They see that, in the long run, whatever cheapens food and reduces human toil serves to elevate the living standard. Hardship arises only in the transition from the Old Order to the new.

Now just who are the reactionaries? And why? By direct inquiry all over the country, I find the 'Dirt Conspiracy' draws heavily on the following classes: the marginal farmers, the half-successful tillers of good soil, large farmland owners (especially the owners of marginal land), country merchants and bankers, rural politicians and lawyers, county-seat newspapers circulating heavily up the back roads, state and federal farm bureaus, nearly all county agents, fully two thirds of the faculties in state agricultural colleges, and a sizable majority of the owners and editors of the periodicals read by 'dirt farmers.' With this horde to sway them with its clamor, is it to be wondered at that state legislatures and the United States

Congress are to be found at the head of the Great Dirt Conspiracy, commanding the economic tide to turn back?

TOO MANY FARMERS

At bottom, we have to do here with another evil of overpopulation. As Wheeler McMillen has shown, we have far too many farmers and a dangerously inflated agriculture. The surplus farmers till millions of acres of inferior land which might better revert to forest and prairie. The first move toward a finer rural civilization must be to abandon about 70,000,000 of the 390,000,000 or more acres tilled last year. For on that immense area nobody can make a dollar, while those who try to do so only glut the market with underpriced commodities, thereby robbing everybody else of fair profits. At least five million farmers — men, women, and children — must be forced out of their futile occupation; and the faster the better for all concerned, in spite of the quick pangs of change. As super-farming spreads, another five million must slowly shift to other work. For the super-farm can feed a man with the yield of three acres, whereas our noble quarter-section grubber must work nearly five acres to accomplish the same result.

Naturally everybody out in the country who earns a living by serving these ten million mortals in jeopardy will join the Great Dirt Conspiracy, for few can see beyond their own noses when looking at matters touching self-interest. Depopulate a farming county, and the little banker there loses depositors and borrowers; the little lawyer gets no boundary fence disputes or tax-dodging clients; the corner grocer sees his salt mackerel wither in its keg; the landlord beholds his stony, steep hillsides abandoned to crows and rabbits and the persistent sumach; the local editor notes with a sigh that subscribers drop off, while advertising shrinks; and the great Friend of the People, the politician, driving his car up the back

roads just before election, learns with dismay that the
hill-billies who always voted for him have fled their
ancient haunts. So the whole countryside arises to save
the superfluous farmer, the stupid farmer, the bankrupt
farmer, and the rest of the doomed ten million.

This Old Order cannot be saved. But its passing can
all too easily be delayed by chicanery and the indifference of city dwellers to the gravity of the farm crisis.
Our thirty-cent statesmen are busy. They thunder
for farm relief, for higher tariffs on farm products, for
subsidies to farmers, for farm loans, for government
purchase of crop surpluses, and so on. Most of the ora-
tors are, in all probability, hypocrites — like the eminent
Middle-Western Congressman who savagely denounced
to Wheeler McMillen in private the absurd McNary-
Haugen bill and, just ten days later, delivered a gush of
words in its favor on the floor of the House. But some
champions of the downtrodden are honest enough in their
fuzzy convictions, just as the farmers themselves are.
And they may work much harm, unless city voters arouse
themselves.

Already the Kansas legislature has enacted a law aim-
ing to suppress corporation farming. Thirty-cent statesmen have tried to dissolve Bird's super-farm on the
ground that it was insolvent; but in court they were
routed by evidence showing its prosperity even in a low-
price era. Texas solons are also scheming against the
industrialized farm. Suppose all of our major farming
states succeeded in such a movement? They will force
the farmers to become coolies in so far as they compete
for world markets, or else to become pensioners of the
government in so far as they maintain the old price levels
on farm products by subsidies, valorizations, and like
paternalisms. In either event, the country as a whole
suffers to no good end. Let me point out two major evils.

In spite of reactionaries, America is becoming a supercity whose suburbs will be what men once called farms. The county will be the municipal unit, as a rule. Out of every one hundred citizens, at least ninety-five will live in the urban centers of the county; and farming will be carried on along industrial lines so that only a handful of watchmen and garage mechanics will have to stay out in the sticks. The farm managers will motor and fly to their farm work every morning from the towns. Thus the cost of living for the city dweller will be lowered so tremendously that, in the face of steadily rising living standards, our factory workers will be able to produce goods that will sell at or below European prices. Study the food costs in typical family budgets and see for yourself what would occur if only thirty per cent were lopped off. I believe that forty per cent can be lopped off within twenty-five years.

But what if the old prices are maintained by legislation? Then all other industrial countries will outstrip us in short order. For they will buy from Russia, from Sudan, from Argentina; and not wheat alone, but cotton, flax, rice, and many other commodities on which the prosperity of great sections of the United States now depends.

'All right!' retort the Dirt Conspirators. 'If that's the outcome, then let's drop all foreign trade! We've business enough at home anyhow.' This is a tenable position, if held with skill and reason, as W. B. Donham does in 'Business Adrift.' America can thrive without a huge export trade. But to do so we must enlarge our own powers as consumers; and one step in that direction is to release as large a fraction of incomes as possible for the purchase of things other than bare necessities. The current trend to eat less food and to pay less for it must persist. But the Great Dirt Conspiracy will thwart that, thereby paralyzing every industry which looks to growing domestic sales for its prosperity. In effect, our city workers will be carrying the burden of ten million useless farmers. Not even our overrated efficiency can offset such a handicap.

NEW JOBS FOR FARMERS

The strongest argument of the reactionaries depicts the horrors of uprooting ten million people without first finding new jobs for them and otherwise protecting them against heavy losses and misery. Wherever I discuss this subject, men always fling back: 'Corporation farms will make confusion worse confounded. Bigger and better machines will throw millions out of work. The cities cannot care for them. There are millions idle in their streets now. Swell those ranks, and you are merely inciting to revolution.'

I admit that this argument calls for serious inquiry; it cannot be dismissed as ill-founded. Nor is any ready-made answer at hand. Unemployment is a problem still too vast and snarled for us. Nevertheless we can say several things about the matter.

First of all, most of the families driven from marginal farms would not be a shade worse off in town. Their present misery is a hideous thing, whether you see it in the famine regions of Arkansas or in the drought zone of old Virginia or in the stricken black lands east of Dallas, or in Montana's lovely but now worthless valleys. Having seen thousands of such wretches in fifteen states during the past winter, I cannot feel that they would go from bad to worse even if they ended up in municipal lodging houses, most of which are more luxurious than shacks on marginal farms.

Secondly, these people, being as yet unaccustomed to the easy-going ways of the mechanized city worker, would be ideally suited to displace the low-grade un-skilled laborers from Latin and Slavonic lands now in our midst; and it is agreed that everybody would benefit by the return of such workers to their native lands. I am not qualified to estimate the present number of aliens who, without injustice, might be returned to Mexico and Mediterranean areas in the course of the next five years; but I should be surprised if there were fewer than four million. We have about five million aliens over and above the foreign-born who have become citizens; so it seems reasonable that we might refuse to naturalize any more and require the entire alien group to leave our shores within a reasonable period. A realignment of population might take care of all marginal farm workers for another five years. Of the five million individuals who ought to shift cityward, not more than two million are adult workers; the others are children.

Thirdly, immense programs of road-building, waterway construction, drainage, reforestation, and the erection of millions of small homes to replace the jerry-built structures foisted on our sucker public during and after the World War will, in the near future, provide work for millions; and the rudest toil should be turned over to these horny-handed rustics. Fully fifty million acres ought to be planted to trees; and who could do that better than men of the soil? At least ten million acres in the South ought to be drained, not for farming, but as a matter of public health.

Fourthly, shorten all work-days considerably, reduce wages very little, if at all, and employment will be spread over most of the idle classes with scarcely any shock. Consider, please, that a five per cent levy on all incomes would suffice to employ eight million workers at an average annual wage of $560 — a sum far above anything ever received by the marginal farmers we are evicting.

Finally, taking the bull by the horns, we might accelerate corporation farming on an immense scale by loans or guarantees of some kind to farmers of proved skill who undertake to work in units of a million dollars and upward. This would immediately bring to pass what Richard Whitney, president of the New York Stock Exchange, foresees as the next move in agriculture, namely, the underwriting of huge agricultural corporations by Wall Street, which hitherto has shunned all such as the plague.

MR. HOOVER'S VIEWS

At the very least, there are about 200,000,000 acres of high-grade plowland adapted to giant farming in blocks of 20,000 to 250,000 acres. Not one square inch of this empire should be bought but all of it must be operated under lease or on some partnership basis. A safe average sum for such operating is around twenty-five dollars an acre; this would carry the company over two years in any grain crop; and the new business ought to stick to grain until it feels at ease, after which it may tackle costly crops such as potatoes. Were our states and the federal authorities to protect and foster in every legitimate manner the rise of this super-farming, Wall Street would, within a few years, be called upon to invest five billion dollars in basic agrarian industries which would show profits fully as sure and sizable as the oils, the rails, and the utilities.

But the Great Dirt Conspiracy will never permit this. It will fight to the last ditch — which happens to be the White House, in this instance. If ever it reaches that spot, it will probably find fresh defenses and ammunition. For Mr. Hoover has always championed expensive wheat and the quarter-section philosophy of life. Just ten years ago he declared: 'Wheat must hold at least fifty index points advance of comparative commodity prices, if we are to assure supplies for our increasing population. That is, if other commodities should return to 100, wheat must hold 150, or some considerable excess.'

His attitude toward farm relief shows no significant

deviation from this point of view, although it is now antiquated. True, he has opposed the gross Treasury raids proposed by the quarter-section half-wits — and let him receive due applause for that. But he seems never to have glimpsed the deeper trends of agrarian economics. If he does see these, he must be ignoring them for some political reason. Is it because the quarter-section half-wits can turn the next election?

But the Dirt Conspirators will not have to appeal to the White House. They will win, hands down, without that gesture. Several of our billionaires and near-billionaires devoutly worship the Old American Farm Home; witness Henry Ford's mania for collecting the junk of that sorry institution, from churn to wallpaper, with the dirty old backyard pump thrown in for good measure. Some of them, too, are like the famous Henry in that much of their fortune is invested in making things for small farmers. Wipe out the latter, and where would Henry sell his cunning little tractors? No wonder he is a reactionary in matters agricultural! (City folks think him a creative radical because he talks about industrializing the farm; but he means by that the widespread use of twenty thirty-horse-power tractors on individually owned and operated farms of five hundred or six hundred acres. All of which is already antiquated.)

Other rich men mix sentiment with self-interest as J. C. Penney does; they would perpetuate the small rustic because he buys from them — and they are duly grateful for his patronage. These infantilisms still sway Wall Street more or less. They keep alive the idea that our nation will dissolve in ruin if our sturdy rustic stock dwindles to a handful of tractor mechanics and county managers. They assure you that city dwellers are weaklings and cannot perpetuate themselves; the great towns must have a peasantry to breed for them a horde of future taxpayers and white-collar clerks.

Within the past year I have heard that alleged argument a hundred times, if once. And I shall probably go on hearing it as long as my ears function. For — I grieve to say — this favorite theme of the city man who left the farm because he couldn't stand it receives lip service from numberless farm experts, who know they are lying but go right on repeating their lies simply because they draw a salary from public funds which are largely contributed by overtaxed farmers. They dare not tell the truth about the fellows who support them.

Here we reach the heart of the Great Dirt Conspiracy. And such a heart disease we find there! I accuse at least half of our agricultural college scientists of supporting the most unscientific, inhuman, wasteful, and generally dirty phase of American life, the small farmer; not always by open speech, but rather by keeping silent or hinting at dark doubts when somebody suggests that corporation methods might solve all our agrarian problems. From a cosmic point of view, this is preposterous.

Another decade of the Great Dirt Conspiracy, and all the evils of the past will be overshadowed by fresh disasters. Will the city voter open his eyes and act? If so, America will advance into a new and better era.

Chapter X

ACTUALITIES OF AGRICULTURAL PLANNING

By Franklin D. Roosevelt

[AMONG the statesmen of our time who have sought a way out of our agricultural crisis none has dealt with the subject more concretely than Governor Roosevelt of New York. To him the problem is far from simple. It is not to be solved by turning our farm lands over to great industrial corporations to be exploited according to capitalist economy and its system of labor. Nor is it to be met by some bit of legerdemain such as currency inflation, export debentures, coöperative marketing, or equalization fees. It is true that Governor Roosevelt has not yet pressed his way through the tangle of issues to a well-rounded scheme of perfection, but he has been searching for fundamental parts of a comprehensive plan and has been expounding his findings with clearness and precision. In an address before the New York State Agricultural Society, on January 21, 1931, he offered a number of specific measures designed to promote the rationalization of agriculture in his state. Except for a few introductory remarks, this address appears below in full.]

The time has come when, in my judgment [said Governor Roosevelt], the state can lay the corner-stone of a land policy — something that has been done by no other state in the Union; something which is needed by modern civilization and by the social and economic advances made by the present generation.

The big question is, What are we going to do with the

land area of the state? No one has ever asked this question before; no one has ever answered the question.

First of all, what is the land area? About thirty million acres. Of this, about three million acres are used for cities, villages, residential and industrial purposes. That leaves twenty-seven million. About five million acres are today in mountains, forests, swamps, and other lands that have never been cultivated. That leaves about twenty-two million acres which were once in farms. Of this, about four million acres have been abandoned or are no longer used for farm purposes. This leaves about eighteen million acres in farms.

The obvious first question in regard to this farm land is how is it being used for farming, and the first step has been taken to answer that question. Last year the legislature passed, on the recommendation of the Agricultural Advisory Commission and myself, an appropriation for a survey of our agricultural resources, the amount of the appropriation being twenty thousand dollars, though I asked for ninety-six thousand dollars.

However, with this twenty thousand dollars, the College of Agriculture at Cornell University has started several important projects in a study and evaluation of the land resources of the state. As a part of this study, a survey has been made of one whole county, Tompkins County. Very simple and clear maps have been prepared covering every ten acres square in Tompkins County and showing the following:

(a) The type of soil.
(b) The climate; that is, the length of growing season between killing frosts and the amount of annual rainfall.
(c) The present use of the land; that is, whether it is forest land and swamp land or improved land, whether in pasture, in hay, or in annual crops and if so, in what crops.
(d) Who lives on the land, or owns it and how the owner uses

the land; that is, to make his livelihood out of it, or to occupy it only as a home while working away from the farm, in the city, or elsewhere.

(e) An analysis of the people who live on the land; whether they are old people who have always been there, or new people who have recently come; whether they are Americans or foreigners; whether the young people are staying on the land or leaving it; whether the cultivation of the farm is supporting the farmer in accordance with an American standard of living.

(f) A measure of the contribution that each farm makes to the food supply of the nation.

The outstanding net result of this survey proves that a very high percentage of the land now in cultivation has no right to remain as farm land. Several generations of farm experience indicate that farmers cannot make a satisfactory living from this land. This percentage runs as high as twenty-two per cent of the farm land in some of the townships in Tompkins County.

Using all of these data, bringing to bear upon the problem what we know about trends in population, in demand for farm products, in the use of larger, modern machinery, there begins to evolve a real plan for the proper development of the land, in other words, a land policy for the State of New York.

This study of Tompkins County includes a classification of the land in the county into several groups with first-class land that should always remain in farms at one end of the scale, and land that clearly should be reforested at the other end of the scale.

A road system to serve the best interests of these areas is projected on a scientific basis. The plan indicates the roads which should be main thoroughfares and improved accordingly; those which may be a part of the secondary hard-road system, narrower and cheaper but out of the mud; roads that should be kept open only as fire breaks and trails to enable people to reach the reforested areas.

The plan also includes a location for electric power lines such as will serve all people of an area and not leave some worth-while farms in pockets which can never be economically reached by electricity. You will see that this plan contemplates two things — the development of the best soil areas to the highest possible degree with the objective of ultimately providing farm-to-market roads and electrical power to practically all the farms that should be maintained as economical farm units and as rural homes. The plan also contemplates removing from agriculture and putting to their proper use those soil areas which through this scientific survey and through the experiences of generations of farmers have been shown to be unsuited for farming.

Hand in hand with this survey there should go a reforestation program on a scale that has never before been attempted by any state or nation. These abandoned farm areas are today a blight upon our agriculture and a great state liability. Year by year they become poorer and poorer through erosion, the depletions of nature and uneconomic use. If put to their proper use, the growing of trees and the furnishing of recreational opportunities, they will again become a great state resource of wonderful value to our future New York. I assume that the Hewitt amendment providing for the greater state program in reforestation will again be passed by the legislature this winter. I hope that the people of the state next fall will ratify this proposed constitutional amendment which will make it possible for a great reforestation program to develop.

A scientific land policy will save the state money in that it will remove the necessity for the upkeep of thousands of miles of road. It will prevent the wrong location of electric power lines. It will help to develop a great agricultural industry in the regions best adapted for farming. The work that has been begun in Tompkins County should be extended to all the other counties in the state.

We have proved to our satisfaction that there are large areas in the State of New York where people are attempting to maintain farms without any economic or social justification for maintaining them. I use the word social as well as economic for the very good reason that the continuance of the maintenance of these farms proves a drag on the social development of our rural life, for the very good reason that the families that maintain and operate these farms cannot make a success of them and must necessarily fail to obtain the social advantages and live up to the social standards which we ought to give to all our population.

This, I call the beginning of a real land policy for the State of New York. As leaders of agriculture and of farm thought in the state, I report it to you and commend it to you for your study.

[Taking a still broader view of the agricultural problem, Governor Roosevelt addressed the Conference of Governors on June 2, 1931, in a speech entitled 'Acres Fit and Unfit: State Planning of Land Use for Industry and Agriculture.' In this document, from which extracts are given here, is to be found a consideration of the vital relations between the two branches of our national economy, a larger program, and a specification of measures already taken or in process of realization in the State of New York.]

At a time when our country, in common with most of the rest of the world [said Governor Roosevelt], is suffering from a severe dislocation of economic progress, all of the people are naturally and properly asking questions about state and national navigation. It seems strange to them that, with capacities for production developed to the highest degree the world has ever seen, there should come this severe depression, when many who are anxious to work cannot find food for their families while at the same time there is such a surplus of food supplies and other necessities that those who are growing crops or manufacturing can find no markets.

This situation has suggested to many that some new factor is needed in our economic life and this new factor must come from utilizing our experience and our ingenuity to draft and to organize concerted plans for the better use of our resources and the better planning of our social and economic life in general.

It is not enough to talk about being of good cheer. Frankly, I cannot take the Pollyanna attitude as a solution of our problems. It is not enough to apply old remedies. A new economic and social balance calls for positive leadership and definite experiments which have not hitherto been tried.

Our country was of necessity developed in a highly individualistic way. Hardy and determined men went into a new wilderness to carve out homes, to gain a living for their families, and to build a future for their race. But the settling of all the land on the continent, the development of a highly organized system of industry, and the growth of a huge population have created new and highly complicated problems. In times of booming industry we can overlook defects of organization and danger signals from industry and agriculture, but in times such as the present these symptoms attain a new importance and show us the urgency of the new problems we have to face.

More and more, those who are the victims of dislocations and defects of our social and economic life are beginning to ask respectfully, but insistently, of us who are in positions of public responsibility why government cannot and should not act to protect its citizens from disaster. I believe the question demands an answer and that the ultimate answer is that government, both state and national, must accept the responsibility of doing what it can do — soundly with considered forethought, and along definitely constructive, not passive, lines.

These lines fall naturally into a number of main heads, such, for instance, as a scientific tariff aimed primarily to create a movement of world commodities from one nation to another; such, for instance, as a better thought-out system of national taxation than we have at the present; such, for instance, as a survey and plan to cut the excessive cost of local government; such, for instance, as the extension of the principle of insurance to cover fields of sickness and of unemployment which are not now reached; such, for instance, as the problem of a dislocation of a proper balance between urban and rural life.

It is this last phase that I am concerned with today and the phrase that best covers all its aspects is 'Land Utilization and State Planning.'

Land utilization involves more than a mere determination of what each and every acre of land can best be used for, or what crops it can best grow. That is the first step; but having made that determination, we arrive at once at the larger problem of getting men, women, and children — in other words, population — to go along with a program and carry it out.

It is not enough to pass resolutions that land must, or should, be used for some specific purpose; government itself must take steps with the approval of the governed, to see that plans become realities.

This, it is true, involves such mighty factors as the supply and not the oversupply of agricultural products; it involves making farm life far more attractive both socially and economically than it is today; it involves the possibilities of creating a new classification of our population.

We know from figures a century ago seventy-five per cent of the population lived on farms and twenty-five per cent in cities. Today the figures are exactly reversed. A generation ago there was much talk of a back-to-the-farm movement. It is my thought that this slogan is outworn. Hitherto, we have spoken of two types of living and only two — urban and rural. I believe we can look forward to three rather than two types in the future, for there is a definite place for an intermediate type between the urban and the rural, namely, a rural-industrial group.

I can best illustrate the beginnings of the working out of the problem by reviewing briefly what has been begun in the State of New York during the past three years towards planning for a better use of our agricultural, industrial, and human resources.

The State of New York has definitely undertaken this as a governmental responsibility. Two and a half years ago the state administration, realizing that the maladjustment of the relationship between rural and city life had reached alarming proportions, undertook a study of the agricultural situation with the immediate purpose of relieving impossible and unfair economic conditions on the farms of the state, but with the broader ultimate purpose of formulating a well thought out and scientific plan for developing a permanent agriculture.

The immediate situation was met by the enactment of several types of laws that resulted in the relief of farms from an uneven tax burden and made a net saving to agricultural communities of approximately twenty-four million dollars a year.

First, the state adopted additional state aid for rural education especially in the communities which are so sparsely settled that one-room schools predominate. This state aid gave the smaller rural schools the same advantages already enjoyed by the schools in the large communities.

Second, by a fair equalization of state aid to towns for the maintenance of dirt roads, putting this aid on the basis of mileage rather than on a basis of assessed valuation, thereby running strictly contrary to the old Biblical formula of 'To him who hath shall be given.'

Third, through the gasoline tax additional aid is given to the counties for the development of a definite system of farm-to-market roads.

Fourth, the state is embarked on a definite program of securing cheaper electricity for the agricultural communities. We propose to harness the St. Lawrence River as a part of this program, and the electricity developed is by the new law intended primarily for the farmer, the household user, and small industrialist or storekeeper rather than for large industrial plants.

This was the program to relieve immediate needs, but it has rapidly developed into something which is far deeper and far more important for the future, in other words, state planning. We have felt that if city planning and even county planning are worth while, how much more important is it that the state as a whole should adopt a permanent program both social and economic and statewide in its objectives. In all of this work, it is worth recording that not only the immediate program but also the long-time planning is being worked out in a wholly non-partisan manner. It has, of course, received the benefits of study by the legislature and legislative commissions. Much of the program has been worked out by the Governor's Agricultural Advisory Commission. This Commission consists of representatives of the great farm organizations such as the Grange, the Farm and Home Bureau, Master Farmers, the Dairymen's League, the G.F.L., members of the Legislature, representatives of state colleges and various departments of the state government. It received the hearty coöperation of the Mayors' Conference, and unselfish business men who are willing to give thought to the future of the state and country.

This state program calls for an intensive development of the good land. For the farms that are on a permanent basis, we have definitely embarked on a policy of providing a farm-to-market road that is passable at all times, available electric power, telephone lines, hospital facilities, and a good high school. We believe that as a general state policy, it is better, under present day conditions, to provide these services and use the good land intensively rather than attempt to use the sub-marginal land.

A good many people, I find, from different parts of the country, visualize the State of New York as consisting primarily of the City of New York, but it is worth while remembering, I think, that nearly six million people in the state live outside of that city, and it is worth while remembering, I think, that New York has always ranked high among the states of the Union in the total value of its agricultural products. In recent years we have ranked somewhere between third and seventh in that value among all the states in the Union, and this in spite of the fact that the State of New York is only twenty-ninth in area.

In spite of this high rank in agriculture, we believe that there is still a large amount of land now being tilled that is better suited for other purposes than for farming.

When we came to the definite acceptance of responsibility for state planning, the first obvious step was to find out what the land area of the state consisted of. I am going somewhat into detail for my colleagues on this for the reason that a great many other states are beginning to embark on the same kind of program, reforestation, drainage, all looking toward the proper use of land, but I hope you will bear in mind that all of this planning for the details dovetails into the larger ultimate picture.

We know, for example, that out of thirty million acres, three million were in cities, villages, residential, and industrial areas; five million were in mountains and forests, and, by the way, of this five million the state itself has about two million acres of the great Adirondack and Catskill preserves; four million were once farmed but are now abandoned, leaving a total of eighteen million acres for agriculture, divided into one hundred and sixty thousand farms.

The first definite step was to start a survey of the entire state. This involved a study of all the physical factors both above and below the surface of the soil, and a study of economic and social factors, such as market possibilities, what the area is now being used for, for what it is best adapted, and how people live, and so detailed that it gives separate data for each ten acre square. Already one whole county has been thus surveyed and we expect to cover the entire eighteen million acres involved within the next ten years or less.

Why is this survey being made? We are proceeding on the assumption that good economics require the use of good materials. For example, fifty years ago, the State of New York every year mined thousands of tons of iron ore and turned it into iron and steel. The discovery and development of vast fields of a more economical grade of iron ore in Minnesota and other sections of the country forced the closing of the New York State iron mines. The raw materials didn't meet the economic standard. By the same token it may have been profitable when land was first cleared to farm this land, but today, with the tremendous competition of good land in this country and in other parts of the world it has become uneconomical to use land which does not produce good crops.

Therefore, we propose to find out exactly what every

part of the state is capable of producing. From the surveys already made we have come to the belief that a certain percentage of the farm land in the state now under cultivation ought to be abandoned for agricultural purposes. I shouldn't be surprised if that percentage ran as high as somewhere between twenty and twenty-five per cent. We are faced with a situation of hundreds of farmers attempting to farm under conditions where it is impossible to maintain an American standard of living. They are slowly breaking their hearts, their health, and their pocketbooks against a stone wall of impossibilities and yet they produce enough farm products to add to the national surplus; furthermore, their products are of such low quality that they injure the reputation and usefulness of the better class of farm products of the state which are produced, packed, shipped, along modern economic lines.

If this is true in the State of New York, it is, I am convinced, equally true of practically every other state east of the Mississippi and of at least some of the states west of the Mississippi.

What then are we to do with this sub-marginal land that exists in every state which ought to be withdrawn from agriculture? Here we have a definite program. First, we are finding out what it can best be used for. At the present time it seems clear that the greater part of it should be put into a different type of crop — one which will take many years to harvest but one which, as the years go by, will, without question, be profitable and at the same time economically necessary — the growing of crops of trees.

This we are starting by a new law providing for the purchase and reforesting of these lands in a manner approved by the state, part of the cost being borne by the county and part by the state. Furthermore, a constitutional amendment will be voted on by the people this autumn providing for appropriations of twenty million dollars over an eleven-year period to make possible the purchase and reforestation of over one million acres of land, which is better suited for forestry than for agriculture.

We visualized also the very definite fact that the use of this sub-marginal agricultural land for forestry will, in the long run, pay for itself (we will get that twenty million dollars back many times over) and will from the very start begin to yield dividends in the form of savings from waste. For instance, the farms to be abandoned will eliminate the necessity of maintaining hundreds and even thousands of miles of dirt roads leading to these farms, the maintenance cost of which averages about one hundred dollars a mile a year. The reforestation of these farms eliminates the need for providing thousands of miles of electric light and telephone lines reaching out into uneconomical territory. The reforestation of these farms will eliminate the existence and upkeep of many small scattered one-room schools which cost approximately fourteen hundred each per year to the state government.

That is why we are confident that over a period of years this state planning will more than pay for itself in a financial saving to the population as a whole.

Modern society moves at such an intense pace that greater recreation periods are needed, and at the same time our efficiency, state and national, in production is such that more time can be used for recreation. That is increasingly evident in this particular year. By reforestation, this land can be turned into a great state resource which will yield dividends at once. The Conservation Commissioner has just issued an order throwing open for hunting and fishing the twenty-five thousand acres recently purchased under this program and all additional reforestation areas when they are purchased.

These reforested areas are largely at the higher eleva-
tions at the headwaters of streams. Reforestation will
regulate stream flow, aid in preventing floods, and provide
a more even supply of pure water for villages and cities.

We are asked what will be done for the population now
residing on these sub-marginal lands? The answer is
twofold: In the first place, most of the comparatively
small number of people on these farms which are to be
abandoned will be absorbed into the better farming areas
of the state, and, in the second place, we are continuing
the idea of the state-wide plan by studying the whole
future population trend. That is where there is a definite
connection between the city dweller and the population
engaged in industry, between the rural dweller and the
city dweller, between the farmer and the people engaged
in industry.

Experiments have already been made in some states
looking to a closer relationship between industry and
agriculture. These take two forms — first, what may
best be called the bringing of rural life to industry;
second, the bringing of industry to agriculture by the
establishment of small industrial plants in areas which
are now wholly given over to farming.

In this particular connection the State of Vermont
through a splendid commission seems to be taking the lead
in seeking to bring industry to the agricultural regions.

For example, one of the large shoe manufacturing
companies was established in a small New York village.
Many of the workers live in this village and many others
live in the open country within a radius of ten miles or
more. Another example is a valley in Vermont where a
wood-turning factory for the making of knobs for lids
of kettles has already been so successful that the trend
of the rural population to the city has been definitely
stopped and the population of the valley finds that it can
profitably engage in agriculture during the summer with

a definite wage-earning capacity in the local factory turning out kettle knobs during the winter months.

As a nation, we have only begun to scratch the surface along these lines and the possibility of diversifying our industrial life by sending a fair proportion of it into the rural districts is one of the definite possibilities of the future. Cheap electric power, good roads, and automobiles make such a rural industrial development possible.

In other words, there are without question many industries which can succeed just as well, if not better, by bringing them to rural communities and at the same time these rural communities will be given higher annual income capacity. We are restoring the balance.

It is for these reasons that I have spoken so definitely of a third and new type of American life. The rural industrial group. It is my thought that many of the problems of transportation, of overcrowded cities, of high cost of living, of better health for the race, of a better balance of population as a whole, can be solved by the states themselves during the coming generation.

I have said 'by the states themselves' because these experiments should and will be worked out in accordance with conditions which vary greatly in different sections of the country. We should not put all of our eggs into one basket. Some of the state methods of approaching the problem may not be economically sound in the light of future experiences, whereas, others may point the way toward a definite national solution of the problem.

I remember many years ago when James Bryce was Ambassador in Washington, I as a young man had the privilege of attending a dinner, and after dinner the discussion came to the permanence of the American form of government. Lord Bryce, I remember, said this:

The American form of government will go on and live long after most of the other forms of government have fallen or been changed, and the reason is this: In other nations of the world when a new problem comes up it must be tested in a national laboratory, and a solution of the problem must be worked out, and when it is worked out that solution must be applied to the nation as a whole. Sometimes it may be the correct solution and other times it may be the wrong solution. But you, in the United States, have forty-eight laboratories and when new problems arise you can work out forty-eight different solutions to meet the problem. Out of these forty-eight experimental laboratories, some of the solutions may not prove sound or acceptable, but out of this experimentation history shows you have found at least some remedies which can be made so successful that they will become national in their application.

So, as Lord Bryce says, the American people have forty-eight laboratories and with all of that competition and coöperation you stand in no danger of falling before the false solution of problems.

In all of this, the states require, of course, the sympathetic coöperation of the National Government as an information-gathering body. The National Government can well act as a clearing-house for all of us governors to work through and I think that is the correct and most useful function of Washington. Instead of trying to run the whole works and to dictate methods and details to all of the states along some hard-and-fast program which may or may not apply in the different sections of the country, the National Government can help us in the several states to work out solutions which, in the long run, will get us somewhere.

I am very confident that during the next few years state after state will realize, as we have begun to do in New York, that it is a definite responsibility for government itself to reach out for new solutions for new problems. In the long run, state and national planning is an essential to the future prosperity, happiness, and the very existence of the American people.

[Making sharper and more explicit his blue-print of a planned social order, Governor Roosevelt, in an address before the Country Life Conference at Ithaca, in August, 1931, discussed the enormous waste that occurs in the distribution of agricultural produce among and within distant urban centers and presented a scheme for promoting the decentralization of industries by the rehabilitation of rural communities.]

The question I think we need to examine [the Governor said] is whether we can't plan a better distribution of our population as between the larger city and the smaller country communities without any attempt to increase or any thought of increasing the number of those who are engaged in farming as an industry. Is it not possible that we might devise methods by which the farmer's market may be brought closer to him and the industrial worker be brought closer to his food supply? A farm and a rural home are not necessarily the same thing.

Conditions have changed a great deal since the great rush of workers to the cities began. They have changed materially even since the war period. There have been great changes in means of transportation, changes in the conditions surrounding rural life, and changes in industrial methods and facilities, all of which offer enlarged opportunity for rural living.

One of the most significant transformations is that wrought by the automobile and the improvement in highways that has come along as a consequence. It is a familiar fact that distances have been tremendously shortened in terms of time, effort, and expense. Except for such congestion of traffic as one encounters in and about New York City and in a limited area in the heart of other cities, a distance of ten miles has become only the equivalent of a few city squares under old conditions.

Communities once a day's journey apart have become close neighbors.

It is no longer necessary that an industrial worker should live in the shadow of the factory in which he works, and as a matter of fact many of them do not. Especially where factories are situated on the outskirts of cities or in smaller communities, the worker should have a wide range of choice for his home in terms of physical distance.

Industry, too, has been freed of a great many old restrictions as to location. It doesn't need to be located close to a water power, nor does it need to be located in most cases near a fuel supply. High-tension transmission of electric current has opened a new era in the transportation of power. The application of electric current to industrial uses has made other advancements. It is not necessary any longer to use power in large quantities or units to use it effectively. The typical factory of a generation ago had huge steam engines driving great line shafts belted to a multitude of machines. Today in the typical installation every machine unit has its own motor and can be placed where it can be used most effectively and conveniently in the process of manufacture. Enlargement of a factory often can be accomplished merely by adding new machine units. In many lines of manufacture small factories have become more feasible economically than before and some large manufacturing institutions have found it advantageous to erect in scattered localities branch plants where a portion of their manufacturing processes are carried on.

Improvements in transportation, too, have had an effect on factory locations. Railroad facilities have been extended and improved to the advantage of lesser centers of population and in New York we have the great resource of the barge canal which brings cheap heavy transportation to many communities across the entire state, in effect almost making them seaboard points. The automobile, the bus, and the automobile truck have become as important in the transportation of finished products and in some cases of materials as in the movement of workers. Huge vans of manufactured goods travel great distances from factory to market on the public highways.

Communication time between factory and administrative offices and between factory and market has been shortened by telephone improvement and extension, and in this item of administration the automobile and improved highway again play an important part through the means they afford for quick travel from plant to plant and from an administrative center to a plant. Sources of supply of most raw materials, too, have been more widely developed and there is much better organization of facilities for distribution, this in spite of the fact that, in the case of many other products besides those of agriculture, there is still much too great a spread between production costs and consumers' prices due to the product's passing through too many hands from producer to consumer.

All of these circumstances seem to indicate that industry of its own volition is likely to seek decentralization. They seem to point to the probability that we shall see more factories established in smaller communities and in agricultural regions and fewer comparatively in the largest centers and in old manufacturing communities. Already there has been a trend in that direction. Factories have found it profitable to move from New England to the West and South seeking to divorce themselves from conditions for which their own individual management was partly but not exclusively to blame.

Industry has plainly been feeling its way toward something better in the way of factory location and what has been called for lack of a better term a 'labor market,' an expression whose implications I detest for the reason that it seems to ignore all human considerations. One of the difficulties of old-established industry today, I am convinced, is due to the fact that it has too often ignored social considerations, has failed to consider that success in industry must in the long run be built on coöperation of human beings on terms which will give all its workers a chance to live decently.

Certainly we want nothing more to do, if we can help it, with the factory town of the old type with its miserable tenements and boxlike company houses built in grimy rows on dirty streets — abodes of discouragement and misery — although I could point out examples of the sort in our own state.

There is no doubt that social considerations have had a great part in keeping workers in the cities. City life has had its advantages as well as an attractiveness not based on any actual benefits. Our urban civilization is new enough not to have entirely outworn its lure and its novelty for a population that was once predominantly rural. But the advantages of city life today are less comparatively than they were ten years ago and they will probably continue to grow less, for city conveniences are very rapidly being brought to the country.

We have seen how transportation has reduced distances and made rural living practicable today where it was not a generation or more ago, in the days when the pattern of the factory town of the old style was devised. But there are a hundred other things that contribute to the comfort and practicability of rural living. There are electric lights and electric refrigeration, there are new methods of sanitation for rural homes, there are gas and electric cooking, there is the operation of household power machinery; there is the rural delivery of mail, including the parcels post which puts housewives in close touch with distant shops; there are modern consolidated schools

equipped to supply as good primary- and high-school
education as can be had in the city; there are rural parks
which furnish better playgrounds than city people can
enjoy; there are the radio and the rural moving-picture
house showing the same films that the city workers enjoy,
and there is the opportunity for a freer and more natural
community life than can be found in the city streets.

The country has added advantages that the city cannot
duplicate in opportunities for healthful and natural living.
There is space freedom and room for free movement.
There is contact with earth and with nature and the rest-
ful privilege of getting away from pavements and from
noise. There is an opportunity for permanency of abode,
a chance to establish a real home in the traditional
American sense.

But, more than all this, there would be the great advantages for the worker of the opportunity to live far
more cheaply and with a greater degree of economic security. The materials for healthful living in the country
are cheap and abundant. Established in a country home
in an agricultural district the worker, even if he were to
grow nothing for himself, could buy a week's supply of
healthful food for little more than a day's supply would
cost him in the city.

With a considerable movement of workers from city to
country there is every reason to believe that the total consumption of agricultural products would be greatly increased. City workers pay sixteen cents for a quart of
milk for which the farmer receives just now about three.
It is well known by health authorities that the city consumption of milk is far less than it should be, that adults
and children alike of workers' families would be healthier
if they could afford to use more of it. The city price of
one quart would buy them at least three in the country.
Vegetables whose city price is made up mainly of the
costs of many handlings could be obtained with like sav-

ings. City workers do not eat enough fresh green vegetables, mainly because they cannot afford them. Many families have them no oftener than twice a week when they should have them twice a day, and could have them that often if they were close to the supply.

The condition of the typical city worker is one of speculative living, with practically no safeguards against the disaster of unemployment that has now fallen on so many of his class. I believe our ingenuity ought to be equal to finding a way by which that condition could be swapped for one of stabilized living in a real home in the country.

Today in fact many city workers have become country dwellers. Both our great and our smaller urban communities are spreading out into the country. It is really surprising to find how many of our country villages are largely inhabited by men and women whose business activity is in some fairly distant city. What is painful about this situation is to see in how many cases families are finding rural homes without finding the real advantages of country living. They are paying more than enough for what they need and desire but are not getting it.

When I see the cheaper city type of houses built on narrow lots of some real estate development far out on the highway, many miles from a city limits, it occurs to me that those who have bought them have been betrayed and that there is urgent need of country life planning for city dwellers. Let us cite the instance of a worker in Poughkeepsie who longs for a pleasant home in the country. He listens to the alluring talk of a real estate promoter and goes miles out in the country to buy a lot in a region where land is selling for agricultural purposes for one hundred dollars an acre. An acre is approximately two hundred and eight feet square. The city worker pays five hundred dollars and gets, not an acre, but a plot fifty by one hundred feet, of which it would take eight to make an acre. The gross return to the developer is four thousand dollars for an acre bought for one hundred dollars. Let us hope, for the sake of being charitable, that some considerable part of this four thousand dollars is being spent for development of the property for residential purposes, but even so the man who bought the land is being cheated because he is not getting any of the benefits he should have from a country home. He has bought simply a city lot in rural surroundings. A real estate developer who considered the needs of the people with whom he dealt and who planned wisely could sell full acre plots in such a locality for five hundred dollars each, give them the improvements they ought to have in that location, and still make a handsome profit. That acre would mean eight times as much land as the uninformed buyer now gets.

It seems to me evident that the time has come for public authority to assert jurisdiction over housing conditions in the country and over the character and planning of rural real estate developments. We have precedent for this in the housing and zoning regulations of cities and a beginning of zoning authority in the counties. But I think, with competent advice, we should be able to go much further than this in moving toward an adjustment of the whole problem of distribution of population and the living conditions of workers in the state, which I have been discussing.

With that purpose I propose to appoint a Commission on Rural Homes, to be made up of a group of prominent citizens of the state, all of them having a record of interest in the improvement of social conditions, and to ask the heads of six departments of the state government to serve with them as *ex-officio* members so that advice and data on various phases of the problems to be considered may be made available to the commission. Those whom I have asked and who have consented to serve on this commission include men and women with distinguished records of public service who will bring to their new task experience in dealing with housing problems, with conditions of rural life, and with industrial affairs on a large scale.

The task I am placing before this commission is, broadly, to determine to what extent and by what means the state and its subdivisions may properly stimulate the movement of city workers to rural homes if such a movement seems desirable; to determine what facilities may be furnished by public authority to assist these workers in getting the right kind of homes in the right locations, and to inquire what encouragement may be offered for the movement of industries from urban centers to rural locations or the establishment of new industries in such locations if such a movement of industry seems desirable.

While the commission will govern the course of its own inquiry, I have fixed in my own mind certain definite objectives which will serve to make the undertaking somewhat more concrete. These are:

1. That the commission be prepared to recommend legislation for village, town, and county zoning for the whole state, but on a permissive basis, and for village, town, and county permanent planning commissions.

2. That the commission explore the possibilities of the enlistment of private capital to aid in the establishment of rural homes within a reasonable distance of industry.

3. That the commission make recommendations as to experiment by the state alone or by the state with the coöperation and assistance of private capital in establishing wholly new rural communities of homes for workers on good agricultural land within reasonable distance of which facilities shall be offered for the establishment of new industries aimed primarily to give cash wages on a coöperative basis during the non-agricultural season.

If we find that the movement of workers to rural homes ought to be encouraged, then it seems to me that we ought to find means of meeting the needs of those who wish to establish themselves in the country. Their requirements suggest themselves to me as follows:

1. Information as to the right type of home to build.
2. Guidance and assistance in obtaining the most economical use of funds in acquisition and construction.
3. Advice as to the right area of land to be acquired.
4. Assistance in financing.

The question how best to establish agencies for providing service along this line is within the scope of the commission's task and problem as I have outlined it. I have no doubt that many specific plans for the establishment and organization of rural communities, extending possibly even to suitable types of architecture, lay-outs of roads and sanitary facilities, planting schemes and methods of community coöperation, will be suggested to the commission. These should furnish valuable data for such temporary or permanent agencies as may be set up as a result of the commission's recommendations.

It will be borne in mind that the objective is to furnish rural homes of an inexpensive sort for unemployed workers and those of small earnings, not to provide for the needs of those who are able to invest ten thousand to fifteen thousand dollars in a country home.

I think I scarcely need to say that this plan doesn't contemplate any coercive use of state power or any attempt to force either industry or private citizens into a fixed pattern of conduct. On the contrary, it involves merely coöperative planning for the common good. In that coöperating planning it will be essential, naturally, to seek the advice of thoughtful industrial leaders on the trends of industry as to location, character, and seasons of employment, and to seek the advice of representatives of labor on other features of the proposal.

I shall ask the commission to report to me about

December 1, so that legislation which may be proposed may be placed before the legislature at the beginning of the regular session in January. I shall be prepared to recommend not only legislation but an appropriation if that is found desirable.

While the membership of this commission is representative of the highest type of citizenship and of the sort of expert knowledge that, it seems to me, ought to be brought to bear on the solution of these great questions, I hope sincerely that the problem will not be regarded even for the moment as theirs and mine exclusively. I count upon their being able to call freely on others for advice and aid. I have learned in my own experience that there is a wealth of wisdom and good counsel and willingness to serve the public interest available to any administrator of public affairs who will but ask for it and I expect this commission to be the beneficiaries of that same generous spirit.

Chapter XI

THE STATE PLAN OF
GOVERNOR PHILIP F. LA FOLLETTE[1]

Fellow Citizens of the Legislature:

You have been summoned in extraordinary session to deal with an extraordinary emergency.

We are in the midst of the greatest domestic crisis since the Civil War. In this crisis, people are divided broadly into two groups: one opposes, and one favors, collective action to meet the emergency and to guard against its recurrence in the future.

Those who oppose collective action base their argument on the supposition that any such action would hamper the return of normal conditions in business; they are apprehensive of the interference of government in its conduct. They point to governmental corruption in some of the states, municipalities, and in certain phases of the National Government. This group insists that if business is given an opportunity, it will put its own house in order and restore normal conditions.

Certain business and industrial leaders have taken intelligent and courageous positions for which they are entitled to high commendation. But throughout the nation, business as a whole has failed to put its house in order, either with reference to the immediate depression or with reference to the adoption of safeguards against a recurrence.

The people have in the past allowed capital to have control of our business machine as well as to receive the larger portion of the financial return from its operation. But capital cannot justly expect to remain in control of

[1] Message to the Wisconsin Legislature on Tuesday, November 24, 1931.

both management and the lion's share of financial return if it is not willing to assume the responsibility of keeping that machine in operation.

For ten years our business system has tolerated the deflation of agriculture. For over two years the same process has been doing its work in our cities. For at least two years this system has had every justification for vigorous and energetic action. With a few outstanding exceptions it not only has failed to act, but is making the same arguments of delay and procrastination today that it made in November, 1929.

Business and industry cannot longer expect the public to wait for them to act.

In 1929, the top rung of our federal financial ladder, comprising 504 individuals, reported net incomes of over two million dollars per return. The next rung, numbering 101,000, reported net incomes of sixty-eight thousand dollars per return. These two groups represent the upper crust of our business and industrial ownership. To put the matter plainly, they are not worth to our society two million dollars a year, or even sixty-eight thousand dollars per year, for the kind of leadership they have given us.

Their policy has been tried for two years. It has failed to produce the desired results. They cannot justly blame the rest of society for insisting that its one agency for collective action — namely, government — begin to grapple with the problem.

In order to grapple with this or any other problem, we must first try to understand it.

We have at least one hundred and thirty thousand people in Wisconsin who are completely out of work, and some fifty thousand or more who have only partial employment; at least one hundred thousand farmers in Wisconsin are in financial distress. Thus, one third to one half of our population is at various stages ranging from hunger to the pressing danger of losing homes and farms.

A cursory glance at either agriculture or industry alone gives a picture which might lead one to the conclusion that our problem is one of overproduction. We find the farmer with more products than he can sell. We find the factories shut down because they cannot sell what they make.

But on closer examination we find literally millions of men and women in our cities actually hungry for the products that the farmer cannot sell; we find literally millions of farm homes without the conveniences or comforts produced by our factories.

It is true that industry and agriculture thus both have large stocks of goods which they cannot sell and which are labeled 'surpluses.' There is a vital difference, however, between a surplus which represents goods that cannot be consumed, and a surplus which represents goods that cannot be purchased. At the present time, broadly speaking, our surpluses have resulted from the inability of the consuming public to purchase what they need. They are not surpluses arising because the people have more to eat, more to wear, more to use than they want and need. The farmer cannot find a market for his food products, and suffers for want of industrial products. Millions of industrial workers and their families are in actual want for the very products which the farmer cannot sell....

It is clear that there is nothing wrong with our power of production. We have created a machine on the farm and in the factory that will produce more than enough to sustain us all. This machine has been producing enough to provide the necessities and many of the luxuries of life for one hundred and twenty millions of people. Nothing has destroyed that machine. It could start functioning tomorrow. It would and it will start functioning the moment that the great mass of people can buy and sell the things which they produce.

Our problem arises out of our system of distribution. That system of distribution is founded on the use of money as the medium of exchange. Instead of the farmer exchanging a load of wheat with an individual worker for a piece of farm machinery, the farmer and the worker use money. Since the producers represent at least ninety-five per cent of our population, and since these producers are dependent upon money in order to exchange the products that they need, the problem before us today is the distribution of our medium of exchange so that people can trade with each other.

Putting the problem another way, our industrial and agricultural machine is geared to mass production. Mass production requires mass consumption, and mass consumption requires mass purchasing power.

Analyzing thus the distribution of our purchasing power, have we divided our medium of exchange, money, so that the bulk of people can trade with one another?

The answer is, we have not. Even in the so-called 'boom' period of 1925, the average income of wage-earners in agriculture, merchandising, mining, manufacturing, transportation, construction, government employees, banking, and unclassified was only thirteen hundred and eighty-four dollars per year — or approximately one hundred dollars per month. In the same year 1925 the total income of at least eighty per cent of all of the families in the United States was well under two thousand dollars per year per family.

In 1928, the farmer, representing at least twenty-five per cent of the population, received less than ten per cent of the national income.

The share of the wage-earners and salaried employees in the total production of industry has decreased since 1920. From 1923 to 1927, the total salaries and wages paid in manufacturing industries in this country were practically stationary, while the return to capital increased by about two billion dollars.

In 1920, there were thirty-three people in the United States who reported taxable incomes to the Federal Government of about one million dollars. In 1924, there were seventy-five such million-dollar incomes; in 1929, five hundred and four. In 1929, the five hundred and four persons who had net incomes of one million dollars or more had total incomes of $1,185,100,000, or more than the selling price of all the wheat and all the cotton produced in the United States in 1930.

In 1929, of the four million income-taxpayers reporting to the Federal Government:

Seventy-five per cent received one third of the total reporting income, or approximately twenty-seven hundred dollars per return;

Twenty-one per cent received one third of the total reporting income, or approximately ten thousand dollars per return;

Two and one half per cent received twenty-eight per cent of the total reporting income, or approximately sixty-eight thousand dollars per return;

One tenth of one per cent received four and eight tenths per cent of the total reporting income, or approximately two million dollars per return.

These figures show that year after year the rich have grown richer, and the poor poorer. Putting it another way, a small class of our population have each year received far more income than they have been able to spend. This has gone on to a point where now a small group have such a 'corner' on the medium of exchange, money, that the rest of us cannot get enough money to trade with each other. Being unable to trade with one another, each of us has a 'surplus' of our own particular product, but famishes for the products of our neighbor.

Those who are receiving these large incomes are able to

spend only a small part of what they receive. They cannot use, relatively, more food or clothes or other necessities of life than the rest of us. So being unable to use any large part of their incomes for buying the production of the factory or the farm, they use the unexpended income to buy more factories and farms from the rest of us who have grown too poor to own them. Or they use part of their incomes to build more factories and machines than are actually needed. It is this investment of unexpendable incomes in new productive equipment that is largely responsible for whatever over-building of plants and machines that exists. And it likewise explains in large part why American capital has invested some fifteen thousand millions of dollars outside of the United States. If these great incomes were actually expended here in America, the money might find its way back to the producers and consumers. But it has not been so spent; instead, it has been used to buy ownership of property not only here, but all over the world.

The rich, being unable to spend the income they have been receiving, have been using their unexpendable income to acquire more property, which in turn, like a rolling snowball, again increases their already unexpendable income. It is this condition which has brought about a situation where three great holding companies control our electricity; where one corporation owns more than half of the country's iron resources; where one corporation controls more than ninety per cent of the world's nickel resources; where four great concerns control the major portion of the country's copper; where eight concerns closely allied with the railroads own nearly eighty per cent of the nation's coal; where two corporations control over half of the steel; where two concerns own and control over half of the meat packing; where one per cent of the banks control ninety-nine per cent of the banking resources; and so on.

The monopoly system has at last acquired ownership of so much of our wealth, thereby receiving such a tremendous proportion of the medium of exchange, that the rest of us cannot do business with each other.

The World War is correctly cited as one of the prime causes of the present depression. This, in my opinion, is correct because during the three years of the World War there was a greater concentration of wealth than in any other single period in our history. There was, following the World War, a pick-up in business conditions, which we now see to have been an inflation period. It is quite possible that we may have another such period. Such temporary pick-ups can be effected through pledging of credit, as was done during the World War. But when the repayment of that credit is imposed upon the great masses of people, as was done by our methods of war financing, or by extending the installment-buying plan to every form of short-lived product, it merely accelerates this unsound distribution of purchasing power.

Our problem is the redistribution of our purchasing power to enable our population to receive enough of the medium of exchange, money, to do business.

In trying to solve this problem, both in the present emergency and in the future, it is apparent that we need action by the National Government. Approximately eighty per cent of the net incomes reported for income-tax purposes is paid in only nine states, although much of it was derived in the other thirty-nine states. Thus New York State alone receives approximately thirty-three per cent of the total net income above the subsistence level. For a century, through a policy of internal improvements, tariffs, and taxation, we have deliberately encouraged the growth of a national economic life. It is not sheer perversity that makes many of us urge that a like system for distributing wealth and economic power on a national basis be put in action in the present national and international depression.

But because that national system, both political and economic, has not acted, and apparently does not intend to act, does not relieve us of the responsibility of using every possible effective course within our own control. If we are reasonably certain that we understand our problem and its causes, we can then at least see that every part of the program which we adopt for dealing with it is kept in the right direction. While our action alone will not remedy the situation nationally, or even within our state, we shall know that our action will help and that we are on the right road and will not have to retrace our steps.

It is just as important to understand our remedy as it is to understand the problem for which we are devising it.

At the time of the formation of our government this country was primarily agricultural. In a country which is primarily agricultural, each individual is largely self-sustaining. *He does not have to trade with someone else.* All he requires is a sufficient degree of political government to give him security. With the introduction of machinery following the industrial revolution, our whole economic system has changed. Few, if any of us, are self-sustaining; we have become specialists; we have to trade with one another in order to live.

The men who founded our government devised a system which was highly satisfactory as a political instrument. They did not devise a government with broad economic powers; but in their far-sighted wisdom they did recognize that the one permanent thing in human society is change. They created a system in which that change could take place peacefully and as the result of intelligent action.

They recognized that human experience teaches us that the progress of mankind in every field and at every point has been advanced by the spark of some individual initiative and vision. They devised a society which gave to the individual the greatest freedom and initiative ever vouchsafed him in all human experience. No careful student can seriously question that the development of this country has been more largely due to this than to any other single human factor.

At the time of the formation of our republic a very small fraction of the population in the other countries of the world — the nobility — had the extreme degree of liberty, namely, license to do what they pleased, but the great bulk of human beings in all of these countries had no liberty whatever. The founders of our republic recognized that in order to give liberty to the great mass of human beings, there had to be restraints and controls upon the selfish and powerful few.

Today a small fraction of our population at the very top have complete economic license to do as they please, but the vast proportion of our people are without adequate economic liberty. The passing of free land in 1890 closed the only door of escape for the mass of people. Unless our generation devises some economic control, some reasonable restraints, we shall have missed both the opportunity and the crying need of our time.

As we look over the world today, we see other nations devising this machinery for economic government. Unfortunately for the progress of the world, most of those attempts are duplicates in the economic field of the political autocracy that prevailed a century ago. We in America should blaze a trail in this economic field as we did in the political field; we should devise instrumentalities for the control of our economic life that will be democratic and in keeping with the experience and traditions of our republic.

I suggest four definite courses that we may pursue:

(1) The direct control and ownership by the people through their municipal, state, and national governments of enough of those instruments of common necessity to pro-

tect the public against extortionate charges, to ensure
efficient service, and, to the extent of the ownership thus
to effect a better distribution of the earning power of
those facilities.

(2) The provision of machinery by the state that will enable
business — and I use business in its largest sense — to
govern itself. I am not here suggesting that the state
should take over the problem of running business. I am
urging that the state enable business to govern itself intelligently, reserving at all times to the Government both
the power and the duty to protect the public from extortion or from combinations for other than sound public
purposes.

(3) The provision of machinery for undertaking and carrying
on the profound research we need as a society; for the
taking of economic and social counsel, and the definite
attempt to plan continuously both for the present and
the future of our communities.

(4) The equalization of the burden of taxation. The intelligent and courageous use of the taxing power is the most effective thing that can be done immediately in the present
emergency. The taxing power is organized and established. We do not have to wait to devise and establish it.
Taxes represent the largest single expenditure for farmers
and for many of our workers who own homes. The use of
the taxing power in those states that have been far-sighted
enough to adopt income and inheritance taxes is an effective instrument with which to redistribute money to
enable workers and farmers to trade with one another. If
the Federal Government would adopt the financial
measures recommended in this message for Wisconsin, it
would at once redistribute over two and a quarter billions
of dollars of purchasing power, which would be almost
the identical sum by which wages and the same sum by
which farm prices have been deflated since 1929....

There will be introduced into both houses of the Legislature proposed laws, which, taken together, present a
definite and specific program for dealing with the present

emergency and for devising instrumentalities for the future. These measures, coupled with what legislation has already been adopted by you, would if enacted into law lay the foundations for a definite attempt upon our part to meet the demands of our time, so far as it lies within our power to act within a single state and one session of the Legislature.

This program divides itself naturally into two parts: that dealing with the present emergency and that relating to an effort on our part to begin to lay down safeguards against recurrences of depressions such as the present one.

Our first responsibility is to enable the towns, cities, villages, and countries of this state to provide the necessities of life for our fellow citizens who are in want. These people cannot wait while we create some ideal system of distribution of either income or the necessities of life. It seems to me clear, therefore, that we must use the local governmental agencies already established, reserving to the state supervisory control over the funds which it provides.

The towns, cities, villages, and counties of this state will expend approximately six million dollars more for providing food, shelter, and clothing for our needy citizens this year than it was necessary to provide in 1928....

I recommend that this Legislature immediately appropriate three million dollars to be paid to the several towns, cities, villages, and counties of the state as they submit evidence to the state of the excess of their 1931 expenditures for relief over 1928, thus providing each town, city, village, and county immediately with one half of the excess of 1931 over 1928.

I recommend an appropriation of another three million dollars to the towns, cities, villages, and counties of the state to be paid to them upon a showing to the state of their compliance with such reasonable standards as the State may provide.

It is far preferable to provide work than to provide charity, whether public or private. It is therefore sound and proper that the State should provide that its funds should be used:

(a) Preferably for the direct labor costs of public works, not exceeding fifty per cent of the entire cost of the project.

(b) For poor relief when public works cannot be practicably provided.

(c) Subject to requirements that will provide work for citizens of our own state under proper working conditions and standards.

In order to provide for special emergencies in those localities where the burden now is or may become excessive, I recommend an appropriation of one million dollars to an agency of the state to be used as a fund to provide relief in localities which find themselves in special distress.

Just as many of us feel that it is a glaring injustice to impose the cost of this national emergency upon a locality irrespective of its wealth, and are convinced that we should meet the problem as a nation with all of the sources of national wealth being required to bear a proportionate cost of the burden, so we feel that, even with the failure of the National Government to act, we as a state should apply the same fundamental principle, namely, that this emergency will be met as a community and that those who are best able to carry the burden shall carry a proportionate amount of it.

It thus becomes manifest that if the total relief burden of this depression amounts to some twelve millions of dollars, the state should provide additional aid for the reduction of taxes upon general property. Since the tax-rolls for the towns, cities, and villages have already been made up, the best and fairest method of affording tax reduction to the individual taxpayer in 1932 is for the state to appropriate funds to the several counties to enable them to reduce their county tax....

In order to enable the towns, cities, villages, and counties of this state to build in this period of low prices and to provide work rather than charity, I recommend the revision and amendment of the existing statutes with relation to bonding to enable the several localities to issue promptly, if they so desire, their general bonds for relief and for public works. However, before such bonds can actually be sold, I recommend that each locality be required to submit the definite project to be thus financed to an agency of the state in order that the state may be assured that the project is necessary and economical and will afford the maximum of employment for the dollar expended, and likewise in order that the state may be assured as nearly as practicable that such bonds can be retired without increasing the tax upon general property. The state should appropriate a sum sufficient to enable the state to aid localities in the doing of such works.

In everything that has been done publicly or privately, the younger unmarried man has been overlooked. We have some twenty-five thousand of these younger unmarried and unemployed men in Wisconsin. I do not need to point out that they are quite as important a part of our citizenship as any other element, and in some ways they are more important for the future than those who are older. Many of them have had less experience with life and are in their formative years. It would be both cruel and unwise to neglect them. I know that it will appeal to the people of this state if we make a constructive effort to make some provision for them. It is not possible for us within our financial means to provide work for them all in public works.

We have, however, a vast area in northern Wisconsin that is in urgent need of reforestation and better fire protection. If we can induce some substantial part of these younger men to coöperate with the state in the doing of this necessary and valuable public work, we may be able to do something for them and a great deal for the future spiritual and material wealth of Wisconsin. At my request a tentative program has been prepared. If these younger men are willing to help the state in this long-time enterprise, the state could, within our financial means, provide them the necessities of life and a modest wage in this emergency. It will be impracticable to commence this work, however, until early spring. The principal educators of the state have coöperated in devising a plan for a combination of vocational education and non-competitive works during the winter — that is, upon public works that are desirable, but which the localities and the state could not expect to finance in a competitive market at the present time....

Large numbers of owners of our farms and homes are laboring under great difficulty in keeping those homes with lack of or decreased income, and I therefore recommend, under reasonable safeguards, that the period of redemption in the foreclosure of mortgages and land contracts may be extended in the discretion of the courts on proper showing during this emergency.

Every thoughtful person sees the relationship between the hours of labor and the present depression. Hours of labor are another way of expressing income. The changes that have taken place from doing the world's work by hand to doing it by machine ought to have meant a lessening in the total amount of work that we all have to do. But each individual industrial plant, operating as it does without general economic government, is forced to look upon each new invention, not as a labor-saving device, but as a money-making device. This is why in the thirty-year period from 1899 to 1929 there has been a decrease of only about fifteen per cent in the hours of labor while our production has increased nearly one hundred per cent. We can no longer proceed with the idea that technological changes — that is, the invention of new labor-saving machinery which displaces hundreds of thousands of men — can be entirely ignored as of no public concern.

I am not saying that it is desirable or feasible that we should seek to discourage socially sound inventions. I do mean that, in considering a labor-saving invention, there is no ultimate social or economic gain if the man power displaced from a private industry is shifted to public or private charity.

We must find some basic principle that will act as a guide in this problem of machine production. We have such a principle in relation to taxation, namely, that taxes should be levied in accordance with ability to pay them. Wisconsin's definite attempt to apply that principle to the operation of its government during the past thirty years enables this state to face the present emergency in a better financial condition with less of a tax burden upon those least able to bear it than any other state in America today. If we could find some basic principle to apply to this problem of both cyclical and technological unemployment, it would be an outstanding achievement.

Such a principle has been suggested. That principle succinctly stated is this: that as an economic society we should adopt the standard that whatever work there is to be done shall be done by all of us; if we have a large volume, we all can work more; if we have a smaller volume, we all will do less. We will not willingly submit to a system that makes the farmer work fifteen hours a day while others have no work at all. It is based on our unwillingness to permit to grow up in our society a system which has half of us at work and half of us idle. The application of such a principle in times such as these would mean that those who are now fully employed would have to share that employment with others less fortunate.

But the application of this principle should not and does not mean that anyone should be permitted to work for less than a living wage. Through the application of the principle of collective bargaining, labor has been able to gain for itself substantial recognition of its rights. At the present time many of those standards are being broken down or endangered through the enormous numbers of unemployed who in desperation are ready to accept work upon any terms. Nothing will do more toward protecting labor's achievements than steps that will help to put people back to work.

We are definitely committed and strongly in favor of the principle of collective bargaining. Just as we are not in favor of the Government taking the responsibility of running business, so we are not in favor of Government unnecessarily taking the responsibility of fixing wages. Our problem is to devise machinery that will enable both labor and business to govern themselves, and protect their rights and interests.

Up to the present time our industrial system has been operated with the machine as the central point. We have regulated our shifts, our hours, our whole plant operations in order that the machine could function at its maximum point of efficiency. It seems clear to me that we have to shift that point from the machine to the human beings that operate it; instead of figuring how human beings must work in order to keep the machinery operating, we must figure how we must run the machinery to keep the men at work. Courageous and intelligent industrial leadership has already demonstrated, not only the human value in such a program, but that it pays as an economic venture in ensuring mass consumption.

In order to put this program into action, it requires that business shall be able reasonably and accurately to estimate the demand for its product over a given period. It can then regulate the hours of employment of those normally employed in the industry so as to provide regular and continuous employment. Wage and working standards won by labor would not then be ruthlessly menaced or destroyed by wholesale discharging of employees.

There is no group more interested in or concerned about the problem of unemployment and fluctuations in the business cycle than intelligent business management itself, and there is in my mind a difference between both the attitude and the understanding of our problems on the part of those who are actively engaged in and have the responsibility for business management and those whose only connection with or interest in the business system is solely their ownership of stocks and bonds.

The problem that faces intelligent business management in any attempt to cope with this underlying matter is the lack of any adequate machinery for self-government. Instance after instance could be cited where seventy-five per cent of both the plants and the volume of a given industry were clearly satisfied as to the public necessity of a given course of action only to be frustrated by the selfishness or lack of understanding of a very small minority within that industry.

I am convinced that we have reached the time where we must help business to devise machinery to stabilize itself, for the better protection of the rights of labor and the public interest generally.

A part of the program to be presented to you provides for the creation of Chapter 109 of the Statutes, relating to the stabilization of employment. The purposes of this Act are well summarized in its introductory clause, which reads:

The purpose of this chapter is to promote the stabilization of industry and thereby to prevent the widespread distress and resulting great public expense incident to the ruthless discharge of workmen when industrial depression curtails demand or when improved machinery or processes are introduced. It is declared to be the duty of employers to do everything possible within their control to give steady and full-time employment, and, when this is not possible, to reduce hours of labor so as to equitably distribute the available work. It is the further purpose of this chapter to enable employers to meet this obligation through combinations and joint action, with safeguards to prevent unreasonable restraints of trade.

Section 109.08 would authorize, subject to the approval of the Executive Council and on recommendation of the Department of Agriculture and Markets, 'any group of employers in the same industry or community' to 'associate themselves in a board of trade' for the purpose of stabilizing employment. This section proposes to enable employers in the same industry or community to create, subject to the supervision of the state, organizations for their own self-government. They may establish rules and regulations and agreements for the stabilization of their industry.

Section 109.09 would provide that every such organization shall have a public policy committee consisting of not less than three members who are selected to represent the interest of the consumers, employees, and other groups distinct from, but affected by, the operation of the board of trade.

Section 109.10 would provide that on the direction of the Governor or of either house of the Legislature or on recommendation of the public policy committee of any board of trade that such organization is not functioning in the public interest, the Department of Agriculture and Markets shall conduct a public hearing to determine whether the approval of the state should be withdrawn.

If after such hearing the Department determines that the board has not in good faith complied with the purposes of the chapter, or is not functioning in the public interest, the approval of the state is then to be withdrawn.

Section 109.11 would provide that, so long as such an organization is acting under the approval of the state, that fact shall be *prima-facie* evidence that it is not violating the anti-trust laws of this state, and that such organization, in the event of prosecution under the federal laws, so long as it has approval of the state, shall have the support of the state in any such prosecution.

Sections 109.02 to 109.07 would provide that the Industrial Commission of this state shall from time to time regulate and fix by order the hours of industries and occupations so as to protect the employee and the public from the effects of both cyclical and technological unemployment. However, those employers who in good faith take advantage of the state's offer to assist them in governing themselves are exempted from the provisions. Thus, by this measure the state would aid and encourage industry in its own self-government. In connection with those individual employers or industries which are unwilling to accept any responsibility for their own stabilization, the state, through the Industrial Commission, would undertake the regulation of the hours of employment to equalize as nearly as practicable the effects of both technological and cyclical unemployment.

I do not suggest that we have in some miraculous fashion discovered a cure-all for the problem of unemployment. I do maintain that the only way we have made any progress in the past is from our experience. Out of the experience of recent years we have learned certain things which indicate that certain steps are now necessary. I have no doubt that, as we try the program which we are indicating, we shall discover both weaknesses and strengths where we did not expect to find them. But we shall never discover anything or make any progress unless we try.

During the first nine months of 1930, our national industrial and business system was able to and did pay $432,000,000 more in dividends and $191,000,000 more in interest than it did in 1929; in the first nine months of 1931, the second year of the depression, it paid $374,000,-000 more in dividends and $338,000,000 more in interest than it did in the first nine months of 1929. In the first nine months of 1929, the total interest and dividends paid was $5,559,000,000, while in the first nine months of 1931, the second year of the business depression, it paid $6,279,000,000 in interest and dividends. Our business and industrial machine was able to pay $720,000,000 more in interest and dividends in the first nine months of 1931 than it paid in the first nine months of 1929. A substantial portion of both the interest and dividends paid in 1930 and 1931 has been paid out of reserves built up for those purposes. Business and industry have, then, felt an obligation to and have built up reserves in times of prosperity to meet the obligations of interest and dividends.

The great bulk of industry has not built up these reserves for unemployment in the past. The question of unemployment compensation relates, then, solely to what is to be done as to future depressions. No voluntary or compulsory plan adopted at this time can affect the present unemployment. Whatever is done now will be done as a safeguard for the future, not the present.

The majority of those in control of industry are strongly opposed to any compulsory legislation. Their position is that, if the state will give industry an opportunity, it will establish fair voluntary systems of its own accord.

No one contends that voluntary or compulsory unemployment compensation will actually compensate for any prolonged period of unemployment. The great objective of unemployment compensation is to reduce unemployment. Workmen's compensation does not and was not intended primarily as compensation for loss of life or limb. The purpose of both unemployment and workmen's compensation is to put a penalty on the conditions that cause loss of life and limb or jobs. Workmen's compensation has succeeded, not only because it pays compensation, but because it has made industry eliminate unsafe machines and conditions of work. Workmen's compensation has given Wisconsin the finest record in America for safety.

If industry fails to pay its interest money, it is penalized by loss of the business. If management fails to earn dividends, it hears from the stockholders, and may be and often is discharged. If industry has conditions which cause loss of life or limb, it is penalized. Industry has therefore built protection for interest and dividends and has enormously reduced the causes of accidents. But today industry is under no immediate penalty for failure to eliminate as far as possible unemployment. Unemployment compensation, voluntary or compulsory, purposes to impose that penalty.

Many of us question, not the sincerity, but the feasibility, of industry's establishing a voluntary system. We are convinced that it is not fair to the rest of society for industry to make great profits in periods of prosperity only to turn its employees over to public or private charity in a period of depression.

It seems to me that the fairest method of procedure for us at this time is to adopt a just and sound compulsory unemployment compensation program for Wisconsin, but to make the taking of effect of such legislation conditional upon industry's failure to establish a fair voluntary system in Wisconsin within a reasonable time.

The Interim Committee on Unemployment, after careful study and consideration, recommends what is commonly known as the Groves Bill for unemployment compensation. My study of this subject leads me to the conclusion that the Groves plan is the soundest and fairest compulsory plan yet suggested anywhere. I recommend the adoption of the Groves plan for unemployment compensation, to be conditional, however, upon the failure of industry to adopt a comparable plan for a substantial part of those employed in manufacturing in this state by July 1, 1933.

BANKING

There will be submitted to you two bills relating to the subject of banking. These bills are the products of the hearings by, and are presented with the approval of, the Interim Committee on Banking.

There are people today who urge that this is not a proper time for the enactment of legislation relating to the subject of banking. It is better to call the doctor before someone is sick and avoid the sickness entirely, but, if we have failed to do that and the sickness comes upon us, we need the best medical attention that can be provided. Banking more than any other occupation is founded on confidence. The public generally is fully aware that all of our economic institutions, including banks, have felt the effect of this depression. We do not help the banking situation by attempting either to ignore it or to do nothing about it. We cannot in one year correct the mistakes of the past twenty years. But we can do all within our power to prevent the consequences of the past twenty years from doing any more damage than is necessary, and we can learn by our mistakes in the past and do our best to guard against them in the future.

I believe we can make no greater contribution to the stability of our banking system than for the public to know and understand that we are not ignoring this vital problem. We inspire confidence, not by putting our heads ostrich-fashion into the sand, but by convincing the public that we understand our problem and are applying the best available remedies.

It is just to say that the general condition of the great majority of the banks in Wisconsin is better and stronger than that of any other state similarly situated. It is our duty and our privilege to make that position better, both now and in the future. The two bills presented to you by the Interim Committee on Banking show that that committee faced and dealt with the problem of banking in the attitude which I have described.

The Interim Committee on Banking, composed of able representation from this Legislature and of the banks of this state, presents a comprehensive and carefully prepared program representing their mature judgment. I know of no higher compliment that could have been paid to their efforts than the reception that has been given to the bills which they have prepared. While there are objections to their program, the objections relate to underlying matters of public policy. No question or suggestion has been raised that their program is ill-considered or poorly drawn. If you agree with the objectives which these bills seek to obtain, you will agree with the banking program. If you disagree with the objectives desired by the Interim Committee on Banking, you will oppose one or both of these bills.

The first bill revises and strengthens the supervision and control of the State Banking Department over state banks and provides for the reorganization of the Banking Department. It broadens the definition of banking to include those corporations and individuals who are in fact in the banking business, but are not now under the control or supervision of the Banking Department.... This first bill relates to the revision of this part of the banking law. It recognizes that three factors have been primarily responsible for the difficulties of our financial institutions: (1) the economic depression, (2) management, and (3) over-banking.

This bill recognizes that the Banking Department can do a great deal, if given adequate personnel and authority, in the matter of bank management and over-banking. Heretofore the Banking Commissioner's powers have been limited practically to closing banks. But closing a bank is not a remedy. The proposal in this bill is to improve the personnel of the Banking Department by placing its personnel under the protection of the Civil Service Law, and to provide adequate compensation so that the state can obtain the services of men who have the experience, the character, and the ability to discharge adequately the responsibility of this important department.

This bill gives to the Banking Department wider authority over the management of the banks and over the individuals who conduct them. Recognizing that no one individual should have either the authority or the responsibility to discharge these widened powers, this bill creates an Advisory Council composed of five members to be appointed by the Governor and confirmed by the Senate. This Advisory Council would be composed both of bankers and representatives of the economic interests of the state. It is their duty to advise with the Banking Commissioner and likewise to act as a board of review to enable any bank or individual aggrieved or dissatisfied with the action of the Banking Commissioner to present his case and obtain, if he is entitled to it, a reversal of the order of the Banking Commissioner.

The problem of over-banking has nothing to do with independent banking, chain banking, branch banking, or group banking. Over-banking has been caused by the granting of too many bank charters and by changes in our methods of transportation. Twenty-five years ago a community may have been in position to support one or more banks, while today — with the shortening of distances by automobile transportation — it may not be able to support adequately the number of banks that it now has.

This bill stabilizes the policy of the Banking Department by providing appeals to the courts in the granting or refusing of bank charters.

The Interim Committee on Banking takes the position, with which I heartily agree, that bankers as a profession and the state as a whole owe a joint responsibility in the conduct of banking; that the failure of any bank causes hardship upon not only every other bank, but upon the whole economic life of the community affected. In a large proportion of cases this problem of over-banking can be worked out, without loss to the depositors, by gradual liquidation, consolidation with other banks, or improvement of management. But this problem of over-banking can only be met by some constructive action. If left to itself — without help, supervision, or direction — it means that many banks in the United States will sooner or later close, with the consequent loss to the innocent depositor. This problem is met by giving the Banking Commissioner greater authority over management and by giving him authority, under proper safeguards, to order consolidations of banks.

No one contends that if this program is adopted, there would never be any bank failures. We do contend that if this bill is adopted, together with the bill providing for the establishment of clearing-house associations, there would be far fewer bank failures than if the situation were left without leadership or direction. I commend this first bill of the Interim Committee on Banking to your earnest consideration and call your attention to the fact that it has the almost unanimous support of the banking profession and is free from any partisan question, and that it can be adopted even though two thirds of both houses of this Legislature are not in agreement with our position upon chain banking.

The other bill recommended by the Interim Committee on Banking offers a constructive solution to the problem of the concentration of control of our credit system through chain or group banking....

This bill authorizes and directs the Banking Commissioner to establish in the State of Wisconsin clearing-house associations composed of both state and national banks. This would divide the state into natural commercial and business districts and unite the banks within such natural districts into homogeneous groups with common economic interests.

At the outset, every bank in this state would be eligible to membership, subject to the limitations I shall call to your attention. Once established, it would mean that all of the banks of this state would be grouped together into local associations. Each group is given the machinery and the authority, subject to common supervision by the Banking Department, of governing and regulating the conduct of its members. From time to time these several associations will be able to establish and enforce standards and regulations which will ensure the highest degree of stability and security for the depositor. Through a relatively small contribution by each of the member banks, each will be able to receive and be guided by research, information, advice, and suggestions heretofore limited to only those institutions with great aggregations of wealth. It would enable the member banks to participate in the underwriting and the sale of the safest and most desirable securities at the best possible prices. This plan will give to all of the banks of Wisconsin every benefit and a great deal more than is offered by any program of chain or group banking.

The limitation upon membership in these associations is that no bank may become a member where ten per cent or more of its stock is held by a holding company. This limitation is inserted, first, because the holding company is the device used for the creation of chain or group banking, and, second, because the ownership of bank stock by holding companies is the method by which stock speculation is interjected into banking. If speculation in stocks has any justification in other fields, it certainly has no place in the banking profession.

One of the substantial evils of chain or group banking is that it introduces stock promotion into the ownership of banks. Banking deals primarily with other people's money. Those that are appealed to by speculative profits and various forms of gambling have no place in, and should be ruthlessly excluded from, banking.

In order to encourage and foster independent banking, eliminate stock promotion, and eventually bring about a complete restoration of local ownership and control of credit in Wisconsin, all of the privileges within the control of the state are granted exclusively to those banks that are members of the clearing-house associations.

Putting this program in the simplest terms, its adoption would mean: The state agrees to give those rights and privileges over which it has control to the banks in this state that agree:

(a) That they will coöperate and work one with another to give Wisconsin a strong, safe, and stable banking system.

(b) That so far as humanly possible stock speculation and promotion are to be eliminated from the banking system of Wisconsin.

(c) That they will agree that the ownership of banks should be in the hands of individuals who primarily reside in and are a part of the community life whose money is deposited in their banks.

(d) That they will stand together and discharge the obligations of their profession toward the public by recognizing their responsibility, not only for their own individual banks but for the other banks within their own territory....

The chief objective of the banking program here recommended is to give Wisconsin strong and stable banks and at the same time to keep the control of our own money. If this program is adopted, Wisconsin takes the position that alien ownership and stock speculation are to have no place in the public banking system of this state.

This banking program is in keeping with the basic program we are trying to pursue, namely, of enabling the various parts of our economic life to construct machinery that will enable them to govern themselves. It is again an application of America's experience and tradition to the problems which we face.

The emergency program presented to you calls for the minimum amount of administration by the state. The funds for direct relief are to be expended through the local agencies of government. The funds for tax reduction are paid directly to the several counties and are to be used for the direct reduction of taxes. I am sure you will agree that, for a program dealing with an emergency, that administrative discretion is reduced to the minimum.

But reduced as it is to a minimum, there is nevertheless necessity for a highly important duty of administration. In order to ensure both the state and the communities against wasteful and uneconomic expenditures as well as provide the proper care for our needy citizens, supervisory control over the state's own funds should be reserved to some agency of the state. The fairness and efficiency of the administration of any duty require above all other things a centering of the responsibility for that administration. The administration of this program or such program as may be adopted by this Legislature is, at the least, an onerous and heavy task. It is not one that anyone would seek. But administration is naturally part of the executive functions of the government. I therefore recommend that the Unemployment Commission membership be enlarged and that the additional members be appointed by the Governor and confirmed by the Senate, and that the thus enlarged Unemployment Commission be charged with the responsibility and given adequate authority to carry out that responsibility.

We come now to the vital question of financing the emergency program recommended to you herein.

The foundation of any program, whether it be public or private, for dealing with this problem is finance: how much money is to be provided and where is the money coming from? The program recommended to you will require a cash outlay in 1932 of approximately sixteen million dollars. It will require an additional sum which can be financed over a period of several years.

I have heretofore pointed out why it is a manifest injustice for the Federal Government to fail to help. Its present policy means that the rich states get off at the expense of the poorer ones, or rather that the rich people in the rich states get off at the expense of the poorer people everywhere. The failure of the National Government to act simply means that those people of wealth in this state will be required to carry a heavier share of the load than they would if all the wealth in this country should be required to share its proportionate part. In the program I am recommending, provision is made for a proportionate reduction of our emergency taxation for whatever relief funds may be provided by the Federal Government.

In financing this emergency, an important consideration should be the state's credit and reputation for solvency. We are now reaping the benefit of having had the courage to levy a substantial tax to pay our soldiers' bonus obligations in full, while states and other communities are groaning under the burden of levying taxes in these hard times to pay the interest and part of the principal of their soldiers' bonus bonds.

By meeting this emergency with an emergency tax program, we will maintain our leadership in sound governmental finance as compared with our chief industrial competitors....

I recommend an emergency surtax upon individual and corporation net incomes, irrespective of capital gains or losses and from whatever sources derived. I would favor rates even higher than here suggested; but recommend the adoption of rates no lower than:

One per cent upon corporations.

A flat exemption from the surtax of $800 and $1500 for unmarried and married persons or heads of families respectively, and $400 for each child or dependent member of the family.

On the excess income over the exemptions I recommend a surtax as follows: One per cent under $1000; three per cent on $1000 to $2000; five per cent on $2000 to $3000; seven per cent on $3000 to $4000; nine per cent on $4000 to $5000; twelve per cent on $5000 to $10,000; fifteen per cent on $10,000 to $25,000; twenty per cent on $25,000 to $50,000; twenty-five per cent on $50,000 to $100,000; and thirty per cent on $100,000 or over.

This, it is estimated, will produce on this year's individual incomes $13,600,000. The corporation surtax should produce approximately $1,500,000. I recommend a permanent chain-store tax for the reasons stated in my message of June 4. If adopted, this should produce approximately $1,500,000 annually. I recommend the adoption of the gift tax upon all gifts with appropriate exemptions....

If this taxation program is adopted, the state will be taking a sound position. It will require everyone from the lowest to the highest who has a net cash income in 1931, over and above the subsistence level, to make a proportionate contribution to Wisconsin's 'community chest' to meet our community responsibilities.

There has been a great deal of agitation from industrial and other sources for a cut in the wages of wage-earners, 'white-collar' workers, and public employees. There is genuine merit and justice in such a program if it meant a proportionate deflation for everybody. The difficulty with any deflation program that has been thus far suggested is that it deflates the wage-earner and the salaried worker, but there is no proposal to deflate the income of the bondholder, the mortgage-holder, and the recipient of interest on term obligations. For the first nine months of 1931, wages to labor and the farmers' income had each been cut approximately two and one half billion dollars from the 1929 figure. But the total of dividends and interest had actually increased over 1929. The dollar of the wage-earner and salaried worker buys more, but so does the dollar that comes from invested capital. Labor and agriculture have taken approximately a twenty per cent cut in income. But for the first nine months of 1931, capital not only had taken no real cut, but the purchasing power of its income had increased twenty per cent. Hence capital, so far as income is concerned, is forty per cent better off for the first nine months of 1931 than it was in 1929....

The United States Steel Corporation, which took leadership in wage-cutting, showed by its last annual report that it had $117,000,000 of cash on hand and $471,000,000 of undivided surplus. If it was necessary for 'sound' economics to cut the wages of the steel worker ten per cent, why do we find no program for the deflation of this enormous cash and undivided surplus? In the first nine months of this year the American Telephone and Telegraph Company made $5,000,000 in excess of the highest total ever earned by this company in any equivalent period. Why have we had no proposals for the deflation in the charges to the American public by 'the world's greatest corporation'?

If we have correctly analyzed our problem, we now see clearly that any deflation in the earnings of those who receive no more than a decent subsistence level decreases the very purchasing power that we are trying to increase in order to reëstablish decent conditions.

We will not help but hurt our problem if we impose the burden so as to decrease the earnings of those below the subsistence level. In dividing income or jobs or anything else, *there should be no division which reduces people below the standard of living our producing power can easily and properly support....*

If Wisconsin adopts this policy of meeting this emergency, we can in truth say to the United States Steel Corporation and similar business and industrial leadership: 'If there is to be any wage-cutting, whether of public or private employees, we will all take our cuts — the millionaire, the bondholder, and the interest-receiver right along with the farmer, the worker, and the salaried man.'

I am opposed to waste, to overpayment for anything or to anybody at any time, whether in depressions or in prosperity. Wherever and whenever any individual in the public service in any of its forms is receiving more than he is worth, his salary should be cut. But any blanket cutting of salaries in public or private employment is merely another method of making the poor poorer and the rich richer. I am opposed to it. I am in favor of meeting the costs of this depression in accordance with Wisconsin's traditional tax policy of people contributing in accord with their ability to pay. That means that those who have net incomes above the subsistence level must contribute their share in proportion to the size of their income.

Their public needs able, courageous, and efficient servants at any time. It needs such services in the period that lies ahead of us especially. It needs public servants who have the intelligence and the courage to fight the self-interest of some of the greatest corporations in America. Public servants as a class do not expect the high salaries of private business. They are willing to accept reasonable salaries for the opportunity that the public service affords. They are more than willing to do their share in this emergency, but they object and they object on just and fair grounds to be singled out and required to contribute from ten per cent to twenty-five per cent of their gross incomes while some millionaire is asked, under the President's scheme, to give 'what he can afford,' which may be anything from nothing up to a modest fraction of his net income. If the plan here recommended is adopted, all public officials and employees will take a reduction in their incomes above the subsistence level, in the same proportion as others with similar incomes. And this is the essential point, they are not alone asked to contribute. They all take a proportionate cut; they all share equally according to their means. The vast proportion of human beings are reasonable, and are willing to carry a burden that is fair and equitable. Men revolt when they feel they are imposed upon....

THE END

At your regular session you adopted constitutional amendments and enacted statutes which go as far as it is now possible for us to go in carrying out Wisconsin's power program. It is the most basic and far-reaching program on the part of any state in the Union in regaining control for the people of essential mechanical energy — electricity. The execution of that program will go far toward giving the state and its municipalities the direct control and ownership of a sufficient amount of power to protect the people of this state in one of the most vital of their common necessities. Generally throughout Wisconsin we own our water. Control of the substantial part of our electricity will give us light, heat, and power.

You have created a body for the intelligent examination of our common problems in the Executive Council. We have outstanding resources, in character and intelligence, in Wisconsin's industrial, agricultural, and business world. I acknowledge the splendid response that has been given to the state's effort to mobilize that creative capacity. No one should be disturbed for Wisconsin's future with this leadership that exists within our borders, a leadership that is so willing and anxious to bury partisan consideration for our common good. While it may be my lot to be Chief Executive of Wisconsin, I shall continue to call to the state's service the best brains and character, regardless of residence, politics, or wealth, that we can obtain. Wisconsin needs the best. So far as I may be able to influence it, Wisconsin shall have the best.

The adoption of the program herein recommended would give us machinery for inaugurating a definite attempt to enable and require business to stabilize itself in the public interest....

I am fully aware that the program that we have heretofore adopted and that is herein recommended challenges the monopoly system at its foundation. I know the power of that system. I know what it can do to the public and even private lives of men who challenge it. I know the attacks, subtle, open, and under-cover, to which everyone of you will be subjected.

You will be assailed. They will say that you are destructive, although they offer no alternatives themselves. They will tell you that the Government cannot put five million men to work, although they forget that they put four million American young men to work at the business of war; that they squandered forty billion dollars of American money in the most wasteful and futile war of modern history. And still they will say that you are extravagant and wasteful and visionary because you propose to spend millions or billions to build highways and bridges and power plants that will make the farmer's and the worker's life better and happier; you may spend tens of billions to destroy — but nothing to build a richer life.

To fight this fight, you give up security, you give up peace; you may give up your homes, your businesses, and your occupations. And what can you expect in return? Only the inner satisfaction that if you are successful, you will have helped to remake the life of America; that you will have been a part of a determined effort to live up to the highest and noblest traditions of our fathers; that the scars and wounds that you have received and will receive came in a great cause, the age-old struggle of mankind to build a better world.

Chapter XII
PRESIDENT HOOVER'S PLAN

[Although, as indicated in the previous documents, there is a great weight of respectable opinion on the side of planning for the purpose of stabilizing production and employment, it must not be thought that the idea is universally accepted. On the contrary, it appears to many to be an impossible or undesirable ideal — 'an infection,' as President Hoover remarks, 'from the "five-year plan" through which Russia is struggling to redeem herself from the ten years of misery and starvation.' Indeed, President Hoover, in his address before the Indiana Editorial Association on June 15, 1931, poured scorn on projects for large-scale and integrated planning, summarized the opposing philosophy with his customary display of acumen, and put forward what he called 'an American plan' based on certain statistical forecasts and on the assumption that it will be realized 'if we just keep on giving the American people a chance.' Since this address is one of the state papers bearing on the issue raised in this volume, it is reprinted here in full:]

The business depression is the dominant subject before the country and the world today. Its blight stretches from all quarters of the globe to every business place and every cottage door in our land. I propose to discuss it and the policies of the Government in respect to it.

Depressions are not new experiences, though none has hitherto been so widespread. We have passed through no less than fifteen major depressions in the last century. We have learned something as the result of each of these experiences. From this one we shall gain stiffening and economic discipline, a greater knowledge upon which we must build a better safeguarded system. We have come out of each previous depression into a period of prosperity greater than ever before. We shall do so this time.

As we look beyond the horizons of our own troubles and consider the events in other lands, we know that the main causes of the extreme violence and the long continuance of this depression came not from within but from outside the United States. Had our wild speculation; our stock promotion with its infinite losses and hardship to innocent people; our loose and extravagant business methods and our unprecedented drought, been our only disasters, we would have recovered months ago.

A large part of the forces which have swept our shores from abroad are the malign inheritances in Europe of the Great War — its huge taxes, its mounting armament, its political and social instability, its disruption of economic life by the new boundaries. Without the war we would have no such depression. Upon these war origins are superimposed the overrapid expansion of production and collapse in price of many foreign raw materials. The demonetization of silver in certain countries and a score of more remote causes have all contributed to dislocation.

Some particular calamity has happened to nearly every country in the world, and the difficulties of each have intensified the unemployment and financial difficulties of all the others. As either the cause or the effect, we have witnessed armed revolutions within the past two years in a score of nations, not to mention disturbed political life in many others. Political instability has affected three-fourths of the population of the world.

I do not at all minimize the economic interdependence of the world, but despite this, the potential and redeeming strength of the United States in the face of this situation is that we are economically more self-contained than any other great nation. This degree of independence gives assurance that with the passing of the temporary dislocations and shocks we can and will make a large measure of recovery irrespective of the rest of the world. We did so with even worse foreign conditions in 1921.

We can roughly indicate this high degree of self-containment. Our average annual production of movable goods before the depression was about fifty billion dollars. We exported yearly about five billions, or ten per cent. The world disruption has temporarily reduced our exports to about three and one half billions. In other words, the shrinkage of foreign trade by one and one half billions amounts to only two or three per cent of our total productivity.

Yet as a result of all the adverse forces our production has been reduced by, roughly, ten or twelve billions. This sharp contrast between a national shrinkage of, say, twelve billion dollars and a loss of one and one half billions from export trade is an indication of the disarrangement of our own internal production and consumption entirely apart from that resulting from decreased sales abroad.

Some of this enlarged dislocation is also due to the foreign effects upon prices of commodities and securities. Moreover, the repeated shocks from political disturbance and revolution in foreign countries stimulate fear and hesitation among our business men. These fears and apprehensions are unnecessarily increased by that minority of people who would make political capital out of the depression through magnifying our unemployment and losses. Other small groups in the business world make their contribution to distress by raids on our markets with purpose to profit from depreciation of securities and commodities. Both groups are within the law; they are equally condemned by our public and business opinion; they are by no means helpful to the nation.

Fear and apprehension, whether their origins are domestic or foreign, are very real, tangible, economic forces. Fear of loss of a job or uncertainty as to the future has caused millions of our people unnecessarily to reduce their purchases of goods, thereby decreasing our production and employment. These uncertainties lead our bankers and business men to extreme caution, and in consequence a mania for liquidation has reduced our stocks of goods and our credits far below any necessity. All these apprehensions and actions check enterprise and lessen our national activities.

With no desire to minimize the realities of suffering of the stern task of recovery, we must appraise the other side of this picture. If we proceed with sanity, we must not look only at the empty hole in the middle of the doughnut.

We must bear in mind at all times our marvelous resources in land, mines, mills, man power, brain power and courage. Over ninety-five per cent of our families have either an income or a bread winner employed. Our people are working harder and are resolutely engaged, individually and collectively, in overhauling and improving their methods and services. That is the fundamental method of repair to the wreckage from our boom of two years ago; it is the remedy for the impacts from abroad. It takes time, but it is going on.

Although fear has resulted in unnecessary reduction in spending, yet these very reductions are piling up savings in our savings banks until today they are the largest in our history. Surplus money does not remain idle for long. Ultimately it is the most insistent promoter of enterprise and of optimism. Consumption of retail goods in many lines is proceeding at a higher rate than last year. The harvest prospects indicate recovery from the drought and increased employment in handling the crop. Revolutions in many countries have spent themselves, and stability is on the ascendancy. The underlying forces of recovery are asserting themselves.

For the first time in history the Federal Government has taken an extensive and positive part in mitigating the effects of depression and expediting recovery. I have conceived that if we would preserve our democracy this leadership must take the part not of attempted dictatorship but of organizing coöperation in the constructive forces of the community and of stimulating every element of initiative and self-reliance in the country. There is no sudden stroke of either governmental or private action which can dissolve these world difficulties; patient, constructive action in a multitude of directions is the strategy of success. This battle is upon a thousand fronts.

I shall not detain you by a long exposition of these very extensive activities of our Government, for they are already well known. We have assured the country from panic and its hurricane of bankruptcy by coördinated action between the Treasury, the Federal Reserve System, the banks, the Farm Loan and Farm Board systems. We have steadily urged the maintenance of wages and salaries, preserving American standards of living, not alone for its contribution to consumption of goods, but with the far greater purpose of maintaining social goodwill through avoiding industrial conflict with its suffering and social disorder.

We are maintaining organized coöperation with industry systematically to distribute the available work so as to give income to as many families as possible.

We have reversed the traditional policy in depressions of reducing expenditures upon construction work. We are maintaining a steady expansion of ultimately needed construction work in coöperation with the states, municipalities, and industries.

Over two billions of dollars is being expended, and today a million men are being given direct and indirect employment through these enlarged activities. We have sustained the people in twenty-one states who faced dire disaster from the drought. We are giving aid and support to the farmers in marketing their crops, by which they have realized hundreds of millions more in prices than the farmers of any other country. Through the tariff we are saving our farmers and workmen from being overwhelmed with goods from foreign countries where, even since our tariff was revised, wages and prices have been reduced to much lower levels than before.

We are holding down taxation by exclusion of every possible governmental expenditure not absolutely essential or needed in increase of employment or assistance to the farmers. We are rigidly excluding immigration until our own people are employed. The departures and deportations today actually exceed arrivals.

We are maintaining and will maintain systematic voluntary organization in the community in aid of employment and care for distress. There are a score of other directions in which coöperation is organized and stimulation given. We propose to go forward with these major activities and policies. We will not be diverted from them.

By these and other measures which we shall develop as the occasion shall require we shall keep this ship steady in the storm. We will prevent any unnecessary distress in the United States, and by the activities and courage of the American people we will recover from the depression.

I would be remiss if I did not pay tribute to the business, industrial, labor, and agricultural leaders for their remarkable spirit of coöperation. Their action is magnificent proof of the fundamental progress of American institutions, of our growth in social and economic understanding, of our sense of responsibility, and of human brotherhood.

Leaders of industry have coöperated in an extraordinary degree to maintain employment and sustain our standards of living. There have been exceptions, but they represent a small per cent of the whole. Labor has coöperated in prevention of conflict in giving greater effort and consequently in reducing unit costs. We have had freedom from strikes, lockouts, and disorder unequaled even in prosperous times. We have made permanent gains in national solidarity.

Our people can take justifiable pride that their united efforts have greatly reduced unemployment which would have otherwise been our fate; it is heavy, but proportionally it is less than one half that of other industrial countries. Great as have been our difficulties, no man can contrast them with our experiences in previous great depressions or with the condition of other important industrial countries without a glow of pride in our American system and a confidence in its future.

While we are fostering the slow but positive processes of the healing of our economic wounds, our citizens are necessarily filled with anxiety, and in their anxiety there is the natural demand for more and more drastic action by the Federal Government. Many of their suggestions are sound and helpful. Every suggestion which comes within the proper authority and province of the Executive is given most earnest consideration. We are, of course, confronted with scores of theoretical panaceas which, however well intended, would inevitably delay recovery.

Some timid people, black with despair, have lost faith in our American system. They demand abrupt and positive change. Others have seized upon the opportunities of discontent to agitate for the adoption of economic patent medicines from foreign lands. Others have indomitable confidence that by some legerdemain we can legislate ourselves out of a world-wide depression. Such

views are as accurate as the belief we can exorcise a
Caribbean hurricane by statutory law.

For instance, nothing can be gained in recovery of employment by detouring capital away from industry and
commerce into the Treasury of the United States, either
by taxes or loans, on the assumption that the Government can create more employment by use of these funds
than can industry and commerce itself. While I am a
strong advocate of expansion of useful public works in
hard times, and we have trebled our federal expenditure
in aid to unemployment, yet there are limitations upon
the application of this principle.

Not only must we refrain from robbing industry and
commerce of its capital, and thereby increasing unemployment, but such works require long engineering and
legal interludes before they produce actual employment.
Above all, schemes of public works which have no re-
productive value would result in sheer waste. The remedy to economic depression is not waste, but the creation
and distribution of wealth.

It has been urged that the Federal Government should
abandon its system of employment agencies and should
appropriate large sums to subsidize their establishment in
other hands. I have refused to accept such schemes, as
they would in many places endow political organizations
with the gigantic patronage of workmen's jobs. That
would bring about the most vicious tyranny ever set up
in the United States. We have instead expanded our
Federal Government agencies which are on a non-political
basis. They are of far greater service to labor.

We have had one proposal after another which amounts
to a dole from the Federal Treasury. The largest is that
of unemployment insurance. I have long advocated such
insurance as an additional measure of safety against
rainy days, but only through private enterprise or through
coöperation of industry and labor itself. The moment

the Government enters into this field it invariably degenerates into the dole. For nothing can withstand the political pressures which carry governments over this dangerous border.

The net results of governmental doles are to lower wages toward the bare subsistence level and to endow the slacker. It imposes the injustice of huge burdens upon farmers and other callings which receive no benefits. I am proud that so representative an organization as the American Federation of Labor has refused to approve such schemes.

There have been some complaints from foreign countries over the revision of our tariff, and it is proposed that we can expedite recovery by another revision. Nothing would more prolong the depression than a session of Congress devoted to this purpose. There are no doubt inequities and inequalities in some of our tariff rates; that is inherent in any congressional revision. But we have for the first time effective machinery in motion through a Tariff Commission with authority for any necessary rectification. And that machinery is functioning.

An analysis indicates that the large majority of these foreign complaints are directed against added protection we have given to agriculture. I believe that some of these countries do not realize the profound hardship which they themselves — with no malevolent purpose — have imposed on the American farmer. Improved machinery, the development of refrigeration, and cheapening of sea transportation have created for them great resources from their virgin lands and cheaper labor. As a result, these countries have taken profitable export markets from the American farmer.

There have been complaints from older nations which import a portion of their food products and export another portion. Yet these nations look upon their own agriculture as a way of life and as vital to their national security, and have long since adopted protective tariffs against the special farm products of the United States. We do not reproach them, for we, too, look upon a healthy agriculture as indispensable to the nation.

The growth of our industrial population will ultimately absorb the production of our farmers, but our agriculture was attuned to the export business and is of necessity passing a prolonged crisis in its shift to a domestic basis. Our tariff had proved so low that our farmers were being crowded even from the domestic market in many products which by use as diversification they can substitute to take up the slack in export business. From that condition we have given them protection, and we stand upon it.

In this connection I noted with interest that the International Chamber of Commerce in its recent meeting in Washington in effect recommended to the world the adoption of this method of the American tariff, although it was not referred to by name.

Our visitors found the American tariff act unique in the field of tariff legislation, as it defines the principle of our tariff by law; that is, the difference in cost of production at home and abroad. They found in our new Tariff Commission the creation of a tribunal open to every interested party empowered and ready to deal with any variations from this principle. They found a tariff without discriminations among nations. They recommended universal adoption of similar principles. Indeed, such a course would greatly modify tariffs in general. It would promote the commerce of the world by removing discriminations, preferences and uncertainties.

But it is not my purpose upon this occasion to discuss the relations of our many economic problems to the problems of other nations. I am not unmindful of our responsibilities or our vital interest in their welfare. The very first service to them must be to place our own house in order; to restore our own domestic prosperity. It is from increases in our reservoir of economic strength that has and must come our contribution to the development and recovery of the world. From our prosperity comes our demand for their goods and raw materials. A prosperous United States is the beginning of a prosperous world.

With industry as well as agriculture we are concerned not merely in the immediate problems of the depression. From the experience of this depression will come not only a greatly sobered and more efficient economic system than we possessed two years ago, but a greater knowledge of its weaknesses as well as a greater intelligence in correcting them. When the time comes that we can look at this depression objectively, it will be our duty searchingly to examine every phase of it.

We can already observe some directions to which endeavor must be pointed. For instance, it is obvious that the Federal Reserve System was inadequate to prevent a large diversion of capital and bank deposits from commercial and industrial business into wasteful speculation and stock promotion. It is obvious our banking system must be organized to give greater protection to depositors against failures. It is equally obvious that we must determine whether the facilities of our security and commodity exchanges are not being used to create illegitimate speculation and intensify depressions.

It is obvious that our taxes upon capital gains viciously promote the booms and just as viciously intensify depressions. In order to avoid taxes, real estate and stocks are withheld from the market in times of rising prices, and for the same reason large quantities are dumped on the market in times of depression. The experiences of this depression indeed demand that the nation carefully and deliberately reconsider the whole national and local problem of the incidence of taxation.

The undue proportion of taxes which falls upon farmers, home-owners, and all real-property holders as compared to other forms of wealth and income, demands real relief. There are far wider questions of our social and economic life which this experience will illuminate. We shall know much more of the method of still further advance toward stability, security, and wider diffusion of the benefits of our economic system.

We have many citizens insisting that we produce an advance 'plan' for the future development of the United States. They demand that we produce it right now. I presume the 'plan' idea is an infection from the slogan of the 'five-year plan' through which Russia is struggling to redeem herself from the ten years of starvation and misery.

I am able to propose an American plan to you. We plan to take care of twenty million increase in population in the next twenty years. We plan to build for them four million new and better homes, thousands of new and still more beautiful city buildings, thousands of factories; to increase the capacity of our railways; to add thousands of miles of highways and waterways; to install twenty-five million electrical horsepower; to grow twenty per cent more farm products. We plan to provide new parks, schools, colleges, and churches for this twenty million people. We plan more leisure for men and women and better opportunities for its enjoyment.

We not only plan to provide for all the new generation, but we shall, by scientific research and invention, lift the standard of living and security of life to the whole people. We plan to secure a greater diffusion of wealth, a decrease in poverty and a great reduction in crime. And this plan will be carried out if we just keep on giving the American people a chance. Its impulsive force is in the character and spirit of our people. They have already done a better job for one hundred and twenty million people than any other nation in all history.

Some groups believe this plan can only be carried out by a fundamental, a revolutionary, change of method. Other groups believe that any system must be the outgrowth of the character of our race, a natural outgrowth of our race, a natural outgrowth of our traditions; that we have established certain ideals, over one hundred and fifty years, upon which we must build rather than destroy.

If we analyze the ideas which have been put forward for handling our great national plan, they fall into two groups. The first is whether we shall go on with our American system, which holds that the major purpose of a state is to protect the people and to give them equality of opportunity; that the basis of all happiness is in development of the individual, that the sum of progress can only be gauged by the progress of the individual, that we should steadily build up coöperation among the people themselves to these ends.

The other idea is that we shall, directly or indirectly, regiment the population into a bureaucracy to serve the state, that we should use force instead of coöperation in plans and thereby direct every man as to what he may or may not do.

These ideas present themselves in practical questions which we have to meet. Shall we abandon the philosophy and creed of our people for one hundred and fifty years by turning to a creed foreign to our people? Shall we establish a dole from the Federal Treasury? Shall we undertake federal ownership and operation of public utilities instead of the rigorous regulation of them to prevent imposition? Shall we protect our people from the lower standards of living of foreign countries? Shall the Government, except in temporary national emergencies, enter upon business processes in competition with its citizens? Shall we regiment our people by an extension of the arm of bureaucracy into a multitude of affairs?

Our immediate and paramount task as a people is to

rout the forces of economic disruption and pessimism that have swept upon us.

The exacting duty of Government in these times is by use of its agencies and its influence to strengthen our economic institutions; by inspiring coöperation in the community to sustain good-will and to keep our country free of disorder and conflict; by coöperation with the people to assure that the deserving shall not suffer; and by the conduct of government to strengthen the foundations of a better and stronger national life. These have been the objectives of my administration in dealing with this the greatest crisis the world has ever known. I shall adhere to them.

If, as many believe, we have passed the worst of this storm, future months will not be difficult. If we shall be called upon to endure more of this period, we must gird ourselves to steadfast effort, to fail at no point where humanity calls or American ideals are in jeopardy.

Our transcendent momentary need is a much larger degree of confidence among our business agencies and that they shall extend this confidence in more than words. If our people will go forth with the confidence and enterprise which our country justifies, many of the mists of this depression will fade away.

In conclusion, whatever the immediate difficulties may be, we know they are transitory in our lives and in the life of the nation. We should have full faith and confidence in those mighty resources, those intellectual and spiritual forces which have impelled this nation to a success never before known in the history of the world. Far from being impaired, these forces were never stronger than at this moment. Under the guidance of Divine Providence they will return to us a greater and more wholesome prosperity than we have ever known.

Chapter XIII

THE RATIONALITY OF PLANNED ECONOMY

By Charles A. Beard

When the above documents, conceived in the light of the possibilities of planning in economy, are drawn together and their essential features compared, there appears to be an agreement among most of them on a number of fundamental principles. It is important, therefore, that these principles be succinctly restated; they form the basis for further consideration of the whole subject and present the irreducible challenge of planned economy to those who assume that drifting or doing nothing is a preferable and safer course of procedure. At all events here are the issues.

First, the authors of the preceding papers generally agree that the present scene of starvation, misery, and insecurity on the one side and warehouses bursting with wheat and manufactured commodities on the other is absurd, an offense to intelligence. It is immoral in that it imposes needless and frightful suffering upon innocent millions of men, women, and children. It is dangerous to our political and social order because it denies the validity of its claim upon loyalties. Mankind will not indefinitely suffer in patience the ridiculous, the preposterous, and the indefensible. To quote from the Chamber of Commerce Report: 'To an onlooker from some other world, our situation must seem as stupid and anomalous as it seems painful to us. We are in want because we have too much. People go hungry while our farmers cannot dispose of their surpluses of food; unemployed are anxious to work, while there is machinery idle with which they could make the things they need.

Capital and labor, facilities for production and transportation, raw materials and food, all these essential things we have in seeming abundance. We lack only the applied intelligence to bring them fruitfully into employment.' Surely here is a call to action that cannot be met by a confession of defeat. If intelligence can do nothing about it, then the probability is that ignorance will make the attempt, for ignorance will not long endure stupidity and anomaly openly confessed by the wise and informed. That seems to be one of the lessons of history from the fall of Rome to the Russian revolution of 1917.

Can anything be done by human intelligence and will? Is the cycle of expansion, explosion, contraction, and calamity a product of inexorable nature or the outcome of human arrangements and methods, susceptible of modification and control by intelligence and will? The Chamber of Commerce Report explains the process and makes an answer which is direct and carries its own implications:

Our progress is not even or regular. Both here and abroad there are periods of super-prosperity, followed by depressions that bring distress. There are recurrent dislocations of our economic machinery. This is a natural consequence of individual action, when no central coördinating influence is exerted over industry as a whole. Our problem is to retain the benefits of private initiative, and at the same time to supply, if possible, some degree of control or influence that will help to maintain a better balance and thus reduce the severity of business fluctuations.

The magnitude of our present depression is such that there is ground to doubt whether the measures so far considered will suffice either to pull us out now or prevent us from getting into another one like it. Planning by individual concerns, and even by whole industries, may not suffice to remedy such a severe lack of adjustment between production and consumption as we are experiencing.... We lack only the applied intelligence to bring them [capital and labor] fruitfully into employment.

If, then, the periodical industrial crisis is not the outcome of natural law but of human arrangements, it is necessary to inquire into the human causes of this phenomenon. Here again the Chamber of Commerce Report supplies the clue and expresses the hope of those unwilling to accept defeat with resignation:

Men produce for the desire of profit. Possibilities of greater profit induce speculation and overproduction. These, in turn, bring about a surplus of goods, a corresponding lowering of prices, and finally the disruption of business, with resultant underconsumption. The surplus is later exhausted, production is resumed, and consumption is restored to normal, with the return of prosperity and employment; and thus the upward and downward swings are continued. While we cannot expect, with our present knowledge and experience, to prevent recurring depressions, let us hope that the depth of the valleys of the depressions may be reduced by avoiding the erection of high peaks in periods of undue activity.

In other words, by allowing free rein to the profit-making motive, without regard to consequences, society permits the extremes of expansion and contraction which bring ruin in their train; and, since the cause of our troubles lies here, the remedy or at least the mitigating applications of reason are within the power of the public and private agencies which can speak with authority in the national interest.

The next step is clear. The only line of action open before those who believe in action runs in the direction of planning — the adjustment of production to efficient demand, the subordination of the profit-making motive to the larger requirement of stability, and the establishment of security founded on a faith in the continuity of fair earnings for labor and capital. On this, all except the drifters and defeatists agree. The Chamber of Commerce Report summarizes it succinctly:

Only through a proper coördination of production and consumption can a sane, orderly, and progressive economic life be developed. A freedom of action which might have been justified in the relatively simple life of the last century cannot be tolerated today, because the unwise action of one individual may adversely affect the lives of thousands. We have left the period of extreme individualism and are living in a period in which national economy must be recognized as the controlling factor.

In the light of these findings the problem confronting us is not the simple issue of planning or no planning. The question presents aspects more complex: how much planning, by whom, under whose auspices, and to what ends? Planning there is already, on a large scale, by national, state, and municipal governments, by great corporations, and by individuals with reference to particular opportunities. And in advancing on the road to a more integrated and extensive planning of economy, all these agencies come into view. The principal documents cited above contemplate the use of public authorities and private enterprise. Opposed to this assumption, of course, is the communist doctrine that only a centralized and despotic bureaucracy can make economic blue-prints and carry them into execution. Planning by a central board of economists and engineers is easy, to be sure, but the rub is in the execution. If human beings were mere inanimate engines, without affections, interests, vagaries, and wills of their own, to be moved about, put in position, and operated, then something could be said for the logic of communism; a bureaucratic despotism would work. But American citizens are not inanimate engines; they are individuals with at least a modicum of education and independence of opinion; they are associated in various forms of government, central and local; they are members of corporations and trade unions; they have long been accustomed to free participation in self-government in public and private affiliations; and they cannot be moved like pawns on a chessboard by bureaucrats, no matter how wise or despotic. So planning in America must begin with a recognition of the realities of the social scene.

Given this stubborn situation, the plans above presented contemplate the utilization of our great business corporations in the program of stabilization and security. Indeed, these concerns are now so well organized and concentrated that about two hundred of them control from thirty-five to forty-five per cent of the business wealth of the country and within the limits of their operations proceed according to plans.[1] The next step then is to facilitate the further organization of business in the important branches of American economy, such as transportation, steel, electricity, fuel, and so forth. Mr. Swope's project advocates the formation of a trade association in the electrical industry, and by implication a

---

[1] In a review of Laidler's *Concentration in American Industry*, Mr. Stuart Chase presents the following striking table (*New Republic*, October 14, 1931):

INDUSTRY	NUMBER OR NAME OF DOMINANT CORPORATIONS	EXTENT OF DOMINATION
Iron ore	U.S. Steel Corporation	50–75 per cent U.S. reserves
Steel	U.S. Steel Corporation	40 per cent mill capacity
Nickel	International Nickel Company	90 per cent world reserves
Aluminum	Aluminum Co. of America	Monopoly of bauxite reserves
Telephone	Amer. Telephone and Telegraph	80 per cent U.S. service
Telegraph	Western Union	75 per cent U.S. service
Automobile	Ford and General Motors	75 per cent U.S. production
Parlor car	Pullman Company	Virtual monopoly
Agricultural machinery	International Harvester	50 per cent U.S. production
Shoe machinery	United Shoe Machinery Co.	Virtual monopoly
Sewing machines	Singer Company	Dominates field
Radio	Radio Corporation	Dominates field
Sugar	American Sugar Refining Co.	Dominates field
Anthracite coal	8 companies	80 per cent U.S. tonnage
Steel	9 companies	80 per cent mill capacity
Sulphur	2 companies	Most of world's deposits
Oil	5 companies	33 per cent U.S. production
Meat packing	2 companies	Over 50 per cent U.S. production
Bread	4 companies	25 per cent U.S. production
Cigarettes	3 companies	70 per cent U.S. production
Electrical equipment	2 companies	Over 50 per cent U.S. production
Railroad rolling stock	2 companies	Dominate field
Chemical	3 companies	Dominate field
Matches	2 companies	Dominate field
Rubber	4 companies	Dominate field
Moving pictures	3 companies	Dominate field
Aviation	3 companies	Dominate field
Electric power	4 groups	Dominate field
Insurance	10 companies	66 per cent insurance in force
Banking	1 per cent of banks control	99 per cent resources

similar step in other fields. *The Forum* plan, looking forward to an economy more closely knit and easily controlled, provides for the creation of a syndicate of the corporations in each fundamental branch of American industry. The Chamber of Commerce Report, in proposing a modification of the anti-trust laws, assumes that this integration would take place if business concerns were allowed to enter contracts for the purpose of equalizing production and stabilizing economic operations. Such integration is not a novelty. As already noted, it has gone far and if not impeded by legislation and prosecution would undoubtedly reach a grand climax soon; but obviously, if uncontrolled, at great peril to the public interest.

It is this protection of the public interest and the necessity for coördination among trade associations or syndicates that require the participation of governmental authority in the planning process. Mr. Swope's scheme provides that the public interest shall be protected 'by the supervision of companies and trade associations by the Federal Trade Commission or by a bureau in the Department of Commerce or by some federal supervisory body specially constituted.' The Chamber of Commerce Report does not go into details, but proposes that contracts made by business concerns for the purpose of equalizing production and consumption shall be filed with 'some governmental authority' and remain in effect unless that public authority finds them contrary to the public interest. *The Forum* plan places the supervision of syndicates or, to use Mr. Swope's term, trade associations, under the supervision of a National Economic Council. At all events, the several planning schemes contain projects for federal control over economic associations for the stabilization of production and distribution.

Since it is admitted that there must be some kind of federal supervision over the integration of industries in trade associations or syndicates and that there must be

coördination among them in the establishment and maintenance of a balanced economy, this supervision and co-
ordination must proceed according to certain principles
accepted in advance. Both the Swope plan and the
Chamber of Commerce Report supply the formula. It is
'the public interest.' But they do not venture to penetrate this shadowy realm and to fix positive bench marks
for future guidance. *The Forum* plan is more explicit: it
suggests that the integrated industries be placed on the
basis of public utilities affected with public interest and
controlled in accordance with fundamental rules already
in force in this field: prudent investment, standard services, equitable charges, and a fair return on capital. That
the regulation of utilities has not been a utopian success
may be granted, but unless the Government is to assume
the ownership and direction of all integrated industries,
what other choice is possible, except the continuance of
the economic anarchy which has repeatedly landed the
country in the slough of despond?

That this dilemma is recognized by Mr. Swope and the
Chamber of Commerce Committee is evident in certain
collateral provisions of their respective projects. The
former does not think that the federal supervisory body,
in protecting the public interest, can operate in the dark;
so he would require all companies coming within the
scope of his plan to adopt standard systems of accounting
and reporting which will make transparent their operations, charges, and earnings. Mr. Swope would go further; he would have the federal supervisory body and the
Internal Revenue Department coöperate with trade associations in establishing principles for reconciling methods
of reporting assets and income with the basis of values
and income calculated for federal tax purposes. For political economists there is more food for thought in these
suggestions than in half a dozen heavy treatises in the
academic style. Similar principles are implicit in the

statement of the Chamber of Commerce Committee bearing on federal supervision: 'Business prosperity and employment will be best maintained by an intelligently planned business structure which affords a fair opportunity to make a reasonable profit through productive activities; but we emphasize again that if this permission is to be granted it must be accompanied by such reasonable governmental regulations as will prevent extortion and unfair business practices.' In other words, competitive anarchy, unreasonable profits, and underhanded practices are incompatible with intelligent planning. In the permanent stabilization of production rational principles must control.

Granted that we are to abandon the once useful practice of unlimited competition, which is largely responsible for the heights and depths of the business cycle, and are to proceed in the direction of planned economy — the integration of fundamental industries under federal supervision — how is a beginning to be made? Who is to take the initiative? Being a practical man and rightly suspicious of comprehensive projects that smell of the oil, Mr. Swope would start with a single group — the electrical industries and make a realistic demonstration of the feasibility of the idea. The Chamber of Commerce Committee evidently contemplates leadership on the part of business enterprise — the voluntary integration of particular industries through the establishment of contractual relations among them. *The Forum* plan would start at the top, by the establishment of a National Economic Council under government auspices, the abandonment of the competitive anarchy prescribed by the anti-trust laws, and the adoption of the legal and administrative measures necessary to integration in the interest of stability.

At first glance there seems to be a conflict of proposed procedures here, but the conflict is more apparent than real. Both the Swope plan and the Chamber of Commerce Report, either expressly or implicitly, call for a modification of the anti-trust laws and the establishment of a federal body to supervise integrated industries for the protection of the public interest. This being so, the initiative must come from both sides: from industry and government. Industry cannot march resolutely in the direction of planned economy unless the Congress of the United States will establish the requisite legal conditions, set up the supervisory body, and define with some degree of precision the methods by which the public interest is to be guaranteed. Nor can the Government go far with any system of planning unless the fundamental industries will coöperate in the process of integration and stabilization. Hence, for the promotion of economic planning we must look to enlightened statecraft in politics and enlightened leadership in business. There must be courage, intelligence, and interest in the commonweal on both sides and a reasonable meeting of minds.

It is not merely business stabilization which occupies the attention of planners. They all recognize the fact that mass production cannot thrive without mass consumption and that this means the maintenance of high wages and security for labor. In brief the projects presented above contemplate provisions for life, disability, and unemployment insurance, for stabilizing wages and prices, for public and private aid in times of crisis, for a more rational allocation of labor, and/or for the expansion of public works to meet particular crises. Planned economy, of course, assumes that there will be a fair stabilization of production and employment, that the security which it offers will encourage the continuous use of buying power, will prevent undue savings for calamities, and will eliminate the peaks and valleys of depression. But perfection is impossible in human arrangements and limited insurance provisions will have to be made against technological changes and inevitable fluctuations. With respect to these supplementary guarantees there is naturally much difference of opinion, especially in the matter of governmental and private obligations. If the experience of England and Germany is indicative of the future, some kind of a dole is the only alternative to stabilization through planning.

To this point we are led by a study of the logic of the economic pattern already in the process of becoming in the United States. Fundamental industries are at present highly integrated and a more complete union must be effected if we are to avoid the explosions and contractions of the historic business cycle. The principles of competitive anarchy assumed by the anti-trust laws are incompatible with such a complete integration as the exigencies of stabilization demand. Therefore a repeal or drastic modification of those laws is a pre-requisite to any further planning of significance in industry. But it is politically unthinkable and economically inexpedient to abandon the restraints of the anti-trust legislation without establishing new rules in the public interest and creating a federal supervisory body to carry them into force. Obviously these propositions strike deeply into politics as historically practiced in the United States and demand a revision and rational ordering of that chaos of doctrines usually found under the head of political economy.

If the facts stated by the Chamber of Commerce Report are indubitable and if the above conclusions represent the logic of the situation, the people of the United States now confront issues no less fundamental than those faced by the Fathers who framed the Constitution of the United States and are called upon to take action no less heroic than theirs. The Fathers found that the principles of the Articles of Confederation were incompatible with the security and efficiency of the Republic; they announced their beliefs and fought hard for radical changes in the prevailing order of politics and economy;

they were repeatedly defeated but refused to aknowledge defeat; and in the end they transformed calamity into victory. To them obstacles were stepping stones to achievement. That there are enormous difficulties in the way of realizing a more orderly system of economy in the United States today cannot be denied. To those of little faith and less hope they are impossible and insurmountable. But our intellectual and moral climate has been changed. The leadership of the nation has abandoned the philosophy of negation and is putting forward proposals for a better order of economy. To transform these tentative blue-prints into workable plans and to realize them in actuality is the supreme task of this generation.

To some such program the only alternative seems to be the policy of drift, but is there any assurance that drift will not make the difficulties still greater in the future and that the country may not be compelled to take comprehensive action at a time when reasonable discussion may be less feasible than it is now? Are those who propose to do nothing sure of their ground? Whatever the answers to these questions may be, planning is already going forward in national, state, city, industrial, and agricultural economy. Those who are responsible for this planning are, of necessity, drawing together as they are coming to a fuller realization of the implications inherent in their operations, for all departments of planning are actually parts of one body politic. The issue then narrows down to this: is American statecraft bankrupt? Have our civic and industrial leaders the courage of their convictions? Beyond that lies destiny — an inexorable movement of historic forces producing ever larger patterns of national and international arrangement of its own out of the little designs of mankind.

THE END

APPENDIX

THE PROPOSED BILL FOR A NATIONAL ECONOMIC COUNCIL

71ST CONGRESS
3D SESSION
S. 6215

IN THE Senate of the United States, February 17 (calendar day, February 20), 1931.

Mr. La Follette introduced the following bill; which was read twice and referred to the Committee on Manufactures.

A BILL to establish a National Economic Council.

Be it enacted by the Senate and House of Representatives of the United States of America in Congress assembled, That (a) there is hereby established a National Economic Council to be composed of fifteen members to be appointed by the President, by and with the advice and consent of the Senate. The members of the council shall be selected annually from lists submitted by groups of associations and organizations representing the industrial, financial, agricultural, transportation, and labor interests of the United States, but not more than three such members shall be selected from the list submitted by each of such groups. The terms of office of the members of the council first taking office after the approval of this Act shall expire, as designated by the President at the time of nomination, five at the end of the first year, five at the end of the second year, and five at the end of the fourth year, after the date of approval of this Act. The term of office of a successor to any such member of the council shall expire four years from the date of the expiration of the term for which his predecessor was appointed, except that any member of the council appointed to fill a vacancy occurring prior to the expiration of the term for which his predecessor was appointed, shall be appointed for the remainder of such term.

(*b*) The President shall annually designate one of the members of the council as chairman and one as vice-chairman of the council. The vice-chairman shall act as chairman in case of the absence or disability of the chairman. A majority of the members of the council in office shall constitute a quorum, but the council may function notwithstanding vacancies. The members of the council shall serve without salary but may be paid a per diem compensation not to exceed $ —— while engaged upon the business of the council. Each member of the council shall be paid his necessary traveling expenses to and from the meetings of the council and his expenses incurred for subsistence, or per diem allowance in lieu thereof, within the limitations prescribed by law, while attending or traveling to or from such meetings.

SEC. 2. (*a*) The council —

(1) Shall keep advised with respect to general economic and business conditions in the United States;

(2) Shall consider problems affecting the economic situation of the United States and its citizens;

(3) Shall endeavor to formulate proposals looking to the solution of such problems;

(4) Shall make an annual report on or before the —— day of ——, to the President and to the Congress, together with its recommendations, if any, for necessary legislation or for other action; and

(5) Shall, from time to time as it deems advisable, submit reports dealing with particular economic questions, together with its recommendations, to the President, to the Congress, and to the appropriate economic associations and organizations interested in such questions.

(*b*) For the purposes of this Act, the council is authorized to make such rules and regulations, and by itself or through its officers, to make such investigations and to call for such information, as it deems necessary. Any member of the council may sign subpœnas, and members and agents of the council, when authorized by the council, may administer oaths and affirmations, examine witnesses, take testimony by deposition or otherwise, and receive evidence.

(*c*) Such attendance of witnesses and the production of such documentary evidence may be required from any place in the United States at any designated place of hearing. In case of disobedience to a subpœna the council may invoke the aid of any district or territorial court of the United States or the Supreme Court of the District of Columbia in requiring the attendance and testimony of witnesses and the production of documentary evidence, and such court within the jurisdiction of which such inquiry is carried on may, in case of contumacy or refusal to obey a subpœna issued to any corporation or other person, issue an order requiring such corporation or other person to appear before the council, or to produce documentary evidence if so ordered or to give evidence touching the matter in question; and any failure to obey such order of the court may be punished by such court as a contempt thereof.

(d) The council is authorized to appoint a secretary, who shall receive a salary of $ —— per year and (1) in accordance with the civil service laws, to appoint, and, in accordance with the Classification Act of 1923, to fix the compensation of such additional officers, experts, examiners, clerks, and employees, and (2) to make such expenditures (including expenditures for personal services and rent at the seat of government and elsewhere, and for printing and binding, law books, books of reference, and periodicals), as are necessary for executing the functions vested in the council by this Act.

(e) The expenses of the council, including all necessary expenses for transportation incurred by the members of the council, or by their employees under their orders, in making any investigation, or upon official business in any other places than in the city of Washington, shall be allowed and paid upon the presentation of itemized vouchers therefor approved by the chairman of the council.

(f) The principal office of the council shall be in the city of Washington, where its general sessions shall be held, but whenever the convenience of the public or of the parties may be promoted, or delay or expense prevented thereby, the council may hold special sessions in any part of the United States. The council may, by one or more members of the council, prosecute any inquiry necessary to its duties, in any part of the United States.

(g) The council is authorized to adopt an official seal which shall be judicially noticed.

SEC. 3. There is hereby authorized to be appropriated annually the sum of $——, or so much thereof as may be necessary, to carry out the provisions of this Act.

8 x 0
3 0 0